The
HADDINGTON, MACMERRY
AND
GIFFORD BRANCH LINES

by
Andrew M. Hajducki

THE OAKWOOD PRESS

© Oakwood Press and A. Hajducki, 1994

ISBN 0 85361 456 3

Typeset by Gem Publishing Company, Brightwell, Wallingford, Oxfordshire.

Printed by Alpha Print (Oxon) Ltd, Witney, Oxfordshire.

To my son David and his collie dog Rex, both of whom also enjoy exploring
old railways.

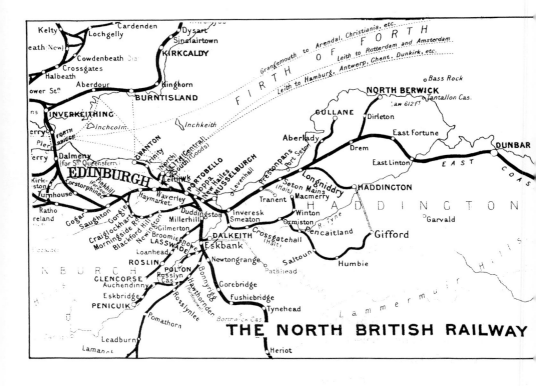

Published by
The OAKWOOD PRESS
P.O.Box 122, Headington, Oxford OX3 8LU

Contents

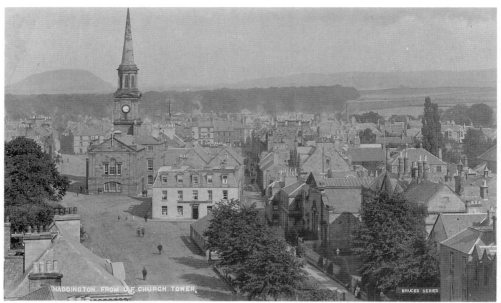

Two postcard views of Haddington before the First War. In the upper picture the Town House dominates the scene while Traprain Law can be seen in the background; behind the Victoria Inn lies the George Hotel. In the lower view, looking westwards, the lack of traffic belies the fact that this road was part of the Great North Road from London to Edinburgh! *Author's Collection*

High Street, Haddington

Introduction

In *The North Berwick and Gullane Branch Lines* the author recounted the history of the two seaside branch lines of East Lothian and, in this volume, he completes this study of the minor railways of the county by narrating the story of the three branch lines that served its landward areas. The Haddington, Macmerry and Gifford lines were an unusual trio which had little in common with each other except for their geographical proximity and the fact that they were all worked by Scotland's premier railway company, the North British, and each of them had its own distinctive and sometimes eccentric character. The first to be built was the short line from Longniddry, on the East Coast main line, to Haddington and it had the honour of forming the first true branch line of the system after the inhabitants of the county town had unsuccessfully sought to persuade the railway promoters to place their burgh on the great trunk route to the south. The line settled down to a peaceful and profitable existence for well over a century and competently served the predominantly agricultural interests of the town with trains for cattle, grain and fertilisers and for the buyers who flocked to the famous Friday market for which Haddington was for so long renowned. The Macmerry line was a very different affair for its *raison d'etre* was the product of the many small pits which were scattered about on the periphery of the Lothian coalfield. The branch line had its heyday when this once highly profitable commodity reached the peak of its production and entered a terminal decline when the mines themselves gave up their fight against quirks of geology and the changing tides of economic forces beyond their control. The third line was perhaps the most unusual of them all for the Gifford & Garvald Railway only barely managed to reach the former place after a series of boardroom disputes and misfortunes and was destined never to reach the latter. Owned by an independent company and worked under a Light Railway Order by the North British, the Gifford line conveyed potatoes, pit props and strawberries and that most Scottish of cargoes, whisky, as

Gifford, c.1905; the 'Goblin Ha' Hotel', whose proprietor operated buses to Haddington, is seen behind the market cross which was featured in the seal of the Gifford & Garvald Railway Company while on the right is the rival 'Tweeddale Arms'. Both establishments received the custom of the eccentric goods guard known as 'the Duke of Gifford'.   *Author's Collection*

The town hall, cross and pump at Gifford in 1909; the poster gives a fairly precise dating! *Author's Collection*

Ormiston between the wars, when market gardening and the relative success of the local mines helped to alleviate the worst of the depression. *Author's Collection*

well as, during that all too brief period between the death of Victoria and the rise of Hitler, passengers. Its often abysmally slow trains were hauled by a selection of superannuated locomotives sent in to serve their last years amongst the woods and vales of Yester and Humbie.

The Haddington, Macmerry and Gifford branch lines have now unfortunately passed into history and the author can only hope that the reader will feel that this book catches something of the atmosphere of these rural Scottish by-ways and the country through which they ran. If he or she is tempted to explore the still surviving trackbeds or visit the varied towns, villages and countryside which surround them then his efforts will not have been in vain. Before doing so, there are two matters which should be mentioned here. For the benefit of those whose chief interest in these branch lines is as part of the East Lothian story it should be explained that the expression 'up' in relation to direction signifies a train travelling eastwards towards the respective branch line termini, while 'down' refers to travel in the direction of Longniddry, Monktonhall Junction and Edinburgh. The second matter concerns the spelling of local place names – unfortunately contemporary documents, maps and the timetables, notices and literature of the North British Railway and its successors neither agreed with each other, nor were even internally consistent, when it came to the rendering of names such as Saltoun, Coatyburn, Lempockwells, Inglefield or Bellyford. The author has, therefore, had to make a decision in each case as to which spelling to adopt and he can only apologise if what seems to have been the preferred railway form of a place name does not conform with the present-day spelling or the reader's own particular preferences!

Edinburgh, August 1993   *Andrew M. Hajducki*

Whisky *en route* from the Glenkinchie Distillery to Saltoun station – today the last remaining distillery in the Lothians still produces a single malt but the horse and railway are no longer used to distribute it.   *Glenkinchie Distillery Collection*

The Lamp of Lothian – a scene from the turn of the century as swans glide along the Tyne past the as yet unrestored St. Mary's.

Author's Collection

Chapter One

The Lamp of Lothian

HADDINGTON AND ITS HINTERLAND

'The green-sward way was smooth and good,
Through Humbie's and through Saltoun's wood;
A forest glade, which, varying still,
Here gave a view of dale and hill . . .'

Sir Walter Scott, 'Marmion'

East Lothian, or Haddingtonshire is, undoubtedly, one of the most beautiful parts of Scotland stretching as it does from the shores of the Firth of Forth in the north and east to the bare Lammermuirs in the south while its western boundary merges imperceptibly with that part of Midlothian which lies on the very edge of the city of Edinburgh. It is a county which presents many contrasts – rolling agricultural land, meandering burns, bosky woodlands, sheep-grazed hills, sandy links and, until recently, pockets of industrialisation where coal was mined, lime was quarried and iron made.

The focus of East Lothian was, and remains, its county town of Haddington, an ancient and picturesque burgh of some 4,000 inhabitants which had an important part to play in the history of Scotland. Close to the town is the windswept and conspicuous isolated hill of Traprain Law where an ancient British tribe, the Votadini, had their capital overlooking the River Tyne, a short but fast-flowing stream which rises at Tynehead on the Borthwick moors of Midlothian, enters East Lothian close to Ormiston, flows through Haddington and reaches the sea near to Dunbar. Haddington itself dated back to at least the time of David I and had the distinction of being not only a place of great strategic importance, by reason of its situation as the bridging point over the Tyne on the main route from Edinburgh to the south, but also as the site of a royal residence and the reputed birthplace of Alexander II. On several occasions the town was destroyed in skirmishes with the English and in 1548 Haddington unwillingly played host to the longest siege in Scots history when, following the battle at nearby Pinkie, the English fortified and garrisoned the town and held it against an army of Scots and French for some 17 months before retreating safely to Berwick-upon-Tweed and taking with them as a trophy the bells of St Mary's.

Haddington was famed for other things too – its market serving the rich agricultural area known as the 'Granary of the Lothians', its importance as a religious centre and its recurrent and disastrous floods. The most important landmark was the great Abbey church known as *'Lucerna Laudoniae'* or 'The Lamp of the Lothians', which was famed for its size and beauty and which acted as a beacon of light shining out in an otherwise darkened world. The lamp was extinguished in the notorious 'Burnt Candlemas' of 1322; the name, however, lived on and was later transferred to the huge parish church of St Mary, described by architectural historian Colin McWilliam as 'arguably the most impressive of the late medieval Scottish burgh kirks'. The floods were a natural phenomena caused by rapid run-off after storms over the Lammermuirs and on 7th September, 1358, the eve of the Nativity of the Virgin, when the Tyne burst its banks and threatened to sweep away the

9

Abbey, one of the nuns took hold of a statue of the Our Lady and threatened to throw it into the swirling floodwaters unless they subsided immediately; by a miracle, they did. This story would not presumably have found favour with John Knox, who was born in the Giffordgait of the town in 1512 and who subsequently dominated the Reformation in Scotland and indelibly stamped his mark upon the character of the nation.

As the centuries passed, and peace was made with England, the town prospered as an important market and staging post on the great highway between the two capitals and there were lively scenes at the Blue Bell and George Inns when the mail coaches arrived to change horses and uplift passengers – the *Royal Mail*, *Union* and *Edinburgh Mail*, all bound for London, the *Magnet* for Newcastle, the *Enterprise* and several others were all coaches which made their first stop at Haddington to change horses. The journey south was, however, still a tedious and hazardous business and the flavour of these days is well caught by John Buchan when he describes the adventures on the Great North Road of the mythical Mr Lammas in his novel *The Free Fishers*.

A good description of Haddington shortly before the arrival of the railway is found in the *New Statistical Account of Scotland* where the two parish ministers of the burgh described it as follows:

> The town . . . is pleasantly situated at the foot of the Garleton range of hills on the north, and bounded by the Tyne to the east, which divides it from the populous suburb of Nungate, to which, however, it is joined by a bridge of four arches. The town consists principally of two parallel streets, running east and west, and a long cross street which bounds one of these and intersects the other nearly at right angles. The high or main parallel street, which is a continuation of the road from Edinburgh, is spacious, and the houses in general regular and handsome. The appearance of the town has, of late, been greatly improved by the erection of a lofty spire to the town-house, 150 feet in height, by side pavements on the streets, and gas lights, and by county buildings on a large and elegant scale for the better accommodation of the Sheriff's court, meetings of the county, and suitable apartments for public records.
>
> The approaches to the town from the west and east are ornamented by a number of beautiful villas with gardens and nursery grounds adjoining. There are nine incorporated trades, having exclusive right to exercise their several crafts within the burgh. There are no manufactures in the town, but there are two breweries and two distilleries in the vicinity; an iron-forge and coach works; a considerable trade in wool, flour milling, in tanning and carrying leather, in preparing bones and cakes for manure, and in supplying the neighbouring country and villages with such goods and articles of merchandise as they may require.
>
> The fairs have gone into desuetude, but there is a good weekly market on Friday, when the several kinds of grain are exposed for sale in bulk for ready money. It is perhaps the largest wheat market in Scotland.

Thus Haddington was a prosperous and flourishing town in the first half of the 19th century and its inhabitants would have confidently looked forward to it having a prosperous future – few would have forseen the radical changes which a new form of transport would bring in its wake.

South and east of the county town the land rises up steadily towards the Lammermuirs and is intersected by the valley of the Tyne and its affluents, the Waters of Humbie, Birns, Coulston and Gifford. Here is a countryside of forests, castles and fields where history was made and reality and myth intermingled and Sir Walter Scott describes these lands well when recounting the journeys of his eponymous hero Marmion. Notable local families included the Fletchers of Saltoun, one of whom was a noted Scots patriot and statesman, the Tweeddales of Yester, the Ogilvies of Winton and the Cockburns and Hopetouns of Ormiston. The lands here were fertile and the farms prosperous, as befitted an area whose landowners had contributed much to the agricultural revolution of the 18th century.

Apart from Haddington there are no other large settlements but several small villages of note. To the west of the county town lies the parish of Gladsmuir ('the moor of the hawks') which includes the small colliers' communities of Penston and Macmerry, while by following the Tyne upstream for a short distance Pencaitland and Ormiston are reached. In 1848 Sir Thomas Dick Lauder described Ormiston thus:

> [It] occupies the central point of the valley, and with the red-tiled roofs of its houses rising here and there over the trees in which it is embosomed. Its main street, running E.N.E., with a row of trees upon either side, has the width of an English village, and from its centre arises a rude old cross, near which at the close of the last century stood a pre-reformation chapel, then used as a parish school house. The village has now a certain air of decay about it, but in our younger days we remember that some of its best houses were inhabited by respectable persons of *demi-fortune*, who came here to live cheap, so that it afforded a quiet, genteel and innocent society. The parish is English in appearance, the Tyne running slowly in a deep alluvial bed through meadows, and the fields being everywhere divided by hedgerow trees, while the extensive and united woods of Ormiston Hall, Woodhall and Fountainhall form a sylvan district of so great magnitude that, when we consider the rich agricultural county in which it is situated, it might be almost termed a forest.

Nearby are the twin villages of the Pencaitlands whose ancient name signifies 'the head or end of the narrow valley' and which were described thus by Sir Thomas:

> The Tyne divides it into two parts, called Easter and Wester Pencaitland. The latter contains an ancient market cross, but the most interesting and picturesque feature of the village is the old church, with its small octagonal belfry in Easter Pencaitland, embosomed in a grove of tall and stately trees. We have long been in the habit of considering the manse as a gem among clergymen's residences of the same kind. Situated on a sunny slope, amid shrubberies and gardens sloping down to the river, it seems to be the very nest of human content.

Here, too, coal was mined from an early age and another peculiarly Scottish product manufactured in the newly opened distillery nearby, where an abundant supply of good water from the Kinchie Burn and the proximity of other suitable ingredients combined to make it the home of a single malt much coveted by the whisky blenders and merchants of Edinburgh and Leith.

Beyond Pencaitland are the Saltouns, East and West, noted as having been the place where pot-barley was first manufactured and where the weaving of a coarse linen fabric known as hollands was initially undertaken in Britain;

here, too, the British Linen Company set up their first bleaching-green. To the south of Pencaitland lay Humbie, a small and scattered settlement situated in a parish which stretched from the edge of the central plain of the county up to the heath and high pastures of the Lammermuirs, while to the east lay the two villages which exuded such an inexplicable charm to the promoters of railways and whose names are forever linked in history as a result, Gifford and Garvald. Set in a wooded vale, and sheltered from the hills, Gifford was a pretty and well planned village with a population of little more than 300 and consisting of two streets, one of which formed a fine avenue leading to Yester House, the seat of the Tweeddales. The first Marquis here founded the village in the late seventeenth century and in the grounds of his impressive house was situated the ruins of an old castle with the Goblin Ha', a strange subterranean chamber where once the sinister Sir Hugo the Wizard held sway. Four miles to the north-east of Gifford is Garvald (whose name 'garbh allt' signifies the rough stream), a tiny village almost lost in a fold of the foothills and consisting of little more than a single street running beside the oddly-named Papana burn. Such was Garvald's lack of importance that even at the height of railway speculation there were few who could understand the commercial logic of trying to build a line to here which might have had even the remotest prospect of ever paying its way.

Behind Gifford and Garvald, and forming an ever present backdrop to the whole of this part of the county lie the Lammermuirs, a long ridge of bracken-clad hills which were for centuries regarded by the lowland Scots as being on the very edge of civilisation, and across which not even the most optimistic of Victorian engineers could have hoped to build a railway. From Gifford an old drove road runs southwards over the hills to Carfraemill and Lauder and a sign still gives the stern warning 'Not passable for motors'. This road climbs steadily past Longyester and eventually skirts the rounded hump of the Lammer Law which, at 1733 ft, may not be the most impressive of summits but nevertheless affords a panoramic view of the whole long sweep of the Lothians from Edinburgh and the Pentlands in the west to Tyninghame and Dunbar in the east, the whole scene being fringed by the Firth of Forth and the distant Kingdom of Fife. From this vantage point the whole of the pleasing countryside once served by the Haddington, Macmerry and Gifford branch lines unfolds beneath the traveller's gaze like a map that has suddenly and unexpectedly come to life. In the solitude of these high wild hills, where the sheep and heather seem to reign supreme, the douce lands of East Lothian finally give way to Berwickshire and the proud Border Country.

Chapter Two
Rails to the County Town

THE ARRIVAL OF THE NORTH BRITISH

'The only opposition comes from Haddington, who do not appear anxious to have a railway at all, but who say that if there is to be one they would rather have a main-line than a branch. The Committee have felt it to be their duty to resist this demand.'
Statement by the North British Railway Provisional Committee, 14th November, 1843

At the beginning of the 19th century a number of schemes were afoot involving the promotion of railways in and around Edinburgh and in the main their purpose was to connect the capital with the coal mines of East and Midlothian and thus to provide a reliable and cheap means of transport of fuel to the city, whose demands for coal seemed to be insatiable. A number of short waggonways were at that time already in existence, including the pioneer Cockenzie & Tranent line which had the dubious distinction of being the first railway in the United Kingdom to have a battle fought over it when, in September 1745, the troops of Sir John Cope and Prince Charles Edward Stuart met at their fateful engagement near Prestonpans. Railways were, however, still something of a novelty and in the Lothians far more primitive methods of transporting coal were being used. As late as 1810 the sight of pit-coal being carried on horseback in sacks and panniers was a common one and carts and wagons were rare owing 'to the miserable and circumscribed state of the roads, or rather want of formed road altogether.'

In 1818 Robert Stevenson* published his *Report relative to the various lines of Railway from the Coal-fields of Mid-lothian to the City of Edinburgh and Port of Leith.* This had been prepared at the behest of a number of landed proprietors, coal owners and others who engaged Stevenson in his capacity as a civil engineer to 'point out a line of railway, the best adapted for leading the coal of the county [of Midlothian] as well as for transporting lime, stone, manure &c &c' and he was particularly directed in making his surveys 'to attend to accomplishing the carriage with the least expence of horses'. Three routes were eventually surveyed; although these were primarily designed to serve the Midlothian coalfield a long loop was projected from the River Esk near to Musselburgh eastwards to circle the Garleton Hills and run on to Haddington via the Tyne valley. Nothing further came of these proposals.

On Wednesday 5th January, 1825 a meeting chaired by the Marquis of Tweeddale† took place in the Royal Exchange Coffeehouse in Edinburgh to discuss plans for a line to be provisionally called 'The East Lothian Railroad'. According to the report in the following day's *Edinburgh Evening Courant* a copy of the prospectus was discussed and,

> It was resolved unanimously that a railroad connecting the towns of Dunbar and Haddington with the proposed Dalkeith and Edinburgh railroad [be undertaken

---

*Robert Stevenson (1772–1850) was a civil engineer from Glasgow who was responsible for the inauguration of the Bell Rock Light and indeed virtually the whole of the Scottish lighthouse system. He was interested in railways and it was at his suggestion that George Stephenson, his near namesake who is rather more familiar in railway circles, adopted the malleable iron rail. His other claim to fame is that he was the grandfather of Robert Louis Stevenson.

†George Hay, Eighth Marquis of Tweeddale (1787–1876) and lord lieutenant of the county of Haddingtonshire. 'He led the way in tile-draining, in deep ploughing and in many bold experiments, in the course of which he incurred considerable expense.' [D.N.B.]

The Subscribers for the Survey of
Lothian Rail Way are requested to meet, wi
Royal Exchange Coffee House, on Wednesday a
inst at three o'Clock P.M. to consider reports o
-mittee, and by Mr Stevenson regarding the s
has been made; - to determine which of the line
way surveyed by Mr Stevenson shall be adop
-rated on the plans required to be lodged in the
Clerks to the peace, - to give instructions to
-garding the Subscription for the Stock reg ___
carrying the undertaking into effect, - and for the
disposal of other business to be then laid before the
Meeting -

  The members of the Committee are requested
to meet one Hour before the above General Meeting, of
Subscribers for the disposal of business preparatory to
the General Meeting.

  It is expected that Copies of an engraved
Sketch of the Railway, and report by Mr Stevenson
will be ready in time to circulate herewith. — But
if not, copies may be had by the Subscribers on appli
-cation to the Clerk.

       Thomas Grahame
         Clerk

27 Windsor Street Edinb
 19th Novr 1825

A circular issued to the subscribers of the East Lothian Railway.

and] an uninterrupted railroad communication may be accomplished between Dunbar, Haddington, Dalkeith, Musselburgh, Edinburgh, Leith, Glasgow, Paisley, Ardrossan and Troon; by means of which grain might be conveyed between Haddington and Glasgow at very little greater expence than is present requisite for its conveyance between Haddington and Edinburgh.

That the expence of the formation of the railroad in East Lothian will, from the nature of the country, prove comparitavely moderate, and the revenue to be derived from the transit of farm produce, coal, lime, manure and other articles, cannot fail to yield a liberal return on the capital invested in the undertaking.

That the committee be empowered to employ Mr Robert Stevenson, or such other person who they may think fit, as engineer, with such assistance as may be deemed necessary to make the survey; and that they be empowered, should they judge it proper, to cause any other eminent engineer to examine the said lines of road, and revise the surveyor's report and estimate.

As can be seen from these ambitous plans an overview was being taken as to the formation of a national railway network for Scotland. At the end of that year Stevenson produced his *Report of a Survey for the East Lothian Railway* which recommended a route some 40 miles in length and according to the following description given by him:

The East Lothian Railway connects at Cairnie with the Dalkeith Railway, 5 miles east of Edinburgh and 1½ miles south of Fisherrow. From Cairnie it proceeds east to the Esk, which it crosses on a bridge of four arches below Sheer Mill, passes Cowpits and Eskfield, St Clements Wells (1 furlong to the north), passes Dolphinstone on the south, Bankhead on the north and enters Tranent by Mr T. Wilson's property. From Tranent it turns south for 2 miles, by Whinbush and North Mains to Wintongate, the summit of the line 350 feet above sea level. Here it turns eastwards and passing Jerusalem on the south and Samuelston on the north it crosses the public road a little east from Hetheryhall and reaches Haddington near the West Toll bar. It proceeds by the south side of Haddington, crossing South Street north of the mills, passes the church yard to the south, crosses the Tyne, passes Amisfield Park on the south side of the public road, Bearfield and Hailes Mains on the north and follows the course of the Tyne on the south side to the vicinity of Linton and Dunbar.

The cost of this line was estimated at £95,082 0s. 7d. but, notwithstanding the considerable sums already expended in producing the report and survey, the Committee did not proceed with the scheme, no doubt due to their inability to raise the necessary capital and the fact that the proposed Edinburgh and Glasgow Railway had also been shelved.

One scheme that did proceed, however, was the Edinburgh & Dalkeith (E & D) Railway. On 7th July, 1831 the 'innocent railway' (so dubbed affectionately by Robert Chalmers on account of its slowness and anachronistic motive power) was opened to goods traffic between Edinburgh and Dalhousie. In the following year passenger traffic was carried for the first time. The E & D* flourished and branches to Dalkeith and Leith were soon opened, all trains being horse-drawn and travelling along wrought iron rails laid to the 'Scotch gauge' of 4 ft 6 in.

In March 1836 a prospectus was issued for the Edinburgh, Haddington and Dunbar Railway (EH & DR). This was intended as a local line which would run between those towns roughly following the line of the London

---

*The full extent of the E & D system was often repeated in the 'bairnie rhyme' or skipping song still used by Scottish children in the playground today – 'Edinburgh, Leith, Portobello, Musselburgh and Dalkeith.

highroad (the A1), with branches proposed to serve the Edinburgh markets. Portobello and the harbour at Dunbar. What is perhaps interesting is that the EH&DR was in reality the precursor of the North British Railway (NBR) which was to form part of the East Coast main line. Two of the proposed officers of the EH&DR were to hold similar positions on the North British Board – John Learmonth, the Chairman, and Charles Davidson, the Secretary; the Engineers were Messrs Grainger & Miller and the Consulting Engineer was the illustrious George Stephenson. In the event two separate lines were surveyed, the 'North Line' and the 'South Line'. The North Line was, in essence, similar to the present main line and ran on the seaward side of the Garleton Hills, while the South Line crossed their western ridge in order to serve the town of Haddington and settlements in the Tyne valley. Both lines were of similar length but the North had far easier gradients while the South involved additional engineering works, a tunnel and steeper gradients – the latter being a major drawback when the steam locomotive was still in its infancy and liable to be defeated by topography. After some reflection the promoters followed Stephenson's recommendations and opted for the South line; this choice was approved by a General Meeting of the County of Haddington held in the following month. The EH&DR company was, however, dissolved without even seeking to obtain the requisite Act of Parliament and once again the matter was allowed to lapse.

Six months after the EH&DR scheme was made public its promoters issued a new prospectus, this time for the 'Great North British or Edinburgh, Dunbar, Berwick & Newcastle Railway' (GNBR). The inhabitants of the county town were now in for a shock for the GNBR line was to embrace the North and not the South line of route. At their own expense the town magistrates obtained the services of George Stephenson to report on the practicability and desirability of having the new line follow the southern route. In a letter dated 11th September, 1838 George Stephenson commented as follows:

> The length of the two lines is nearly the same. From the calculations I have made, it appears that there is a loss of power equal to five miles in length on the line by way of Haddington, when compared to the North line, which is equal to 12 minutes in time and 2½d. per ton extra for the whole distance. The increased expense to the Company for the conveyance of passengers on the south line will not be considerable so far as gradients are concerned. The most important point for consideration against the South line is the expense of execution; if I were making an estimate of two such lines in England, I should consider the cost of the South line £100,000 more than the North line. I have not made any increased calculations for bridges or land on the South line; I have only calculated the expense of earthwork allowing the slopes at 1:1. In making this comparison I have not calculated for a tunnel at the summit at Alderston, as after duly considering this point, I think it would be better to open cut it, so long as you can keep the gradient as low as 16 ft per mile.
>
> As the extra outlay on the South line will be equal to £5,000 per annum, the great point for consideration is, will the increased traffic be sufficient to pay the greater expense of execution; and after fully considering this point I am at present strongly inclined to recommend the South line for adoption, as I think the increased cost of the line will be more than balanced by the greater amount of population as well as the more extensive district of country it embraces and especially as it approaches

the coalfield, where probably such an amount of tonnage may be obtained as would warrant the making of a railway for that article alone.

Over the course of the next century the myth appears to have grown up that, in some way, Haddington was the author of its own misfortunes in failing to persuade the promoters of the railway to build their main line through the town. This was hardly fair for the majority of its inhabitants were in favour of this course and, indeed, there were many who were only too well aware that the railway would supplant the old high road and that there was an all too obvious risk that Haddington would be relegated to being a mere backwater unless it were to form a station on the principal line to the south. As it happened, the Great North British Railway scheme never proceeded for matters were suspended pending the findings of the Smith-Barlow Commission (otherwise the Commission on Railway Communication between London, Dublin, Edinburgh and Glasgow). This was set up to consider the various cross-border railway proposals in an effort to avoid wasteful duplication and provide the United Kingdom with what it was never to get – a rational and properly planned national network.

On 14th January, 1842 a public meeting was held in the Waterloo Rooms, Edinburgh where, being 'impressed with the advantages of railway communication generally and in particular with the great importance of establishing a line of railway to England' the meeting gave its support to the promotion of an Edinburgh to Dunbar line along the route of the GNBR North line. The promoters hit upon a name which was destined to become famous as that of Scotland's greatest railway company, the North British Railway. The scheme caused renewed consternation in Haddington and the inhabitants, seeing that, despite the Smith-Barlow Commission's opting in favour of a west coast trunk route, the North British proposals were attracting widespread support, resolved to petition the Provisional Committee of that company in order to persuade them to change their plans and serve the county town. At the end of the same month another General Meeting of the County of Haddington was held, the Marquis of Tweeddale again being in the chair, and the Magistrates of the town stated that,

> In the event of the proposed railway being carried through the County of Haddington they resolve to give it all the support in their power, on condition that it is to be brought in the immediate vicinity of the burgh, and to give it all the opposition in their power, if the North line is adopted; namely the line to the North side of the Garleton Hills, because that line would be very detrimental to the town.

The Marquis, after stating that 'there is no person in the county more alive than I am to the utility of a railroad passing in this direction', outlined the history of the previous EH & DR and GNBR proposals. Then others took the floor including a Mr Dudgeon of Tyneholm who said that 'were the line to by-pass Haddington then a great injustice would be done' while a Mr Sawers disagreed stating that 'it would be absurd to sacrifice the general interests concerned in the line merely for the sake of Haddington.' Sir Frances Walker Drummond, Bt then spoke:

> I have the highest authority for saying that to bring the line of railway near Haddington would cost an additional expense of £100,000. I do, therefore, think

that the gentlemen who advocate this line of road should either come forward with the money themselves, or be prepared to show that the revenue from Haddington would suffice to defray this additional expense . . . It comes, therefore, to this that if the gentlemen of Haddington will insist that the line near to their town is the only one which they can admit of, the thing must fall to the ground – there will be no railway at all, because I have it from the highest authority that it is the determination of the managers that the railway shall be abandoned if this objection shall be insisted upon . . . If you adopt the resolutions and resolve to oppose this measure in Parliament, the proposers must abandon this undertaking, and you will have no railway at all. But if, on the other hand, you agree to the low [i.e. North] line, I pledge myself to use every exertion – which is perhaps not to say much but to do all I can to promote a branch line to Haddington, and I have the highest authority for saying that such a measure would receive every encouragement from the Directors.

Sir Francis, with his reliance on the unspecified 'highest authority' appears to have carried the meeting for the North British proposals were approved by the County 'with an expression of regret that the railway does not pass through the county town of Haddington'. It was resolved to send a deputation 'to confer with the directors and induce them to agree with the Haddington line'.

On 14th February, 1842 the Provisional Committee of the North British Railway met and resolved to procure a survey for a branch to Haddington,

. . . and if it can be executed for a sum not exceeding £30,000 and the Haddington people will subscribe a fair proportion of that sum towards the expenses of it, it was agreed to make it so as to remove the objections raised by those parties to the presently proposed directions of the main-line.

The Marquis of Tweeddale led the faction of the Provisional Committee who disagreed with this decision and wanted the main line to follow the South route; although the North British Board outwardly presented as being united the internal dispute simmered. Two days later the Haddington deputation met a North British sub-committee and, after repeating the objections which had already been expressed, a number of new points were raised such as that the town would lose its present annual revenues of between £400 and £500 from the corn markets which it was felt would be relocated in East Linton. Provost Lea put forward the somewhat extreme view that the people of Haddington would never use the new line but would use the coach as before, and that the North British would accordingly derive no revenue from the town. Mr Learmonth, on behalf of the Provisional Committee, said that the additional cost of diverting the main line through Haddington had been estimated by Mr Grainger, the Engineer, at £116,000 (the whole authorised capital of the company at that time being only £800,000, although this was subsequently increased). This extra expense would never be compensated for by increased revenue, but he gave them a promise that if the town dropped its opposition then he would try to secure a branch line to Haddington.

In April 1842 the North British issued its proposal for a line from Edinburgh to Berwick-upon-Tweed, from where it would eventually connect with a line to London. Nothing more relating to Haddington was heard until

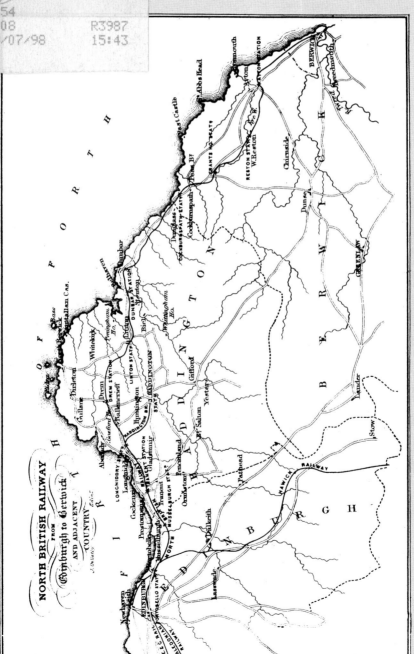

From Thompson's Guide to the North British Railway, 1846.

ANNO SEPTIMO & OCTAVO

VICTORIÆ REGINÆ.

****

Cap. lxvi.

An Act for making a Railway from the City of
Edinburgh to the Town of *Berwick-upon-Tweed*,
with a Branch to the Town of *Haddington*.
[4th *July* 1844.]

WHEREAS the making a Railway from the City of *Edinburgh* to the Town of *Berwick-upon-Tweed*, with a Branch to the Town of *Haddington*, would be of great public Advantage : And whereas the Persons herein-after named are willing, at their own Expence, to carry such Undertaking into execution ; but the same cannot be effected without the Authority of Parliament : May it therefore please Your Majesty that it may be enacted ; and be it enacted by the Queen's most Excellent Majesty, by and with the Advice and Consent of the Lords Spiritual and Temporal, and Commons, in this present Parliament assembled, and by the Authority of the same, That Sir *George Grant Suttie* Baronet, Sir *James Forrest* Baronet, *William Aitchison, John Learmonth, William Mitchell Innes, John Campbell Renton, Alexander Thomson, John Swinton, John Sligo, John Cockburn, John Thomson, Alexander Wright, John Maxton, Henry Maxwell, George Turnbull, John Christison, Hugh Francis Cadell, Robert Allen Harden, George Crosbie, Gilbert Laurie Finlay,* Doctor *George Hamilton Bell, Alexander Sinclair,* Incorporation of Company.

[*Local.*]   33 *C*   Eagle

The Act which authorised the North British Railway main-line and the branch to Haddington.

on 2nd November of that year the North British shareholders were told that, following a re-survey of their main line, a saving of more than £40,000 compared to the original estimate had been made. Accordingly the Provisional Committee announced that:

> This is of itself sufficient to meet the expense of the branch to Haddington so that upon the whole there will be no more expense incurred in making the line and branch than there would have been had the gradients remained as originally laid down had the main-line alone been formed.

Thus the North British were now willing to build the Haddington branch at their own expense, free from any contribution from the town. The burgh was still not satisfied, and further entries in the company minutes record communications from the town expressing their dissatisfaction and repetition of their desire to fight hard before the hearings of the Parliamentary Committee on Railway Bills. Relationships were strained: at a shareholders' meeting on 14th November, 1843 it was announced that now only the town of Haddington was in opposition to the North British scheme and that they were adopting a dog-in-the-manger attitude in their entrenched opposition to the idea of a branch line. A truce was, however, soon reached for the inhabitants of the burgh realised their weak bargaining position and the fact that the choice was really only between a branch line or nothing. Reluctantly, they finally opted for the former and agreed to withdraw their opposition to the Bill on being given a promise that the Haddington branch line would be open for traffic on the same day that the North British main line was opened. The upshot of this was that after the first reading of the Bill, the North British Railway Act was passed, unopposed, on 4th July, 1844.

In the preamble to the Act it was stated that 'the making of a Railway from the City of Edinburgh to the Town of Berwick-upon-Tweed, with a Branch to the Town of Haddington would be of great public advantage' and in Section CCXXIV the company was given authority to make and maintain both the main-line and,

> A Branch Railway commencing by a Junction with the said Main Line of Railway at *Redhouse* in the said Parish of *Gladsmuir*, and passing through the following places or some of them, (that is to say), *Gladsmuir*, *Aberlady* and *Haddington*, in the County of *Haddington* together with all necessary Bridges, Culverts, Approaches, Embankments, Roads, Basins, Towing Paths, Wharfs, Quays, Loading Places and other works and conveniences connected with the said line of intended Railway.

The Haddington Branch, which was to have a total length of 4 miles 60 chains, was to leave the North British main line at the east end of Longniddry station, 13 miles and 20 chains from Edinburgh. Longniddry was described in the *Gazeteer of Scotland*, published in 1844, as 'a decayed, curious and antiquated village. It is straggling and irregular, and but the wreck of a formerly large and important little town.' The coming of the railway did little to enhance the appearance of the village, for the main line was carried almost through the centre of Longniddry on a high embankment which now formed a physical boundary to prevent any southwards development, giving the place a strangely lop-sided aspect. To build this embankment it was necessary to demolish a number of houses and the Minutes of the North British Lands and Planning Committee of 14th July, 1845 contained the following entry:

> A report by the resident engineer was read as to the number of cottages (5) required to be taken down at Longniddry but in respect a greater number of cottages is claimed (by the owner) than is stated by him, on the grounds of their being out-houses and double cottages, it was resolved to offer to compromise by paying for six cottages.

There was, however, a consolation in that as the importance of Longniddry increased by reason of it being a junction station, this had an effect on the development of the village and in time several railway employees were added to the permanent population of the place. *En route* to Haddington the only settlement near the line was Coatyburn (otherwise Cottyburn or Coatieburn) which was described in the *New Statistical Account* as 'a solitary place at the north-eastern extremity of the parish of Gladsmuir' and consisted of little more than a school and adjoining schoolmaster's house and a smithy, all clustered around the railway and, notwithstanding the miniscule size of the place, it was soon to acquire a private siding.

One of the schedules to the Act contains a list of the 'houses and inclosed grounds which were to be taken for the construction of the railway' and it is remarkable that in the whole four and a half miles or so of the branch only a handful of properties were so affected. The decision to build the terminus at Haddington half a mile from the centre of the town was, perhaps, an unfortunate but not wholly unsurprising one and was a cause of continual complaint thereafter, and one of the contributory factors to the eventual withdrawal of the passenger service. But the reason for this was a combination of a desire to avoid the destruction of valuable property, and also to site it at a place where it could be easily extended in a southwards direction if necessary.

The North British put the construction of the Haddington branch in hand with rapidity and on 27th September, 1844, thirteen weeks after the passing of the Act, the contract for the earthworks and other civil engineering needed for the line was, after a careful scrutiny of 10 tenders received at between £10,080 and £16,700, awarded by the Plans and Works Committee to Messrs James McNaughton and J. Feely on the basis of their tender of £12,311 1s. 9d. – a sum which was reduced by some £314 from their original tender. This sum did not include the costs of land acquisition and this was now put in hand. The Lands Committee Minutes record the minutiae of these heritable transactions; although it was relatively easy to deal with the major landowners such as Lord Wemyss, other smaller landowners could often prove troublesome. A certain amount of give and take was necessary and in a Minute entry dated 1st November, 1844 it was reported that,

> In respect of Mrs Ferguson's Trustees at Laverocklaw, it was resolved to offer to purchase the portion of Field No. 19, which is cut off, and excamb [exchange] it with Lord Hopetoun for a similar portion taken from him on the other side of the line. It was also resolved to give a pipe to the well and to offer 37½ years' purchase for the land on 40s. per acre. But no allowance for the proximity of the steading to be allowed.

Construction proceeded at a fair pace and by 5th February, 1845 two interim payments, totalling £1,457, had been made to the contractors. On the 18th of that month a report by Mr Miller, the Consulting Engineer to the North British, was read out to the shareholders at the company's second general meeting:

> On that part of the line under contract to Mr Forbes, the Haddington branch strikes off. The branch, extending to 7,200 yards, is under contract to Mr McNaughton. He has removed a considerable quantity of stuff, and has the work now fully opened out. It is being proceeded with in a satisfactory manner.

Throughout the summer and autumn the contractor was busy at work and further interim payments were made. A new matter, however, now arose. On 1st October, 1845 the *Edinburgh Evening Courant* printed the following notice:

TYNE VALLEY JUNCTION RAILWAY
CONNECTING
DALKEITH AND HADDINGTON
WITH
BRANCHES TO TRANENT AND GIFFORD
and to form a junction with the
NORTH BRITISH, EDINBURGH & HAWICK AND EDINBURGH
& PEEBLES RAILWAYS

CAPITAL £200,000 in 8,000 shares of £25 each
DEPOSIT £2 10s. per share.

This Railway establishes the most direct communication between Dalkeith and Haddington – the two most important market towns for agricultural produce in Scotland. By the junction with the North British, the Edinburgh and Hawick and the Edinburgh and Peebles Railways, it will form an outlet, both towards the important town of Dunbar and the South of Scotland, for the vast mineral and other products abounding in the districts traversed.

The line will commence at the North British branch from Haddington and will proceed by the towns of Pencaitland and Ormiston to Dalkeith, there falling into the Hawick line. It is proposed to extend the line to Linton, and to form branches to Gifford and Tranent.

It thus in its course accommodates the richest agricultural country in Scotland, and opens up for its benefit valuable coal mines, stone and lime quarries, which are situated on both sides of the line, thereby not only securing to the proprietors an extensive market but imparting a fresh impetus to agricultural improvement.

The line is also attended with this great advantage, that it does not compete with any existing railway but on the contrary, will be the source of a great revenue to the lines with which it will be connected.

The survey of the line has to a great extent been completed, and correct estimates of the expenditure and return are in the course of preparation. As the line runs along the course of the Tyne, and through the valley below Elphinstone Tower, it is nearly in its whole extent a dead level and presents no engineering difficulties whatever. No ornamental or house properties will be interfered with, and in consequence it will be constructed at an unusually small expense. The length of the line, including the bridges, will be about 15 miles; and the promoters have received the strongest assurances of support from the gentlemen interested in the district of country.

The application received for SHARES in this undertaking are already so numerous that it has been resolved that the *lists will be closed* on Wednesday the 15th instant.

DAVID WRIGHT, Interim Secretary.

The history of the North British involvement with this scheme is not wholly certain, for although the company appear to have been openly supporting the scheme (which in itself was an amalgam of two quite distinctive lines known as the East Lothian Central Railway and the Tyne Valley Railway) they were most concerned that the East Lothian & Tyne Valley Railway (EL&TVR) was capable of acting as a rival to their own uncompleted line, at least insofar as it served Haddington and Dunbar. The result of this concern was that the North British were forced to co-operate with the EL&TVR; on 10th December, 1845 they agreed that the new line from Dalkeith should be treated as the main line to Haddington and that the existing branch from Longniddry would be merely a secondary route. Subsequently it was proposed that the North British and EL&TVR Boards should have Directors in common and it was agreed that the North British would take 5,000 paid-up £25 shares in the new line. They would advance a further £10,000 in cash as a deposit to the EL&TVR Directors when the contracts were signed for the line's construction, while authority was given to ratify a Joint Agreement between the two companies for the proposed junction of the lines at Haddington. On 17th February, 1846 the North British Board reported to its shareholders at the Half-Yearly General Meeting that 'the locomotive engines, carriages and other plant' for the NBR main line were in an advanced state and that,

> The next project which the Directors conceived it was right to support, was the East Lothian Central and Tyne Valley Railways (now amalgamated). These lines are to diverge from the Dalkeith Branch of this railway at Dalkeith, to cross the country by Ormiston to Haddington, where they were to pass close to this Company's Haddington branch, but not to unite with it, and to proceed from there to East Linton where they were to join this Company's line and station. The intimate connection which those two lines had with the Branch of this Company, and the apparent certainty that they would sooner or later be required for the public accommodation, induced your Directors to watch the progress and ultimately they were able to make an arrangement by which the two lines, i.e. the East Lothian Central and the Tyne Valley Railway, amalgamated together and agreed to join the Haddington branch of this Company at Haddington, where there will be a joint station.
>
> The advantages of this arrangement will be apparent to every one who knows the District, for although at the outset their traffic may not be sufficient to pay a large dividend on their capital, yet viewed as a feeder to this Company's main-line, as well as their branches in every direction, its importance is indeed very considerable, and the connection cannot fail to be profitable to this Company.

The East Lothian & Tyne Valley Railway was not, however, destined to see the light of day and on 1st April, 1846 the North British resolved to concur in the winding-up of the former company. This did not happen immediately and three weeks later the EL&TVR Directors agreed that they would not proceed with their scheme without the direct consent of the NBR. The North British now began to distance itself from the EL&TVR and within months the whole scheme had faded into oblivion, no doubt a victim of the bursting of the railway mania bubble which ended a year of intensive promotion of railways, both practical and ludicrous, throughout the Kingdom. It was ironic, however, that the threat of the resurrection of the EL&TVR or the promotion of a similar line to form an incursion into what the North British felt to be its exclusive fiefdom, was to cause that company much worry for many years.

By the spring of 1846 both the North British main line and the Haddington branch were nearing completion and on 23rd May a tender for the station at Haddington, that of the local firm of Messrs Dorward and Farquharson in the sum of £837 12s. 7d. was accepted. The Haddington branch was laid as a single line with 16 ft rails weighing 70 lb. to the yard, and sleepers were provided at four feet intervals. It is interesting that, having gone to the trouble and expense of providing a trackbed and bridges to double-line clearances throughout, only a single line was laid and this decision, along with the sub-standard track specification, was soon to be regretted. Notwithstanding the weather and the considerable labour problems which the North British contractors were facing, the main line and branch was duly completed 'although a considerable time must elapse before the banks are properly finished, along which numbers of workmen are busily engaged.'

Following upon a successful inspection of the whole North British works by General Pasley, the government Inspector of Railways, at the end of May 1846 the Directors resolved to open their lines to the public as soon as possible. On Saturday 20th June, 1846 the *Edinburgh Evening Courant* carried the following report:

OPENING OF THE NORTH BRITISH RAILWAY

Improvement progresses at a rapid rate in the internal intercourse of this country, insomuch that journeys which were formerly counted by months, and weeks or days, are now counted in a few hours by the miracles of modern science, ingeniously fashioning the powers of nature to the various purposes of life. Steam is the agent which has affected so great a revolution . . . we really cannot refrain from expressing admiration of this astonishing improvement when we have to record the addition of another important link in the chain of internal communication by the opening of the North British Railway, which took place on Thursday last, and is a great and we may add nearly the last step that remains to complete a continuous line between the great capitals of London and Edinburgh.

It will open up the rich districts of East Lothian and Berwickshire, and will admit their product to the metropolitan markets through Dunbar, Haddington, Prestonpans, Musselburgh and Portobello . . .

We congratulate the Directors and Shareholders generally of the North British Railway on the happy circumstances under which their line has been opened and trust that it is a harbinger of that success and reward which their exertions and enterprise so fully merit, and which we have no doubt they will receive.

Two days later, on Monday 22nd June, 1846, the North British Railway opened its Edinburgh to Berwick and Longniddry to Haddington lines to the public for the conveyance of passengers and goods and thus the county town finally had acquired its railway, albeit not the line that its inhabitants had wanted.

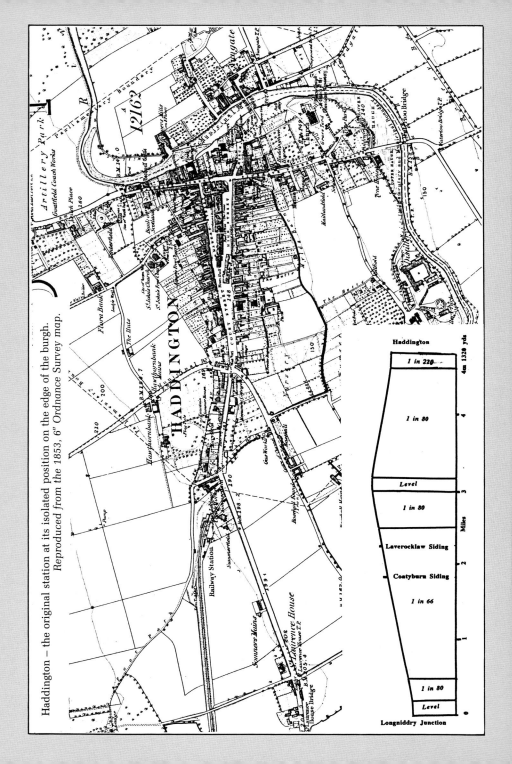

Haddington – the original station at its isolated position on the edge of the burgh.
Reproduced from the 1853, 6" Ordnance Survey map.

Chapter Three

Of Trains and Turnip Fields

EARLY DAYS ON THE HADDINGTON BRANCH

'The engine gave a sudden leap off the line, lurched heavily first to one side and then to the other, and came to rest in the adjoining turnip fields'

Railway Commissioners' Report on the Accident on the Haddington Branch,
14th October, 1850.

The initial passenger service on the Haddington branch consisted of five mixed trains running between the terminus and Longniddry, with three having onwards connections both for stations to Edinburgh and for stations to Berwick-upon-Tweed, the fourth having an Edinburgh connection only and the fifth, the 9.40 pm, connecting with a Berwick train only; the pattern of return journeys was similar. On Sundays two return journeys were made between Haddington and Longniddry each having connections both for Berwick and Edinburgh. No through carriages ran beyond Longniddry and all passengers had to change there. The first weekday train left Haddington at 8.35 am and the connection arrived in Edinburgh 65 minutes later, thereby providing a convenient commuter service for the handful of regular passengers who would contemplate travelling up to the capital on a daily basis. It is interesting to note that annual season tickets were being issued between Edinburgh and Haddington from the outset, albeit in very small numbers. A horse-drawn bus was provided to convey passengers between the station and the centre of the town, and this gave a regular connection to and from every weekday train.

Single fares from Haddington to Edinburgh initially ranged from 3s. 0d. (15p) first class to 1s. 6d. (7½p) for the third and fourth classes, the latter being equivalent to the 'Parliamentary' class which came about by virtue of Section 6 of the Regulation of Railways Act, 1844. This imposed a duty on all railways in Britain to operate at least one train daily carrying passengers at a fare of one penny per mile at an average speed in excess of 12 mph. Other special fares subsequently offered included those for excursionists, 'pic-nic parties', week-end travellers, scholars and residents; this latter facility was designed to induce persons to build substantial villas close to North British stations in return for heavily-discounted annual season tickets, the cost of which depended on the value of the villas.

From the outset the company resolved that Sunday trains would operate on both the main line and the Haddington branch for reasons of commercial efficacy. This was something of a bold decision in an age when the Scottish sabbath was not regarded as a day upon which decent Christians would travel – indeed at a very early stage several North British shareholders challenged the moral right of the Board to operate these Sunday services. They were backed up in this view when in October 1846 the Haddington Presbytery lodged objections to the continuation of the Sunday service on the branch line. This opposition was not, however, successful and the Haddington branch (unlike many subsequent North British lines such as the North Berwick branch) was to carry Sunday trains throughout its lengthy life.

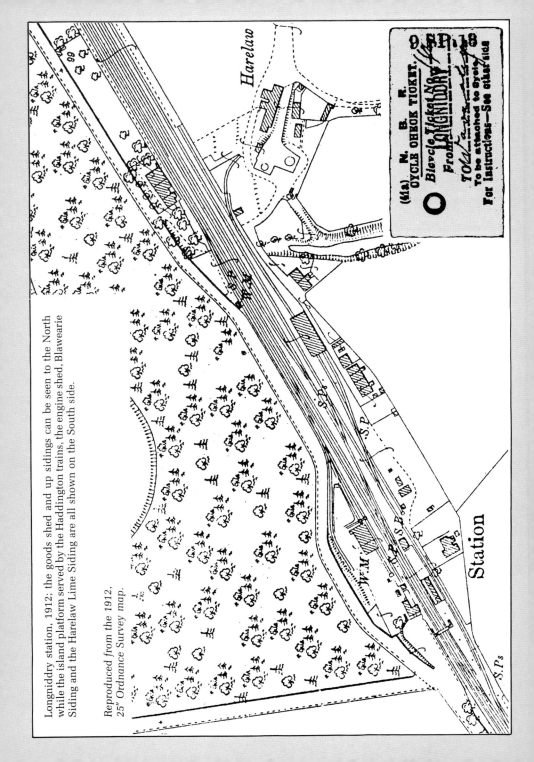

Longniddry station, 1912; the goods shed and up sidings can be seen to the North while the island platform served by the Haddington trains, the engine shed, Blawearie Siding and the Harelaw Lime Siding are all shown on the South side.

Reproduced from the 1912, 25" Ordnance Survey map.

Harelaw

Station

(41a) N. B. R.
CYCLE CHECK TICKET.
LONGNIDDRY
From
O
To be attached to cycle
For instructions—See other side

In the first decade of operation the branch trains were not, on any view, well patronised and it would appear that both the predictions of the inhabitants of Haddington and those of the North British Board with regard to the potential of the branch line were over-optmistic. Shortly after the opening F.P. Oakshott, an officer of the Stockton & Darlington Railway who was journeying in Scotland, remarked that only five passengers had alighted at Longniddry from the main line train in which he had been travelling in order to change. He concluded that the branch must have been built solely for the public good and not for commercial reasons. Indeed this view is supported by other evidence which also tended to suggest that passengers were not numerous. As late as 1856 an average of less than 10 persons per train were using the branch, making it debatable as to whether the line would ever have been built if the inhabitants of the county town had not put such pressure on the North British. This being so, it is extraordinary that the NBR Board were to inform their shareholders at the Half-Yearly General Meeting held on 27th August, 1846, barely two months after the branch opened, that they had provided double track on another branch line and that

> ... they have acted in the same way in regard to a portion of the Haddington branch but they find that from the extent of the traffic already on that branch and the certain prospect of its largely increasing that it will be very desirable to lay it with a double set of rails the whole way. They therefore recommend that it be done and with a view to a greater accommodation of the town of Haddington and that the probable ultimate extension of the branch southwards, they also recommend that it should be extended farther into the town.

The extension of the branch line into the town itself was, perhaps, not such a contentious matter and indeed had been the subject of a Memorial from the Magistrates of Haddington received by the Board in the previous month, but the doubling of the track was another thing altogether. Perhaps the real key to this decision was the threat which the moribund East Lothian & Tyne Valley Railway still presented. The spectre of an independent and unfriendly rival to the North British caused John Learmonth to later comment that when the Haddington branch was doubled 'we were under very pressing circumstances and the shareholders were not aware of the causes of this'.

The Haddington branch was operated by a single train set consisting of one third class, one second and one first class four-wheeled wooden coach and a van for luggage and parcels, although composite carriages were to appear within a few years. First class was reasonably comfortable, the carriages being of three compartments the shape of which emphasised the origin of their design as eminating from the contemporary stage coach. They were trimmed internally in drab cloth, had curtains at the windows and were lit with an oil pot-lamp while the second class compartments were similar but less luxurious in a plainer trim. The third class carriages were, however, a different matter having only a single central door on each side and four fixed windows and in a report in the *Scotsman* of 20th June, 1846 the following comments appeared:

> We must give the directors a hint about their third-class carriages. They will never do in summer. There is an entire want of circulation of air in them, and the closeness and heat rise to suffocation. To save time, we travelled from Dunbar to

Edinburgh in one of them, and never in our life experienced such a stew. No air can get in except by the upper half of the door, and each of the two doors was constantly blocked by two mannerless fellows, who got fresh air for themselves by shutting up their aperture through which alone others could get a mouthful. The windows, which are fast, should either be made to open, or taken out altogether, and their size is too small for a box which contains seats for 24 or, at a pitch, 32 persons.

As railway historian Hamilton Ellis somewhat caustically remarked, 'probably they were draughty in winter as well as fuggy in summer' but at least the third class passengers were provided with a roof over their heads although this was more a result of government legislation than because of the munificence of the NBR Board. The carriage vans were plain and were used to convey passengers' luggage, parcels and other miscellaneous traffic booked by passenger train and, from 1847 onwards, mail bound for Haddington and the outlying districts served from its post office.

The first locomotives to work the Haddington branch were the original North British 0–4–2 engines built by R. & W. Hawthorn of Newcastle for the opening of the system. These locomotives, 16 in all and appropriately carrying on their boilers the numbers 1 to 16 on a large brass plate sandwiched between the words 'NORTH' and 'BRITISH', were built to the specifications of the NBR Engineer, John Miller, and had coupled wheels 5 ft in diameter and trailing wheels of 3 ft 6 in., a large heavy dome on the centre of the boiler and a safety valve on the firebox casing. Both engine and tender were heavily double-framed and weighed, when in full working order, 28 tons. These locomotives, and another 10 roughly similar goods engines, were constructed for the sum of £1,650 each and this was regarded as being an extremely good price. Hawthorns, being the builders of locomotives for a number of English and Scottish lines were therefore able to enjoy economies of scale which were reflected in their ability to tender competitively; they were later to build locomotives for the Scottish market at their new works in Leith.

Apart from the passenger services, goods were also carried. Initially, this was by means of attaching goods wagons to passenger trains when and if required and thereby running mixed trains. Although loadings were not high* there was apparently sufficient traffic to justify the running of a special weekly train to serve the Friday grain market at Haddington. The grain market was of extreme importance to the town and indeed formed one of the largest and most important markets for that commodity in the whole of Britain. Held traditionally on a Friday, the market initially received a boost from the construction of the railway and in 1854 a new Corn Exchange was built in the centre of the town 'at a cost of upwards of £2,400 after designs by Mr Billings. This spacious edifice, said to be exceeded in size in Scotland only by the Corn Exchange in Edinburgh, measures within walls 128 ft in length and 50 in breadth.' The market opened with the sale of oats at 12 noon, barley at 12.20, beans at 12.45 and wheat at 1 pm and was supplemented on the first Friday in February by an outdoor hiring market for farm servants, by an autumn fair in October and by certain miscellaneous

---

*The 1856 returns for the branch stations are printed in Appendix 4 at the end of this book and show a weekly average of 352 tons of merchandise and 44 tons of minerals being handled at Haddington.

fairs. In order to serve this grain traffic a special mixed train was run on Fridays only from Edinburgh at 9.30 am, arriving at Haddington at 10.45. The return working from the county town at 7.30 pm arrived at the capital two hours later, while the 3.45 pm goods train from Haddington conveyed first and second class passengers to Edinburgh on Fridays only, thus breaking the long afternoon gap between trains.

Two sidings were provided between Longniddry and Haddington, namely Coatyburn and Laverocklaw. Both were constructed at the expense of the North British and served local farms, the former those at Setonhill and Coates while the latter served the farm of the same name (which was derived from the Scots words 'laverock' meaning skylark and 'law' meaning hill) and lime, grain, seed potatoes and oats was all handled here. Neither were staffed and Coatyburn was open continuously until 1964 while Laverocklaw, although designed as a 'public delivery siding', appears to have seen only limited use and was closed on several occasions.

Longniddry station was initially a small affair with a platform on each side of the main line and served by both through trains and the branch services. The main station building was a two storey rubble stone structure with overhanging eaves entered from the up platform at first floor level; other facilities consisted of goods sidings, a loading bank and a water tank. On the south side of the line was a single-storey stone house for the station master. Some hundred yards to the west of the station was situated the West Siding opened in June 1847 and also known as West Seton Mains or Longniddry Manure Siding (or, more prosaically by the inhabitants of the village, as 'the dung lye'). This was used, as its name suggests, for manure traffic which consisted of horse dung gathered from the streets of Edinburgh and the separate Burgh of Leith and then sent by rail to be used to enrich the fields of East Lothian. It was sometimes referred to as 'Police Manure' in reference to the fact that the proceeds of sale went towards the costs of running the Burgh Police functions then exercised as a form of local government. One tends to overlook nowadays this important (if anti-social) source of revenue to the railway, in the days before artificial fertilisers and the motor vehicle killed off the trade completely.

Haddington was a more impressive station. Here there were goods sidings and a shed, a turntable for locomotives, and a small two-storey stone building built at right-angles to the single passenger platform and consisting on the ground floor of a booking-office with the other offices situated on the first floor at rail level. In accordance with normal practice a bell was rung prior to the departure of each train so as to enable any stragglers who intended to catch the train to hurry along. Additional sidings were provided for the grain traffic and gradually improvements to them were authorised and alterations made in October 1850. Three years later a plan was approved to extend the goods shed and to provide a covered stairway to enable passengers to climb up from street level to the platforms without getting wet when it rained. In 1859 a tender for £70 was accepted from Andrew Dickson of Haddington for the latter work but, for some reason, it was never carried out.

Staff records for these early years are rather perfunctory but at Haddington the original station agent (a post equivalent on the North British to the more familiar 'station master') was C.H. Davidson. At Longniddry the first agent was George Tait, appointed in April 1846 at an annual salary of £80. Later on Edward Sladen was appointed to Longniddry at a reduced salary of £60 but his position was made precarious when, according to the NBR Minutes for 13th February, 1857:

> On a report from the managers as to various instances of excess monies collected at Longniddry being unaccounted for, it was resolved that George Neill, Clark, who received the excess be dismissed and that Mr Sladen, Agent, who appears to have been very remiss, have notice to leave.

At the following Board meeting, held two weeks later, it was recorded that Mr Sladen was not to be dismissed after all but that he was to be under a 'strict caution'. Other employees at Longniddry included a clerk, two porters, a van driver, a pointsman and a gatekeeper with a total annual wage bill of £264 8s. 0d. while at Haddington, to which George Tait had been promoted, there was a staff of eight including both a salaried and a waged clerk, four porters and a watchman employed at an annual cost of £305 16s. 0d. With regard to the latter station, the number of porters appears to have been insufficient for grain traffic and in 1857 a Memorial was received by the North British from farmers and others attending the markets at Dalkeith and Haddington as to the shortage of hands and the lack of sacks for hire at both stations, and these defects were attended to. Other employees who worked on the Haddington branch included two platelayers and a 'gauger' to look after the track, all of whom lived locally, and the train crews who were based at the locomotive sheds which the company had established at St Margarets on the then outskirts of Edinburgh.

Rather unusually, two early accounts of travel on the Haddington branch have survived. The first of these is contained in a letter which Jane Welsh sent to her husband Thomas Carlyle on 20th July, 1849.* She had been born in Haddington when it was still a flourishing staging-post on the Great North Road and was now returning to her native town for a first visit after 23 years. Her letter, after describing her trip from Morpeth ('a journey of only four hours') puts her

> . . . at Longniddry, where I had to wait some fifteen minutes for the cross-train to Haddington, 'there came to pass' a porter! who helped me with my things, and would not leave off helping me, quite teased me in fact with delicate attentions.

This was apparently as a result of confusion on the part of the porter who mistook her for a scion of a family with which his brother had once been in service, due to the fact that she had used as a luggage label the back of an old visiting card from a member of that family. She continues,

> A few minutes more and I was at the Haddington station, where I looked out timidly, then more boldly, as my senses took in the utter strangeness of the scene;

---

*Jane Welsh Carlyle (1801–1866) was an inveterate correspondant with the literati and famous persons of her times and her *Letters and Memorials*, from which the above account is taken, forms a fascinating contemporary record; her birthplace in Haddington is now a museum. Another famous native of the town was Samuel Smiles (1812–1904) whose works including *Self-Help, The Lives of the Engineers* and *George Stephenson* achieved worldwide fame.

THE GEORGE HOTEL

HADDINGTON.

THE PRINCIPAL HOTEL IN TOWN.
FULLY LICENSED.

Large Stock, Commercial, and Billiard Rooms.

Good Bedrooms and Bathroom.

LARGE BANQUET HALL.
DINNER, SUPPER, MARRIAGE, PICNIC, AND DANCE PARTIES PURVEYED FOR.

Posting in all its Branches. Stabling and Lock=up Coach=Houses.
HOTEL 'BUS AWAITS ALL TRAINS.

Dinner Daily from 12.30 to 3.30.
Charges Strictly Moderate.

The 'dusty little omnibus' which took passengers from the Haddington station to the George Hotel in the centre of the town.
Author's Collection

and luckily I had the 'cares of luggage' to keep down sentiment for the moment. No vehicle was in waiting but a dusty little omnibus, licensed to carry any number, it seemed; for, on remarking that there was no seat for me, I was told by all inside 'never heed! Come in! that makes no difference!' And so I trundled to the George Inn.

The same evening she took a nostalgic walk around the town and echoed the sentiments of many who had feared what would happen to Haddington once the road was supplanted by the railway. After remarking that the town looked quieter than when she had left it in 1826 she commented that:

> Where are all those living beings one used to meet? What could have come to the place to strike it so dead? I have been since answered – the railway had come to it, and ruined it. At any rates it must have taken a great deal to make the place so dull as that.

The other account is of an altogether more unusual journey, that of the 6.50 pm passenger train from Haddington to Longniddry on the evening of 14th October, 1850. The train, drawn by a Hawthorn 0−4−2 and consisting of a van, a third-class carriage and two composites, came to grief near to Laverocklaw; in the words of Lt Douglas Galton of the Royal Engineers in his Official Report to the Commissioners of Railways, dated 31st October, 1850:

> The train ... appears to have left Haddington at its right time and to have proceeded, according to the statement of the engine driver, at its ordinary speed. According, however, to the statement of some of the passengers, its speed was excessive. On commencing to descend the incline towards Long Niddry, the engine driver states he shut off his steam, and had proceeded for about half a mile, at a rate of perhaps thirty miles per hour (the line being perfectly straight there, and raised two or three feet above the adjacent fields), when the engine gave a sudden leap off the line, lurched heavily first to one side and then to the other, and came to rest in the adjoining turnip fields. The coupling between the tender and the carriage-truck went into the field without sustaining much damage. The couplings of the third-class carriage were broken at both ends, and it was thrown across the hedge and turned upside down, and the body knocked to pieces; the two composite carriages remained on their wheels, just off the rails. The guard was in the last carriage with his back to the engine. He states he felt the carriage going off the rails, and that it came to rest almost immediately. The passengers who were injured were in the third-class carriage and they, in describing the accident, state that there was first a shock or jar, then a sudden rush forward, and violent oscillation, and then the overturn. The engine and tender suffered no injury beyond the sand and feed-pipes being carried away, and were at work on the line when I arrived.

The cause of the accident was eventually thought to have been a broken rail, perhaps resulting from the fact that the track itself was too lightly constructed and that an additional sleeper required to be inserted underneath each 16-foot length in order to provide a firmer support. Ironically this strengthening work had been taking place at the time of the accident and much of the down line had already been dealt with. Lt Galton went on to remark,

> It may be observed, that it is possible that the empty carriage-truck, being next to the tender may, when the engine driver shut off steam on descending the incline,

have been overrun by the carriages in rear and, being lighter than they are, have been forced up off the rails, and so caused the marks on the rails and chairs; it may thus by some jerk have either forced the engine off the rails or caused it to break the rail. This, however, is only a surmise.

The North British had Lt Galton's remarks 'on the apparent necessity of strengthening of the permanent way' drawn to its attention and in a formal acknowledgement of the receipt of the report, the company told the Commissioners that 'the matter has already occupied their attention.' The sequel to this accident is recorded in the Board Minutes when claims were intimated by James Bell Ballinger and Robert Darling (the latter described as a 'grocer from Haddington') in respect of injuries sustained in the accident; on 4th November, 1850 the Board resolved 'to consider and delay any settlement'.

The early history of the Haddington branch comes to a close in 1856 when, on 26th September of that year, the North British Board ordered 'the lifting of one line of rails on the Haddington branch . . . to be proceeded with immediately' and it was subsequently reported that 'the branch has been worked as a single-line service since 7th October'. The work took the form of the lifting of the up line although a certain amount of realignment took place of the remaining track. Other economies were put into place, namely the discontinuance of the carting contract at Haddington and its replacement with the NBR's own van – this was all against a general background of financial stringency on the North British which included matters such as a clamp-down on station agents' use of coal and the replacement of steam trains by a horse-drawn service on the North Berwick line. At the North British Half-Yearly Meeting held on 15th March, 1857 the shareholders were informed that:

> One of the lines of rails on the Haddington branch has been lifted and one of the lines on the Duns branch is in the process of being lifted. Both are now worked as a single line, which answers the purpose well, at the same time making a reduction on the cost of maintenance.

Thus did the first decade of the Haddington branch end upon a somewhat austere note.

The earliest known ticket issued at Haddington – a yellow card Edmonson of c.1850.
S.R.O. Collection

Two views of Longniddry in 1974 showing the original up buildings with their incongrous extension and (*lower*) the curious boarded footbridge which existed prior to electrification and the realignment of the platforms.   *John Hume*

The outer face of the island platform at Longniddry, looking west on 16th May, 1956 – from here the Haddington branch trains started their twelve minute run.

RCAHMS, Rokeby Collection

Longniddry shed looking west towards Edinburgh – the Haddington branch is the line to the immediate right of the signal and the shed wall. *J.E. Hay*

A North British five compartment third of *c.*1870 in its final resting place at Longniddry in 1961. *J.E. Hay*

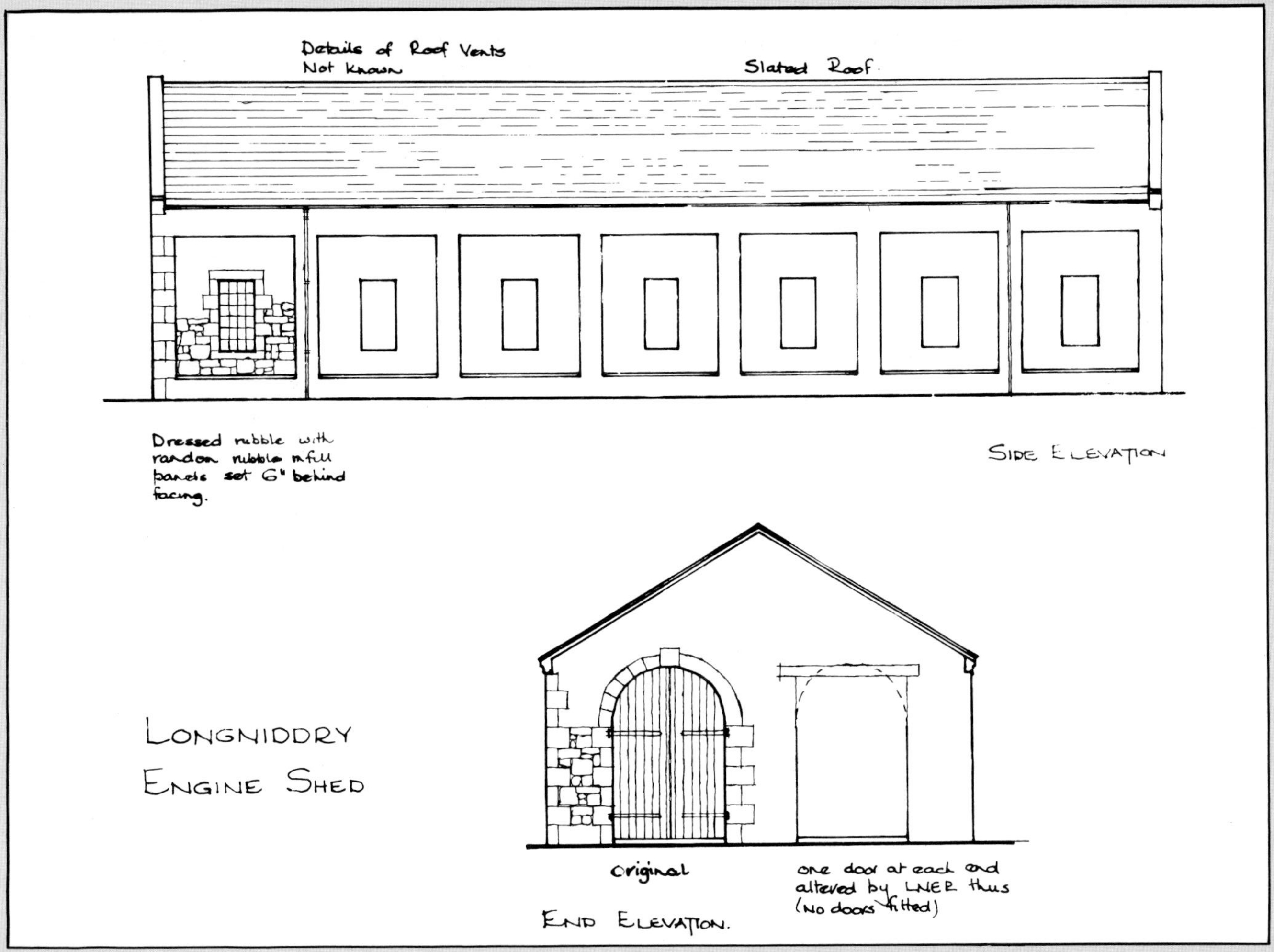

Details of Roof Vents
Not Known
Slated Roof.
Dressed rubble with random rubble infill panels set 6" behind facing.
SIDE ELEVATION
LONGNIDDRY
ENGINE SHED
original
one door at each end altered by LNER thus (no doors fitted)
END ELEVATION.

Drawing of Longniddry Locomotive shed — J.F. Hay

An unusual view of Longniddry showing signalling details, the goods shed and the up sidings; in the foreground are (*left*) Mr Traynor, the storeman at the goods depot and (*right*) W. McAdam, the manager of the small John Menzies shop at the station.

George Angus

The small engine shed at Longniddry on 9th July, 1952 – here the Haddington branch locomotive was stabled and in this view the branch itself runs directly in front of the shed while to the left are the Blawearie Sidings and the main line.   *A.G. Ellis*

Longniddry, seen as Reid 'B' class No. 9188 drifts through the station with a down freight while passengers from Haddington await an Edinburgh connection at the island platform, *c*.1930. *RCAHMS Rokeby Collection*

An NBR 'M' class 'Yorkie' arrives at Longniddry with the Haddington branch set, *c*.1928. *A.G. Ellis Collection*

Two postcard views of Longniddry, *c.*1920. The upper picture shows part of the Scottish War Veterans Garden City; the shop is still a familiar port of call to modern commuters and the station gates can be seen in the right background. The lower picture shows the accommodation level crossing at Blawearie to the east of the village and next to the Haddington branch – today InterCity 225's cross this lane which is little changed.   *George Angus Collection*

Haddington at the turn of the century – a down train arrives hauled by one of Matthew Holmes' 0–6–0 locomotives. *Lens of Sutton*

A Drummond 'terrier' – No. 20 *Haddington* in its later guise as plain No. 1348. *A.G. Ellis Collection*

Chapter Four
Off the Main Line

THE HADDINGTON BRANCH 1858–1922

'Haddington is off the main-line of the railway, and possesses no guide-books. Neither Cook nor Gaze has ever set eyes upon it, and seldom indeed an excursion train comes roaring and hurrahing up to its junction line from a distant city . . . The town wakens from its slumbers once a week, on market day . . .'

Robb's Guide to the Royal Burgh of Haddington, 1890

The latter half of the 19th century was a time of both expansion and contraction for the burgh of Haddington and its branch line and this period illustrated well the hopes and fears which the people of the town had expressed when they were first made aware that the railway would be coming to their town. Initially the grain market, in its new building, flourished and although its national predominance was eclipsed by that of Edinburgh, largely as a result of the later town being at the hub of an ever expanding Scottish railway network, it remained of great importance. Other markets still took place including the hiring fairs, produce market and livestock sales and a certain amount of industrial development had taken place. By 1890 the town could boast a couple of woollen mills as well as breweries, foundries, a coach works (situated close to the station), corn mills, agricultural implement makers and a tannery. All of this provided traffic for the railway and in the half century between 1850 and 1900 the tonnage of goods handled at Haddington increased by some 50 per cent – a rise which, while not spectacular, was nevertheless creditable given the extent of the severe agricultural depression which affected Scotland in the 1870s and 1880s. This hit areas like East Lothian and its county town particularly hard and the local population figures remained static or in decline for many years.

In 1881 there were two purely goods services daily, one of which ran 'as required' and the other on Fridays Only for the market but the majority of passenger trains, including the 12.50 pm Haddington to Longniddry, which also worked Coatyburn siding, conveyed goods wagons when necessary. The two sidings *en route* continued in use but at Laverocklaw the siding was lifted in July 1874 with the proviso 'that should the landowner so require on one month's notice, the Company shall be bound to replace it'. The notice was duly given and the siding was reopened to traffic as from 9th October, 1875. Few details of traffic are available, since no traffic returns for the sidings were kept, but it was noted that following upon the discovery of a rich vein of haematite of iron in the Garleton Hills in 1866 Coatyburn was used as the railhead therefore.

Passenger traffic on the Haddington branch showed a more encouraging rise with the number of people booked to the station more than doubling in the latter half of the century. By 1881 seven passenger trains were operating on the branch with an additional Friday market train, the 11.55 am which, along with the 5.55 pm 'residential' were both worked as through trains from Edinburgh. The standard journey time for passenger trains was 15

Three Victorian documents found behind the panelling at Haddington station during renovations in 1943.

East Lothian District Libraries

minutes, which gave a start-to-stop average speed over the branch of 31 mph – no mean feat considering the gradients! The fastest trains were booked to take 12 minutes, but the 15 minute timing continued for as long as mixed trains operated on the branch.

Throughout its history, the Haddington branch could never lay claim to have been operated by unusual or exotic motive power and, in consequence, seems to have attracted little in the way of comment, favourable or otherwise, either from enthusiasts or the operating authorities. In the 1860s and early 1870s the variety of locomotives working branch services would have included one or more of the rather trim Wheatley 'E' class 0–6–0 passenger saddle tanks. In 1877 a new locomotive appeared and had the distinction not only of being the sole engine to be built specifically for the branch but also the only engine to be named after the county town. No. 20, built at the NBR Cowlairs locomotive works in Glasgow, was one of 25 'R' class 0–6–0 tank engines designed by Dugald Drummond and closely based on the 'Terrier' (or 'Rooter') tank engines built for the London Brighton & South Coast Railway and designed by William Stroudley, to whom Drummond had acted as assistant. The North British 'Terriers' were larger and more powerful than their Brighton counterparts but they were nevertheless similar in appearance. Drummond followed Stroudley's practice by giving the engines local names and No. 20 (its low number resulting from the NBR policy of keeping a single set of numbers in which new locomotives were substituted for withdrawn ones) proudly carried the name 'HADDINGTON' on its side tanks.

For a number of years, this locomotive worked the branch and would have been a boon to passengers when it was operating its intended service. Difficulties arose however when it worked away from home or when other named engines worked the line. The confusion caused to passengers by inappropriately named engines (not uncommon when the NBR had been giving engines 'local' names) was partly responsible for names being abandoned so that, in time, No. 20 became anonymous. She was reboilered in Edwardian times and renumbered 1348 before being withdrawn in 1925, by which time she formed part of the LNER 'J82' class. Passenger stock in late Victorian times tended to be of the 4- and 6-wheeled variety and, in a process of cascading, some of the more venerable examples of NBR main-line stock ended their days on the Haddington branch. The riding qualities of this stock, however, tended to leave much to be desired and there are still people who can remember the jolting and swaying of these elderly vehicles as they traversed the Gifford and Macmerry branch lines as late as the 1920s!

Towards the end of the century goods trains on the branch were in the hands of the 0–6–0 tender goods engines designed by Matthew Holmes. These were of two classes, the 'D' class 17-inch light goods locomotives which were introduced into service from 1883 onwards and the 'C' class 18-inch heavier goods locomotives put into service from 1888 – the designations 'light' and 'heavy' perhaps over-emphasised the difference in weight for the 'C' class weighed 72 tons 4 cwt and had a tractive effort of 17,901 lb while the 'D' class weighed 69 tons 16 cwt and had a tractive effort of 15,967 lb. Both classes became stalwarts of the Haddington line and they survived not only to become LNER classes 'J33' and 'J36' but even lasted until virtually the end of steam on British Railways, the last 'J36' being withdrawn in June 1967. When, on Thursday 20th October, 1898, the North British carried out a system-wide survey of all goods workings on that day, it was recorded that the 'D' class locomotive No. 170 was in charge of the 6.25 am Longniddry to Haddington goods, a train which consisted of a brake van and one loaded wagon, while the 6.30 am Portobello to Haddington goods and the 10.15 am return working were in the hands of 'C' class No. 680 (one of the locomotives built for the NBR by Sharp, Stewart & Co), this time however with a much more respectable load.

The small two-road engine shed at Longniddry, situated on the down side adjacent to the branch, was classed as a sub-shed to St Margarets and it was here that the Haddington branch engine was kept together with any shunting engine provided on an 'as required' basis. For operating convenience the Gullane branch engine was, however, kept in a small shed at the terminus.

Passenger facilities at both the junction and the terminus left much to be desired and in the 1880s a new passenger station building was erected at Haddington, the original building being made over to the exclusive use of the station master, Walter Grafton, as a house. The new building was situated on the passenger platform to the east of the old building and was a most impressive affair described by the *Haddingtonshire Courier* as 'being commodious and convenient and built in a design of red and white brick which presents . . . an imposing frontage to the main thoroughfare at the west end of the town'; a large clock on the gable end became a familiar local landmark. In front of the new building, and connected to it by a long covered staircase was a wide semi-circular forecourt for road vehicles setting down or uplifting passengers and their luggage and this was backed by a retaining wall in a matching polychromatic brick style. The inhabitants of the town approved and in the words of a contemporary guidebook:

> The station is rather an extensive one for a town so small as Haddington. You see the inhabitants had been grumbling. They wished to have the railway extended through Haddington to Gifford, they wished the station nearer the town &c. &c. The Railway Company, to make peace, built this large station, yet some people are not satisfied.

The reference to a line to Gifford related to the abortive plans outlined in Chapter 6, while simultaneously with the provision of the new station building new cattle loading banks were built and the goods shed was doubled in size. Eventually the station was to boast a separate grain shed, weighbridge, goods office, store, stables and crane – quite an impressive array of facilities for what was, after all, a relatively insignificant location.

At the turn of the century the Haddington branch appeared to be in good shape. In the year 1900–1 a total of 72,000 passenger journeys were recorded there, in contrast to figures of 58,000 for North Berwick, 21,000 at Gullane and 35,000 at Longniddry. The majority of passengers were bound for Edinburgh and consisted of a small number of professional persons travelling first class and a much greater number of clerks, shopworkers and others travelling third while in the up direction there was a much smaller traffic

The impressive red-brick passenger terminus at Haddington from a photograph taken by W.F. Jackson, the General Manager of the North British Railway, in 1913.

Glasgow University Archives

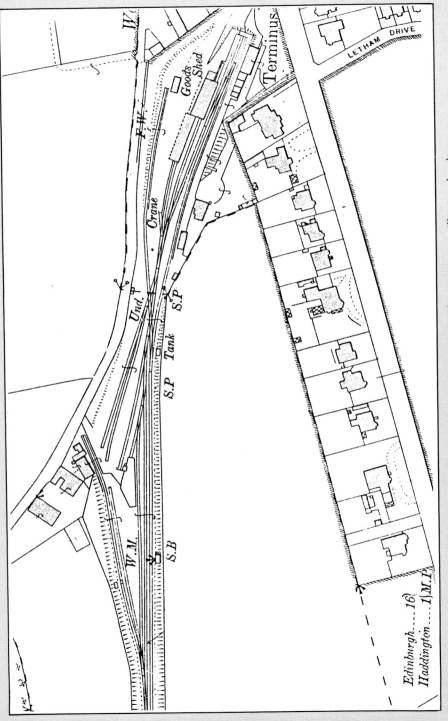

Haddington after the rebuilding of the station in the 1880s; new villas are already spreading westwards along the main Edinburgh road.
Reproduced from the 1895, 25" Ordnance Survey map

The entrance to Haddington station seen from the platform – the brick pillars with their handsome gas lights flank the main Edinburgh road while the villas in the background, ideal for the railway commuter, are still with us.

W.F. Jackson, *Glasgow University Archives*

which included persons attending the market, travelling representatives and some daytrippers as well as a number of schoolchildren attending the Knox Institute who came from Prestonpans, Aberlady, Gullane and Longniddry. The inhabitants of Haddington used the branch to visit the seaside resorts on the Forth and for shopping and pleasure trips to Edinburgh but even at this time there was a marked difference in loadings between the well filled business trains and the quiet off-peak services. There was now a service of eight up weekday services leaving Edinburgh at intervals between 7 am and 10.25 pm; remarkably the single fare was unchanged from that charged in 1846; return tickets were 5s. 0d. (25p) first class and 3s. 0d. (15p) third; second class had been abolished by this time.

Goods traffic was equally buoyant. In 1900 Haddington handled over 32,000 tons of merchandise, 6,000 tons of minerals and nearly 10,000 tons of coal, the latter being intended for domestic use, for the mills and other industrial premises and for the works of the Haddington Gas Light Company which, in 1911, carbonised 1,500 tons of coal and produced 15 million cubic feet of gas. These works were not directly rail-connected and so the coal had to be taken from the station by one-ton load horse-drawn carts operated by George Patterson, a local hauler. There were several coal merchants having offices at the station yard and these included John Samuel, the Ormiston Coal Company and James Beattie, the latter two having their own fleet of private owner wagons for this traffic. Livestock formed an important source of traffic and in 1900 10,857 cattle, 30,322 sheep and 242 pigs were handled. Many of these animals would have been destined for farms in the area but a considerable number would be unfortunate enough to be making their last journey to James Thomson, a butcher with premises at 10 High Street, who owned an abbatoir and private siding next to the station.

At Longniddry the accommodation was proving to be inadequate and, as far back as the 1860s, it was said that the only shelter provided for passengers was a shallow wooden shed which faced north-east and was known locally as 'the bathing machine'. The down platform was extended in length in July 1894, after a Mrs Sheriff, a third class passenger on the 4.20 pm train from Haddington, fell when alighting from her carriage which was unable to be drawn up next to the platform because of the latter's short length. New facilities were provided in 1898 when Longniddry became the station at which passengers changed for the Aberlady and Gullane branch, and an island platform was provided on the down side and the Haddington branch trains thereafter used its outer face. In 1903 the Clerk to the Dirleton Parish Council complained to the North British that passengers 'were frequently inconvenienced by the want of shelter and general comfort' at Longniddry station; this complaint was repeated by the Manager of the British Linen Bank in Haddington. Staff difficulties were also evident and in an intriguing entry in the Minutes of 3rd February, 1902 there is a reference to a telegraph clerkess stating 'the less she has to do with the Ticket Collector in question, the better'. In 1906 the inhabitants of Haddington sent a memorial to the North British with specific comments about the height and length of the platforms at Longniddry and complaining that 'the accommodation for passengers is deficient throughout the whole station and anything but in keeping with its importance as a junction. Three years later the Member of Parliament for West Fifeshire, who lived locally, complained to the Board of Trade 'as to the disgraceful condition of this station' and in 1910 Mr Hope of Luffness wrote to the NBR about Longniddry station in the following terms:

> On the North side there is no shelter of any sort on the platform and an open shed with the two ends closed and fitted with plain wooden benches would really be sufficient. The platform on the south side is nearly as bad, the only shelter there is a narrow platform between the waiting room and the trains, there is hardly room for two persons to pass one another.

The North British rejected these criticisms stating that,

> The waiting accommodation at Longniddry is fairly adequate on both platforms now that there are through carriages on all trains to and from Haddington . . . We do not think that the platforms are wide enough for any more buildings . . . The lengthening and heightening of the up platform has removed one of the most important grievances that used to be complained of.

Nevertheless a new brick building with a canopy was provided on the down island platform and on the up platform a single-storey extension to the original building was made; an unusual open truss footbridge with wooden matchboarded sides also made an appearance here at about this time. The goods sidings were also a cause for complaint. It was said that on market days at the turn of the century 'it was impossible to walk down the main street of the village because of the vast quantities of dung scattered on the road by the constant procession of livestock and cart houses heading for the station, which went on from dawn until late in the morning'. In 1900, 6,500 tons of goods were handled here as well as 7,000 tons of minerals, 18,000 tons of coal and nearly 17,000 heads of livestock and the siding accommodation was proving inadequate. In 1904 a Mr Shields of Dolphinstone (described in the NBR Minutes as 'an agriculturalist of great influence') complained that the Manure Siding was inadequate; on 20th December of that year the North British Chief Goods Manager reported that:

> The 100 manure wagons present at Longniddry on 10th December, 1904 was an unusually large number . . . if [the siding] is extended as pressed by Mr Shields the sure tendency will be to keep the traffic mentioned upon the rail otherwise carting by road necessarily follows. Mr Shields is an agriculturalist of considerable authority in connection with the Highland Society and apart from the working of the traffic concerned, it may be a good policy to meet his wishes as far as possible.

The 'Dung Lye' was duly extended although the District Goods Manager commented that 'the estimated cost (£192) is out of proportion to the little extra dislodging accommodation to be provided'.

Passenger services continued to improve and after the introduction of through trains to Edinburgh some of the business trains became overcrowded. In 1909 a deputation from Haddington Town Council headed by William Davie, an ironmonger and seed-potato grower who had formerly been a Dean of Guild of the Burgh, made a formal complaint about this to the North British and W.F. Jackson, the NBR General Manager, replied that,

> While I find the carriage accommodation on the 4.02 pm train from Edinburgh is

sufficient for the traffic, there is no doubt that the 5.15 pm is somewhat limited. I have, therefore, given instructions that an additional third-class carriage is to be attached and continue to run until further notice. The staff are quite alive to the necessity for excluding Portobello passengers and every effort will continue to be made to prevent them from gaining access to the Haddington carriages.

In late Edwardian times larger passenger tank engines, those of the Reid 'M' class 0−4−4s (LNER class 'G9') made a brief appearance on branch services. These seem to have been the locomotives which operated the very reduced branch service during the six-week miners' strike of March 1912, by which time the first of the 'Yorkies' was appearing on the branch. These locomotives, which derived their nickname from the fact that, unusually for the North British, they had been built to tender by the Yorkshire Engine Company of Sheffield, were also designated as 'M' class and were the first 4−4−2 tanks designed for the NBR by Reid. They were joined on the branch in 1916 by the similar Reid 'L' class of superheated 4−4−2T locomotives built under contract by the North British Locomotive Co. of Glasgow at their Atlas Works; both classes (designated by the LNER respectively as the 'C15' and 'C16' classes) began to work regularly to Haddington and were destined to enjoy a long period of operation on the line.

On the evening of Monday 3rd November, 1914 the Haddington territorials, after being addressed by the statesman and former prime minister A.J. Balfour who lived nearby at Whittingehame, marched to Haddington station and were entrained there in two detachments, there being two separate troop trains which departed within an hour and a half of each other. Four years later a rather lesser number of the territorials were to return to their home town, Haddington having lost 110 of its young men in the service of their King and country. The war was felt in other ways − a general staff shortage led to the wider employment of women on duties which previously they would not have undertaken, and price inflation and rising wage levels were to cause some concern to the Executive appointed by the government which had assumed control, for the duration, of the North British in common with all other railways in the country. By 1917 widespread economies and a general raising of fares was in operation and although the Haddington branch service was hardly affected, the timetable ominously warned that:

In consequence of the European War, the Train Coach and Steamer services shown in this timetable may be altered or curtailed without notice, and the Companies will not be responsible for any loss, injury and damage, or delay through any failures to afford their ordinary services or any modified services.

Towards the end of the War, life began to revert to normality and the North British made plans for its peacetime prosperity, notwithstanding the rumours that the government was to nationalise or regroup the railways of Britain. By 1921 it was clear that the North British was to be grouped into an Eastern amalgam of companies; although these were to remain in private ownership the NBR began to lobby hard for its independence.

Proposals to make Longniddry a principal stopping place for East Coast main line services, first put forward in 1915, were not followed through, but Longniddry did, in fact, start to assume a new significance when Lord

Return of 1/8 Royal Scots, Haddington 730/4/19/)

Photo by C. Bruce Haddington.

The Royal Scots arrive home to a 'land fit for heroes' – two scenes at Haddington station, 30th April, 1919. *George Angus Collection*

Wemyss first began to feu his land next to the village for private housing development, both public and private, and for the ambitious and charitable 'Scottish Veterans' Garden City Scheme' – an estate of houses for disabled sailors and soldiers; thereby began the metamorphosis of the 'decayed place' into a railway commuter suburb.

On 16th October, 1921 a petition was received from 37 Haddington season-ticket holders complaining about the lack of a train with a Haddington connection from Edinburgh between 5.19 and 8.50 pm. The NBR responded by putting on an extra train at 6.10 pm. In a letter of thanks from Mr Scroggie, one of the petitioners, he added

> Whilst on the subject, I should like to take the opportunity of drawing your attention to the deplorable state of the carriages on the Haddington line. They are of a very old-fashioned type, mostly very dirty, not heated and on occasions I have even seen them not rain-proof. As may be imagined, therefore, during the winter evenings, travelling is very uncomfortable and looking to the fine up-to-date carriages supplied on the Gullane and North Berwick lines, I trust that you will see your way to do something in this respect for Haddington passengers.

Undoubtedly the general standard of North British maintenance and cleanliness of carriages had slipped badly during the war years but the company remitted the matter to their Chief Mechanical Engineer at Cowlairs, to investigate and he duly reported that:

> The train on the above branch is composed of four-wheeled stock, which is not heater fitted. I have had it thoroughly examined, and find the roofs and paintwork in good condition and no signs of leaking. The upholstery in some of the third-class compartments is somewhat worn, but still quite serviceable. Of course, as you are aware, it has been decided that the trimmings of four-wheeled stock should only be renewed when absolutely necessary. With regard to cleanliness, there is little cause for complaint. I quite agree, however, that this train set does not compare favourably to the up-to-date stock on the Gullane and North Berwick services. I understand that this train is to be sent to Edinburgh every fortnight for gassing [i.e. filling up with gas-oil the tanks which fed the gas lighting in each compartment] and I would suggest that it might be sent to Craigentinny Cleaning Sheds thereafter, when something might be done to freshen up the upholstery with a vacuum cleaner. Of course the Operating Superintendent would require to provide a spare train set to allow of this to be done.

Subsequently it was decided that vacuum cleaning would not freshen up the upholstery because of its generally worn and run-down condition but in a less than forthright reply Mr Scroggie was informed that 'arrangements have been made as will, I think, effect an improvement.' It was, perhaps, unfortunate that the North British should have been so complacent in this matter for already the chill winds of competition were being experienced as passengers were discovering the delights of the Scottish Motor Company's new rival bus service from Haddington to Edinburgh, and the slow haemorrhage which would eventually lead to the demise of the passenger service was about to begin. But it was early days yet and the Haddington branch could still look forward to a future as the end of the pre-grouping era approached.

Chapter Five
Coal, Carberry and Cousland

THE ORMISTON, DALKEITH AND MACMERRY LINES 1838–1922

'The running of the passenger trains on the Macmerry branch will be a great accommodation to the district, and we have no doubt that the Company will find the result not unprofitable to themselves.'

Haddingtonshire Courier, 4th May, 1872

The failure of the East Lothian and Tyne Valley proposals created only a brief hiatus in the development of the East and Mid Lothian coalfield and within a decade the North British found itself once again involved in a scheme to provide improved railway facilities to the area. This time the plans for this new set of lines relied not only on Robert Stevenson's earlier proposals but also upon a number of existing horse tramways which had been built to serve the pits and mines already in production.

The most extensive of these tramways was the Buccleuch Tramway, a 4 ft 6 in. gauge horse-worked line which was begun in 1838 and opened in 1840. In the words of *The New Statistical Account:*

> The Dalkeith Branch [of the E & DR], which is the exclusive property of His Grace the Duke of Buccleuch,* and was intended solely for the benefit of that town, was opened in the end of 1838. However desirable, it seemed, for some time, impracticable to extend this branch to His Grace's coalfields, in the neighbourhood of Cowden. But these obstacles were soon surmounted; the intervening properties were purchased, and a magnificent viaduct has been erected at great expense over the vale of the South Esk. This bridge consists of six arches; the two arches at the extremities of the bridge are each of 110 feet span; and the four intervening arches are each of 120 feet span. The arches are built of the best Dantzick timber, and rest upon stone piers of hewn ashlar. The height, from the ordinary water-mark to the road-way, is 78 feet; the whole length is 830 feet; and the entire width of roadway between the railings is 14 feet. The whole structure is of the most tasteful architecture, and imparts a highly picturesque character to the surrounding scenery.

The tramway began at Dalkeith station, the terminus of the short branch to the town from the E & D line (at the site now occupied by Dalkeith bus depot) and ran north-eastwards literally through the streets of what, at that time, was one of the most important market towns in the south of Scotland. After threading between the houses it reached Elmfield, where a siding was constructed to serve the ironworks of William Mushet. The tramway then continued past market gardens before reaching the South Esk River, a major obstacle which was bridged by a large and impressive structure referred to above and known as the Victoria Viaduct, named in honour of the new Queen who stayed at the Duke's residence, Dalkeith Palace, during her visit to Scotland in 1842. The architects responsible for the design of the Victoria viaduct were J. & B. Green and the builders were Messrs Lawrie & Mitchell; the Clerk of Works in charge of the project was W. Ker.

Having crossed the viaduct the Buccleuch Tramway reached Thorneybank, a farm and works belonging to the Duke, where there was a siding situated close to the junction at a point which the Cowden branch of the

---

*Walter Francis Montague Scott Douglas, Fifth Duke of Buccleuch, (1806–1884). 'The magnificent works which he has undertaken, will transmit his name to posterity, as one of the most enterprising and public-spirited noblemen of the age.' – *New Statistical Account*

The original Victoria Viaduct, which carried the Buccleuch Tramway over the South Esk on a series of slender Danzig timber arches – a contemporary print showing Midlothian, the lost Elysium!

RCAHMS

Tramway diverged from the Smeaton line. The Cowden branch ran for half a mile eastwards to serve the extensive coal pits at the place which were opened in 1837. 'Dwelling houses for the colliers of a very superior description have recently been erected at Whitehill and Thorneybank, and impart an air of elegance and comfort to the neighbourhood.' The Smeaton branch swung abruptly northwards from Thorneybank for a distance of one mile to Smeaton Head where the Dalkeith Colliery was served by sidings. There were various pits on sites in this vicinity known under this title, which was somewhat confusing given the fact that they were some distance from the town of Dalkeith, and in addition there was the Smeaton Colliery owned by the Marquis of Lothian. The terminus of the tramway was at the Smeaton Brick and Tile Works at Newfarm which were opened by the Duke in 1837 and where, according to *The New Statistical Account:* 'it yields an ample supply of bricks and tiles, which are formed with astonishing, rapidity by a very ingenious machine, contrived by the present Marquis of Tweeddale'.

The Buccleuch Tramway seems to have enjoyed a relatively long and uneventful life remaining independent of the Edinburgh & Dalkeith and its pattern of operation did not alter when the latter concern, including the Duke's branch line to Dalkeith, was acquired by the North British for £113,000 in 1845 and subsequently converted into a standard-gauge conventional steam-hauled line. Part of the tramway was subsequently relaid so as to permit steam locomotives to use it but this reconstruction did not apparently involve the strengthening of the Victoria viaduct. It was soon rumoured locally that the wooden arches of the bridge had deteriorated to the extent that they had become unsafe.

By the middle of the century, interest began to be expressed locally in the idea of building a conventional line or lines to serve the area lying between Dalkeith and Haddington. The attractions of such a proposal were similar to those which had caused the earlier schemes, namely the traffic which could be generated by coal, lime and agricultural produce. At first the North British showed comparatively little interest in the matter, being apparently more concerned at that time in pursuing the enduring rivalry with its neighbour the Caledonian Railway. However, coal consumption was rising steadily as the emergent industries of central Scotland, the expanding towns and the increasing number of railway locomotives in the country were all hungry for this very basic necessity which provided the only real source of power and fuel. By the end of the decade the local farmers and the owners of land under which coal deposits lay were all solidly behind the idea of a railway being built; in addition there was a great deal of agitation amongst the inhabitants of Dalkeith for a new line as they felt, with some justification, that their town had been unfairly be-passed by the North British and that they deserved a better deal.

The North British now put forward more concrete proposals for the area and sought support for a series of local lines, namely a 'main' line to run southwards from the original Edinburgh to Berwick line near to Musselburgh and to serve Dalkeith, and a further line to branch off from that line at Smeaton and to run eastwards to Ormiston and the parish of Gladsmuir.

Agreements were reached with the landowners over whose lands it was hoped that the lines would pass and the company began negotiations with the Duke of Buccleuch in his capacity as the principal proprietor in the locality. Meetings were now held to gauge local opinion and in Dalkeith the ebullient Chairman of the North British, Richard Hodgson MP, outlined the proposals to a large audience, explaining that the company were 'anxious to secure the countenance and aid of the mercantile and manufacturing inhabitants of the town'. He appears to have been successful in this aim as the folk of Dalkeith in general welcomed the proposals with pledges of support coming from the Provost, Magistrates and other local worthies such as Alexander Mitchell and William Mushet the ironfounder. Hodgson stressed that the line would 'confer upon the town the advantages of a more direct connection with the south and west'; indeed this seems to have been a real attraction to the North British itself as it intended to run through trains between Edinburgh, Leith and Portobello in the north and Peebles and Hawick in the south as well as providing an alternative route for traffic on the outer suburban lines to Penicuik and the villages of the Esk Valley.

Although local support for the North British scheme was virtually unanimous, and Messrs Mitchell and Mushet actually went to the length of travelling down to London so that they could address the members of the Parliamentary Select Committee on Railway Bills in person, there arose a determined and virulent opposition to the proposals from Andrew and John Wauchope, the proprietors respectively of the estates of Niddrie Marischal and Edmondstone. This not wholly unexpected turn of events arose from a quirk of recent history in that the Wauchope estates had been crossed by the original main line of the Edinburgh & Dalkeith. When the North British had tried to acquire the E&D in order to reconstruct it as a conventional steam railway, the Wauchopes managed to extract from the North British annual wayleaves and tonnage charges for all traffic passing over the line crossing their estates as the *quid pro quo* for abandoning their opposition to the Bill needed for this purpose. Quite naturally the Wauchopes now regarded the new proposed lines with dismay, since, given their promotion as a through route between the Berwick and Hawick lines, they undoubtedly had the potential to deprive the Wauchopes of their revenue from the North British. A fierce battle ensued and the North British, being unwilling to give in to what it saw as in effect little more than blackmail, almost got to the stage of renouncing the whole scheme and probably would have done so had it not already been so committed to the Duke of Buccleuch. In the event it was the Wauchopes who once again triumphed and the North British had to climb down by agreeing to pay the Wauchopes the then not inconsiderable annual sum of £1,000 in all time coming 'in full of all claims of wayleave and tonnage duties.'

On 3rd June, 1862 the North British Railway (Branches) Act finally received the Royal Assent and in section 2 thereof the construction of the following lines was provided for:

A Railway (hereinafter called the *Monktonhall* Branch) commencing by a junction with the *North British* Railway in the Parish of *Inveresk* in the County of

ANNO VICESIMO QUINTO

VICTORIÆ REGINÆ.

◆∗∗∗

Cap. xlix.

An Act to authorize the *North British* Railway Company to make certain Railways from their Main Line in the Parish of *Inveresk* to the Farm Steading of *Smeaton,* and thence to near *Macmerry* and to their *Hawick* Line at *Hardengreen ;* and for other Purposes.

[3d *June* 1862.]

WHEREAS by " The *North British* Railway Consolidation Act, 1858," the Acts relating to the *North British* Railway Company were consolidated and amended, and by the Local Acts Twenty-second and Twenty-third of *Victoria,* Chapters Fourteen and Twenty-four, Twenty-third and Twenty-fourth of *Victoria,* Chapters One hundred and forty, One hundred and fifty-nine, and One hundred and ninety-five, and Twenty-fourth and Twenty-fifth of *Victoria,* Chapters One hundred and two and One hundred and fourteen, further Powers were conferred upon the *North British* Railway Company : And whereas a Railway in the Parish of *Inveresk* from the *North British* Railway to the Farm Steading of *Smeaton,* and Two Railways therefrom, One to near *Macmerry* in the Parish of *Gladsmuir* in the County of *Haddington,* and the other to the *Hawick* Line of the *North British* Railway at *Hardengreen* in the Parish of *Dalkeith* in the County of *Haddington,*

21 & 22 Vict. c. cix.

[*Local.*] 7 O

Edinburgh, and terminating at or near the Farm Steading of *Smeaton* in the same Parish;

   A Railway (hereinafter call the *Ormiston* Branch) from the *Monktonhall* Branch at or near the Farm Steading of *Smeaton* to a point in the Parish of *Pencaitland* in the County of *Haddington*, near *Macmerry* in the Parish of *Gladsmuir* in the same County;

   A Railway (hereinafter call the *Dalkeith* Branch) from the *Monktonhall* Branch at or near the Farm Steading of *Smeaton* to the *Hawick* Branch of the *North British* Railway at or near the point of junction between the said *Hawick* Branch and the *Peebles* Railway at *Hardengreen* in the Parish of *Dalkeith* in the County of *Edinburgh*.

The Monktonhall branch left the Edinburgh to Berwick line at the point where it crossed the River Esk a mile to the south of Musselburgh and ran for one mile southwards to Smeaton. Here, remote from any real settlement other than the farm and Steading mentioned in the Act, was situated Smeaton Junction; the Ormiston branch ran from here eastwards to Crossgatehall (a row of houses so named because four roads met there). From here the line led through the Cousland gap before passing north of the village of that name and, following the course of the Bellyford Burn, reached Ormiston where it turned to the north and crossed the Tranent to Pencaitland road (B6355) where a station was later to be built close to the Jacobean mansion of Winton. The line continued to the terminus at Macmerry, a small and unimportant mining village on the main London road, having a population, when the railway reached it, of only 330.

   The Dalkeith branch was three miles long and ran southwards from Smeaton Junction to Thorneybank where it turned west, crossing the South Esk, and then south-west passing by the eastern outskirts of Dalkeith and, close to Strawberrybank, entering a cutting which terminated at Hardengreen, just to the north of the junction of the Hawick and Peebles lines.

   In the case of both the Ormiston and Dalkeith branches the trackbeds of former tramways were used for at least part of their lengths. Between Winton and Macmerry the line was laid alongside a horse tramway which had been constructed in about 1850 to link the pits in the Winton and Penston areas with a shipment point on the coast near to Cantyhall, as well as carrying pig-iron from the furnaces of the Christie Brothers at Macmerry, the latter giving the village the nickname of 'The Blast'. This tramway seems to have survived the opening of the North British line as there are references in the Board of Trade reports to the NBR line having tramway crossings although there are no references to it after 1872, by which time it had presumably been abandoned.

   At Dalkeith the position was more complicated and Section 5 of the 1862 Act provided that:

   The Company may, by Agreement with His Grace the Duke of Buccleuch, but not otherwise, purchase the private Tramway belonging to the said Duke leading from *Dalkeith* to *Smeaton* Brick and Tile Works, or Parts thereof, and appropriate the site of All or Parts thereof to the Purposes of the Undertaking; and in constructing the *Dalkeith* Branch thereof . . . through or over any Property of the said Duke, it shall not be lawful for the Company, except with the Consent in Writing of the said

Duke first had and obtained, to deviate from the central line of the Railway laid down upon the deposited plans, nor to construct the said *Dalkeith* Branch without acquiring the said Private Tramways, unless with the Consent in Writing of the said Duke as aforesaid.

In the event, the route of the Buccleuch Tramway was followed between the Dalkeith Colliery at Smeaton and the South Esk but the remaining parts of the tramway, including the part that ran through the streets of Dalkeith, were abandoned.

A long delay now ensued and it was only at the beginning of 1865 that the North British were actually in a position to seek tenders for the construction of the lines. In June 1865 the NBR Engineer, Charles Japp, reported to the Board that 'matters concerning the tenders were progressing satisfactorily' and, on 14th July, 1865, the offers by the North Shields firm of contractors Rosser & Smith in the sum of £17,256 2s. 3d. for the Ormiston contract and £39,453 15s. 1d. for the Dalkeith contract were accepted – the discrepancy in prices being accounted for by the fact that the latter contract included the reconstruction of what was referred to in the Minutes as 'the large viaduct'. The cost of land acquisition was said to be £647 4s. 0d. – a low sum but perhaps not remarkably so given the largely rural nature of the country through which the lines would pass.

On 27th July, 1865 a deputation was received from the residents of Dalkeith who requested that the North British reconsider their decision to build the Dalkeith branch only as a single line, since 'this could not efficiently serve the purpose of the Company or accommodate the public.' The North British replied that all of the bridges and the structures, with the exception of the Victoria viaduct, were being constructed to double line clearances but that the line was only be laid as a single one so as to expedite its completion. A pledge was given that when the suburban lines to Lasswade and the Esk valley were opened then the increased traffic, which would naturally be generated, would lead to a doubling of the Dalkeith branch.

The construction of the branch lines caused little difficulty and the only major feat of engineering required was the reconstruction of the Victoria bridge. The original arches were now removed and the piers were altered – the disparity of colouring between the old and new masonry was apparently so marked that it could be seen right up until the piers were finally demolished. The original abutments were retained but a new superstructure of twin wrought iron main girders of the double system laithie type 11 ft wide and braced 8 ft apart was manufactured and installed by the contractors. A new deck of 7 inch thick timber planking was provided. When the bridge was completed there were no weight restrictions placed upon it and it was deemed to be suitable for all types of traffic.

The section between Monktonhall Junction and Thorneybank was brought into use on Sunday 23rd December, 1866 and a circular in the following terms was issued to staff:

OPENING OF MONKTONHALL BRANCH, Between Monktonhall Junction and Thorneybank for Goods and Mineral Traffic.

This branch, consisting of a single line of rails of about 3 miles in length, is now open for goods and mineral traffic; As, however, the Contractor's men and engines are still working over a portion of the line now used for traffic, it will be necessary for all parties to adhere to the following instructions:

1. Only one engine, and that of the NB Company's Engine, employed in the working of the goods and mineral trains, will be allowed to run over that part of the Monktonhall branch or extending from Monktonhall Junction to the safety switch near Carberry Colliery siding.

2. This safety switch will be under the charge of one of the men employed at Inveresk station who will (except at the moment of allowing the goods and mineral trains to pass) keep it properly set and locked, so as to throw any run-away wagons off the line.

3. It is now intended that this man shall remain longer at the Safety Switch than during the times the goods and mineral trains are daily employed working the Monktonhall Branch and he will employ the rest of his time at Inveresk station taking care that it is properly set and locked, as required by Clause 2.

4. Between the Safety Switch hereinbefore referred to and Thorneybank, the Goods and Mineral Trains will be worked by timetable attached and the contractors are required to have their Engines, Horses, Wagons &c entirely clear of that part of the line at least 15 minutes before the Goods and Mineral Train is due at the Safety Switch, when on its way to Thorneybank; and thereafter nothing whatever must be allowed to enter upon or in any way obstruct the line between Safety Switch and Thorneybank until the goods and Mineral Trains have done their work and arrived back at the Safety Switch from Thorneybank.

5. The contractors will be held responsible for the points on that part of the line between Safety Switch and Thorneybank being left shut and properly set for Goods and Mineral Traffic to pass safely over the line.

THOMAS K. ROWBOTHAM
General Manager

The Timetable adopted is as follows:

PORTOBELLO .... dep 6.00		DALKEITH COLLIERY ...... dep 9.30
Monktonhall Junction .... dep 8.20		Safety Switch .... arr 9.45
Safety Switch .... arr 8.25		Monktonhall Junction 9.50
DALKEITH COLLIERY .... arr 8.45		PORTOBELLO .... arr 10.53

It is MOST IMPORTANT that these TRAINS be worked PUNCTUALLY!

On 1st May, 1867 the section between Smeaton Junction and Ormiston was brought into full use for goods and mineral traffic and this was followed on 19th March, 1868 by the opening of the line between Ormiston and Macmerry. In the case of Ormiston station the North British were compelled to rename an existing station on the Jedburgh branch from 'Old Ormiston' to 'Kirkbank' in order to avoid confusion and this change took effect on 20th May, 1868. Attention was now turned towards completing the Victoria viaduct works and at 11.30 am on Sunday 31st July, 1870 the line between Thorneybank and Hardengreen Junction was finally opened to traffic.

As yet the service consisted solely of goods trains serving the public goods depots at Smeaton, Ormiston and Macmerry, the colleries at Smeaton, Belly-ford, Carberry and Penston, the lime quarry at Cousland, the Elmfield and Gladsmuir iron works and a private siding near to Winton. Later two additional public sidings were provided, namely at Winton (brought into use in December 1869) and at Thorneybank.* No passenger services were provided and no attempt was being made to run any through trains via Smeaton and Hardengreen, despite the considerable expenditure on the Victoria viaduct and the assurances which had been given to the people of Dalkeith. As events transpired, the line south of Smeaton never did carry any regular passenger trains or through services and the reason for this does not, in retrospect, seem clear. Perhaps the North British had been over optimistic in their estimates of the traffic potential of the line and it never saw the level of service originally envisaged. At the end it was very definitely something of a white elephant. Writing many years later, Alexander Mitchell commented of this period that 'the idea of conveying through traffic along the line was given up, and with that all that had rendered the undertaking interesting to the people of Dalkeith ceased to exist.'

Although the North British had originally intended that the line east of Smeaton should carry passengers, no positive steps were taken for a couple of years and then the following notice appeared in the *Haddingtonshire Courier* of 4th May, 1872:

PASSENGER TRAINS TO EDINBURGH. On Wednesday last (1st May) the directors of the North British Railway opened their branch line for passenger traffic between Edinburgh and Macmerry. The train, as might have been expected, was up to time at Ormiston, but was behind time a little in returning. The running of the trains will be a great accommodation to the district, and we have no doubt the Company will find the result not unprofitable to themselves.

The passenger service over the Macmerry branch was never lavish, consisting of a basic three trains each way which covered the distance of 14 miles from Edinburgh in between 40 and 45 minutes and serving *en route* the stations at Winton, Ormiston and Smeaton and, on the main line, New Hailes, Joppa and Portobello. There was no Sunday service and towards the end of the century the mid-day train became Saturdays Only, leaving only the weekday departures from Macmerry at 8.10 am and 6.15 pm. Fares for the journey to Edinburgh were 1s. 2d. (6p) for a third class single and 2s. 4d. (12p) for first class. Facilities for passengers were spartan – at Smeaton an island platform with a waiting room was provided although passenger trains normally only used the eastern face of the platform. At Ormiston a small brick building containing a booking office and waiting area was available. Winton consisted of a rudimentary wooden building next to the level crossing there (the crossing itself having been replaced to all intents and purposes by the reconstruction of the Pencaitland to Tranent road alongside it) and at Macmerry (Gladsmuir), as it was officially known, a short platform with a brick waiting room was built. Clearly the North British did not expect any great amount of passenger traffic from the branch, although Ormiston did generate some local and commuter traffic and Winton, despite its seemingly isolated situation with only the small village of New Winton and the estate of Winton House in the vicinity, was the railhead for the villages of Pencaitland and Humbie while also being a popular destination for picnickers and ramblers.

---

*For a fuller treatment of goods yards and public and private sidings, and a map showing their location, see Chapter 11.

The usual motive power on the Macmerry branch for many years was No. 230, one of the Wheatley 'E' class (LNER 'J81') 0−6−0 saddle tanks, built in 1871 and allocated to St Margarets for use on the branch. These small engines were admirably suited to lines where axle loadings were not too great and No. 230 was a regular performer for many years; a sister locomotive, No. 39, was allocated to the North Berwick branch.

In contrast to the modest amount of passenger traffic, goods and mineral receipts were more than satisfactory. A number of public and private sidings carried both inward and outward agricultural traffic and in season a heavy traffic in soft fruits including produce from the famed strawberry fields of Ormiston was carried. The lime quarry at Cousland provided further revenue as did the numerous colleries which, from the profits point of view, were undoubtedly the jewel in the crown. In the last quarter of the 19th century the output of the Lothian coalfields more than doubled and, as new and bigger colleries were opened such as the Fleets pit and the Ormiston Coal Company owned mines, coal both for domestic destinations and for foreign destinations via Leith docks became the staple traffic of the Ormiston and Macmerry line.

In the 1890s alterations to signalling and stations had to be carried out in order to comply with new Board of Trade requirements and on 28th November, 1894 Major Marindin reported on these alterations, commenting that he had inspected additional waiting room accommodation for ladies at Smeaton, Winton and Macmerry stations, and that he was satisfied with what he had found there.

Curiously, however, the Smeaton to Hardengreen line did not share in the prosperity of the Macmerry line and by the 1880s a slow terminal decline had begun. By the end of the century only one regular daily pick-up goods train used the line; in 1896 the intermediate signal box at Thorneybank was closed and the whole line worked as one section. After the closure of Mushet's ironworks and the virtual cessation of originating traffic from Thorneybank the only remaining traffic was provided by the Dalkeith gas works and by the North British Railway's own Telegraph Pole Depot which it established close to the junction at Hardengreen. Occasional special excursion trains used the line but there were never any regular scheduled passenger services, and, after July 1913, no booked good services either.

The Lothian coalfield production continued to expand at a phenomenal rate and, in common with the rest of Britain, coal production peaked in the years immediately prior to World War I. By 1910 traffic was so heavy, and the profits to be gained by transporting coal so great, that serious proposals were being put forward by a number of colliery owners for a series of lines known as the 'Lothian Lines', the purpose of which was to provide a direct and independent link between the mines and Leith docks, thereby bypassing the North British. In these proposals new lines were to be constructed between Newtongrange and Leith, which would have had the effect of parallelling the existing Hardengreen to Monktonhall line of the North British and between Smeaton, Dalkeith and Ormiston. Eventually the North British defeated these proposals and completed its own Lothian Lines, but no new lines were constructed in the area south of Monktonhall Junction although the junction there was modified and a new signal box provided. One upshot of this heavy traffic, though, was that it was decided to double the section of line between Smeaton and Monktonhall Junction and the contract for this was let out to Hugh Symington & Sons, contractors from Caotbridge, who completed the works in December 1912. The necessity for this work can be neatly demonstrated by the fact that in 1900 Smeaton station and its subsidiary sidings handled some 189,000 tons of coal annually, whereas in 1912 this figure had risen to a staggering 740,000 tons. A regular shunting engine was now stationed at Smeaton on double shift from 7 am on Mondays to 10 pm on Saturdays; its duties included the shunting and trip workings to Carberry and Dalkeith Collieries in addition to providing banking for coal trains as far as Dalkeith Colliery signal box.

Another change in the early years of the century was brought about by the through running of trains from the newly constructed Gifford & Garvald Light Railway over the section between Ormiston and Monktonhall. Although the additional trains did not seem to boost the passenger figures at intermediate stations (and, in fact, led to a sharp fall at Ormiston and Winton stations which had both formerly acted as railheads for several surrounding villages now better served by the Gifford line), it gave a renewed impetus to demands for a station to break the long section between Ormiston and Smeaton. In particular these demands were most vociferously made by the inhabitants of Cousland who felt quite isolated as the railway ran close by their village but trains did not stop there. Accordingly, in January 1913, they petitioned the North British to provide them with a station and this was duly constructed on the north (up) side of the line at Crossgatehall close to the junction of the Dalkeith Colliery branch and the bridge which carried the Musselburgh to Pathhead road over the line. The station was a modest one due to 'the meagre passenger traffic on the line' and that fact that 'any station would be unremunerative for a long time and that therefore the North British could only justify the construction of a cheap station'. The Board of Trade gave provisional approval to what Major Pringle suggested should be called 'Crossgatehall Halt' and on 1st August, 1913 the station was duly opened, all Macmerry and Gifford trains being scheduled to stop there. The station had a single platform 120 ft long with a small wooden building situated thereon – the building was 36 ft long, consisting of a waiting room 20 ft by 10 ft and a booking office 16 ft by 10 ft, the ticket window being into the waiting room area. There were no goods facilities and the halt was intended only to handle passengers and parcels.

Crossgatehall Halt seems to have been something of a success, for in its first complete year of existence some 5,000 passengers booked from here and receipts totalled £250 compared with, say, Smeaton which handled only some 2,800 passengers and had receipts of only £90. Unfortunately World War I intervened and the halt was closed as a temporary measure so as to releaso manpower for the war effort on 1st January, 1917 and not re-opened until 1st February, 1919.* This closure would seem to have been in defiance of any commercial logic since it appears to have been making a profit when

---

*The single member of staff, the station agent employed at a salary of £80 p.a., was transferred to Gartshore. Upon re-opening an NBR internal memorandum states 'there will be no difficulty in finding a station master to take this job'.

compared to the likes of Smeaton, Winton and Macmerry whose total *combined* number of passengers did not even equal that of Crossgatehall. Happily this temporary closure did not appear to have acted as a deterrent and the halt managed to regain most, if not all, of its former passengers once the War was over.

Monktonhall Junction signal box, where the Macmerry and Gifford lines left the East Coast main line.   *N.D. Mundy*

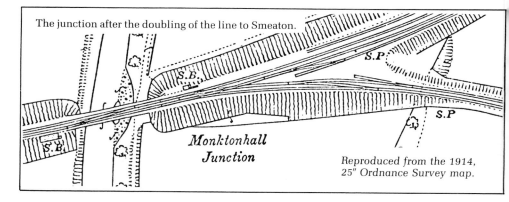

The junction after the doubling of the line to Smeaton.

Monktonhall Junction

Reproduced from the 1914, 25" Ordnance Survey map.

Two NBR class J37's earning their keep with trains of empty mineral wagons on a return working from Leith South to the Dalkeith Colliery Sidings. The upper picture was taken at Carberry Colliery Junction; note the steeply graded Carberry Colliery Branch behind the locomotive and the scorched paintwork on the smokebox door. The lower picture is at Smeaton, immediately north of the road bridge. Both photographed on 27th March, 1959.   *W.S. Sellar*

Smeaton station on 17th April, 1955 with the west sidings in the foreground and the Dalkeith washery and colliery in the background. The Macmerry and Gifford lines diverged to the left at the end of the platform while the Hardengreen line continued southwards. *A.G. Ellis*

Smeaton looking north on 22nd March, 1959 – the west sidings are in the foreground. This face of the island platform was rarely used for passenger trains. *W.S. Sellar*

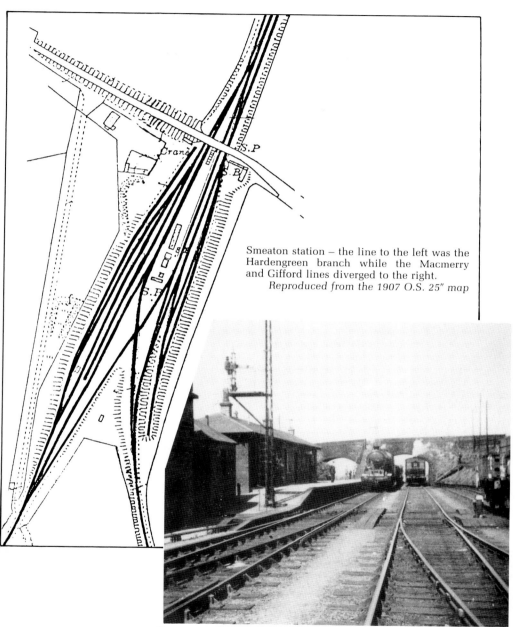

Smeaton station – the line to the left was the Hardengreen branch while the Macmerry and Gifford lines diverged to the right.
Reproduced from the 1907 O.S. 25″ map

Smeaton in the 1920s, with a coal train passing the passenger platform.
S.R.O. Collection

Two views of the rebuilt Victoria Viaduct, taken in 1938 and some two years before it was demolished for scrap. The upper view is looking towards Thorneybank while the lower view looks in the opposite direction – note the fence to keep out trespassers and the presence of the New Cow Bridge which still carries the A6094 Dalkeith to Wallyford road over the South Esk. *G.N. Heathcote*

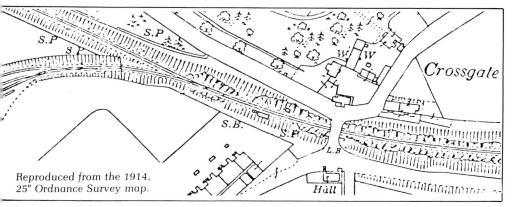

Reproduced from the 1914, 25″ Ordnance Survey map.

Crossgatehall – the halt was on the north side of the line to the left of the over-bridge while the signal box shown was Dalkeith Colliery, the branch to which diverged at this point. The football ground and the cottages in the left and mid-foreground were later engulfed by a coal bing.

A Reid 'B' class J35, No. 64532, coasts through the Cousland Gap and down the bank to Crossgatehall with a coal train on 16th April, 1956. *D.L.G. Hunter*

The site of Crossgatehall Halt in July 1959 – the stairs led down to the long vanished wooden platform of a station that, curiously, does not appear to have been photographed during its 17 year life. *M.B. Smith*

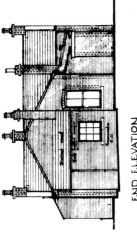

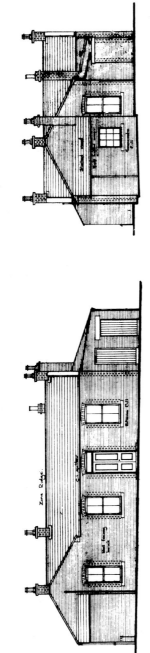

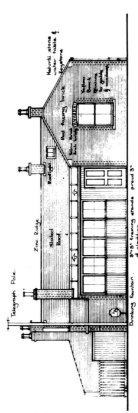

Ormiston Station Buildings Plan.

J.E. Hay

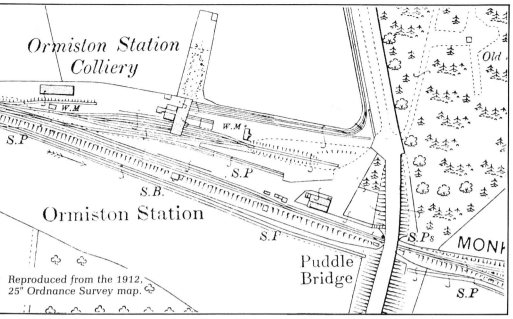

Ormiston station; to the right of the Puddle Bridge the junction of the Gifford and Macmerry lines can be seen.

Ormiston at the time of a Stephenson Locomotive Society special in June 1960 – the surprisingly rural surroundings give little indication that a coalmine once existed here. *Harold D. Bowtell*

191 Ormiston Station, East Lothian

Ingram Gordon & Co.

Ormiston in the 1920s – the junction of the Macmerry and Gifford lines can be seen through the arch of the bridge.   *R.W. Lynn Collection*

Ormiston looking westwards towards the loop and signal box, 9th July, 1952.
                              A.G. Ellis

The view from the Puddle Bridge at Ormiston in June 1961 with the Macmerry line on the left and the Gifford line on the right — by this time the respective termini were Winton Mine and Saltoun. The fine North British style interlaced turnout reflects permanent way practice of a former age.   *M.B. Smith*

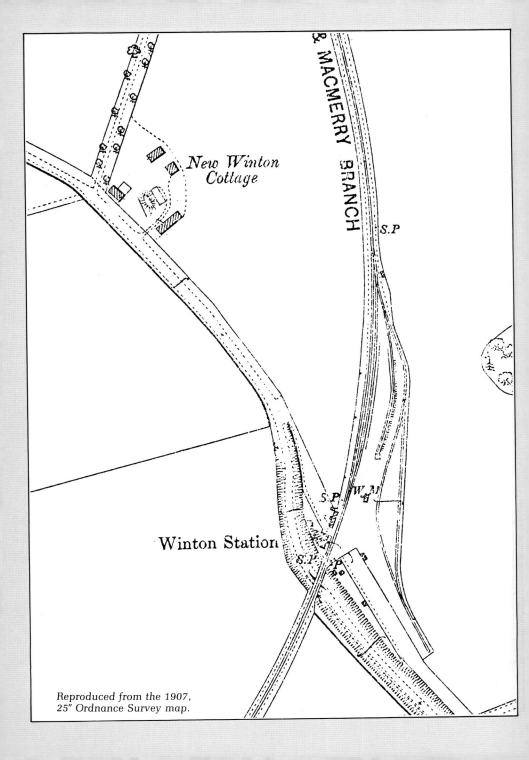

Reproduced from the 1907,
25″ Ordnance Survey map.

The rarely photographed station at Winton, looking north, c.1920. In the foreground is the level crossing while to the right lie the Winton Sidings.

S.R.O. Collection

Guard Charlie Dodds surveys the scene at Macmerry on a gloomy day in July 1959 — the locomotive is BR Standard 2MT No. 78048 and, not unusually, the train carries no load.

M.B. Smith

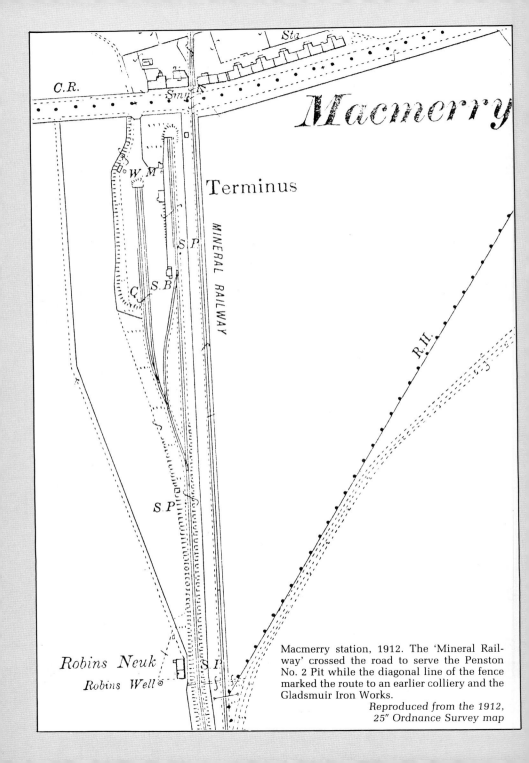

Macmerry station, 1912. The 'Mineral Railway' crossed the road to serve the Penston No. 2 Pit while the diagonal line of the fence marked the route to an earlier colliery and the Gladsmuir Iron Works.

Reproduced from the 1912, 25″ Ordnance Survey map

The terminus at Macmerry looking north, in about 1932; behind the fence lay the main London road (A1).   *S.R.O. Collection*

A deserted Macmerry station on 17th April, 1955.   *A.G. Ellis*

Easter Pencaitland looking towards Haddington, *c*.1925; only a motor lorry disturbs the rural tranquillity. *Author's Collection*

A Victorian view of Pencaitland, showing the cross and a row of cottages in the typical vernacular style of East Lothian. *Glenkinchie Distillery Collection*

Chapter Six

Into the Lap of the Lammermuirs

THE PLANNING AND CONSTRUCTION OF THE GIFFORD & GARVALD RAILWAY

'So quietly is the construction of the new Gifford and Garvald Railway proceeding that most folks will need to be reminded that unless some unforseen hitch occur, the early months of the new century will see the locomotive an institution by the hillfoots.'

Haddingtonshire Courier, 12th December, 1899.

The countryside lying to the east and south of Ormiston would seem to have offered few possibilities for profit to the promoters of railways and yet several schemes to open up this wild and beautiful area were put forward, one of which eventually came to fruition. As the 19th century wore on many of the inhabitants of the more remote areas in Scotland began to press for connections to the national railway network and there was a considerable feeling amongst them that a branch line could make all the difference between rural prosperity and decline. In the case of the area to the south of Haddington this may well have been true, for the railway had effectively by-passed the rich agricultural parishes of Pencaitland, Saltoun, Humbie, Yester and Garvald and the movement of farm produce and agricultural machinery along the poorly maintained country roads was a slow and tedious business. Intending passengers were not well served, the nearest railheads being Winton and Haddington; although the eastern parishes could gain access to the latter place by the horse omnibuses operated by George Anderson, a local carrier who advertised that 'he takes passengers and parcels to and from Gifford and the Haddington railway station', the inhabitants of Pencaitland and Humbie parishes had to make do with a long walk (eight miles in the case of Humbie) to Winton station.

After the failure of the East Lothian & Tyne Valley scheme there was some talk of providing a branch line to serve Gifford but nothing materialised until February 1889, when the *Haddingtonshire Courier* reported that plans had been published for a proposed Haddington & Gifford Railway. This was to have run eastwards from a junction with the North British at the existing newly rebuilt passenger station, which was to be relegated to use as a goods depot since a new station was to be provided north of, but much closer to, the centre of the town. The new line was then to pass through the park at Amisfield and then run generally south and west (the exact route not having yet been chosen) to a terminus in the centre of the village at Gifford. It does not appear that these proposals were ever seriously followed up and there is no evidence of a proper survey having been carried out; the Haddington & Gifford scheme rapidly faded from public interest.

An alternative scheme was now put forward, that of a line to be called the Gifford & Garvald Railway. This new line was to be some 12 miles in length and was projected to run south-eastwards from a junction with the North British Macmerry branch at Ormiston and to cross the River Tyne on its way to Pencaitland. Here it would enter the estates of John Fletcher of Saltoun and, half a mile south of West Saltoun village, abruptly turn north-east to a

CHAPTER lxxxv.

An Act to incorporate the Gifford and Garvald Railway Company and to empower them to construct a railway in the county of Haddington and for other purposes. A.D. 1891.

[3rd July 1891.]

WHEREAS the construction of the line of railway from Ormiston to Gifford and Garvald in the county of Haddington herein-after described would be of public and local advantage :

And whereas the several persons herein-after named with others are willing to carry the undertaking into execution on being incorporated into a company (in this Act called "the Company") for the purpose :

And whereas it is expedient that the Company and the North British Railway Company be empowered to enter into and carry into effect working and other agreements as herein-after provided :

And whereas plans and sections showing the lines and levels of the railway authorised by this Act and also a book of reference to such plans containing the names of the owners and lessees or reputed owners and lessees and of the occupiers of the lands required or which may be taken for the purposes or under the powers of this Act were duly deposited with the principal sheriff clerk for the county of Haddington and are herein-after referred to respectively as the deposited plans sections and book of reference :

And whereas the purposes of this Act cannot be effected without the authority of Parliament :

May it therefore please Your Majesty that it may be enacted and be it enacted by the Queen's most Excellent Majesty by and with the advice and consent of the Lords Spiritual and Temporal and Commons in this present Parliament assembled and by the authority of the same as follows :—

1. This Act may be cited as the Gifford and Garvald Railway Act 1891. Short title.

[*Price* 1s. 6d.]

point just past East Saltoun village before turning almost due east to Gifford. It would then swing north-eastwards to a terminus at Tanderlane in the parish of Garvald and Bara. Although one might question the logic of building a line to serve Gifford and Garvald, the route chosen was both sensible and reasonably direct. Had the line been built to this original plan then it is just possible that its economic position would have been marginally less disastrous than that of the line which was eventually built.

In an explanation of the background of the affair given by the Directors of the Gifford & Garvald Railway Company at the First Statutory Ordinary Meeting held on 25th November, 1891 it was said that:

> The desirability of railway accommodation from Ormiston to Garvald had long been felt in these districts and in the spring of 1890 the beneficial character of and necessity for such an undertaking became so evident as to induce some of the local proprietors to take up the matter. Accordingly a survey was made and a plan prepared showing the most expedient route. This plan was submitted to and readily approved by the proprietors whose lands would be affected by the proposed line and it also received the approbation of the North British Railway company.
>
> In furtherence of the promotion of the scheme a meeting was held of the principal owners interested in the line within the North British Railway offices on 6th August, 1890 at which it was unanimously agreed and resolved that a Bill should be promoted in the then coming session of Parliament for the incorporation of a Company to construct the railway and to that end an influential committee was appointed.
>
> The Committee appointed Solicitors, Parliamentary Agents and Engineers and the necessary preliminary procedures being duly carried out a Bill containing all powers necessary for the construction of the railway was lodged. The North British Railway had all along acted in a friendly manner towards the scheme and had expressed their willingness to give a Working Agreement.

The 'influential committee' consisted of John Fletcher of Saltoun, Mr Hamilton Ogilvy of Biel, Walter Wingate Gray of Nunraw (an estate close to Garvald) and Mr W. Black Trevelyan. The Chairman was William Montagu Hay, Tenth Marquis of Tweeddale, whose family seat was at Yester House in Gifford. He was no stranger to railway matters since he also served as the Chairman of the North British between 1890 and 1899. Also involved were James Reid, Writer to the Signet (W.S.)* (a solicitor and partner in the Edinburgh firm of Reid & Guild, W.S.) and two engineers who were responsible for surveying the line, namely Patrick Walter Meik and M.A. Pollard Urquhart of Thomas Meik & Sons, Consulting Engineers of London and Edinburgh. From the outset it was clear that the line would be built as a result of the amalgamation of interests between the local landowners and the North British; in March 1891 an agreement was reached between on the one hand the Marquis and Mr Gray, representing the Gifford & Garvald company and on the other hand the North British Railway. Thereby it was agreed that the smaller company would construct the railway and stations and provide all the necessary apparatus and the North British would appoint the staff, provide locomotives and stock and operate the line themselves in return for 50 per cent of the gross revenues of the line, with a guaranteed minimum

---

*Writer to the Signet — a member of an exclusive and ancient society of solicitors in Scotland.

return to the Gifford & Garvald shareholders of four per cent per annum on their capital.

On 3rd July, 1891 the Gifford & Garvald Railway Act 1891 was passed giving the new company powers to build the line, raise capital of £111,000 and to use compulsory purchase powers for a period of three years. Provision was made for stations at Pencaitland and Saltoun to satisfy the demands of, respectively, Mary Georgina Nisbet Hamilton Ogilvy of Winton and John Fletcher. At the outset relationships between the Board of the Gifford & Garvald and that of the North British were amiable, and Alexander Guild, W.S., the Secretary of the Gifford & Garvald, attempted to negotiate with a contractor, James Young of Glasgow, who had offered to build the whole of the line for £10,000 in cash and £80,000 in fully paid-up shares. The problem, however, was that the North British were not willing financially to underwrite the project; while local landowners were happy to sell their land to the company, often at a substantial discount, and the Marquis was willing to seek sources of finance, no one was willing to commit themselves by actually providing any money.

At the Gifford & Garvald Directors' meeting, held on 4th December, 1891, Alexander Guild resigned his position as Secretary and his job was taken by George Bradley Wieland, the somewhat unpopular Secretary of the North British. The Marquis now proposed that an agreement should be made with another firm of contractors, Messrs Pauling & Elliot, who had offered to construct the line between Ormiston and Gifford for £45,000 in cash and £22,000 in paid-up shares; Mr Gray should then be left to raise the £11,000 or so which would be needed to extend the railway to Garvald. Negotiations continued against a backdrop of increasingly vociferous conflict within the Gifford & Garvald Board. The Directors began to complain that they were effectively being 'frozen-out' by Wieland who was being characteristically autocratic, failing to keep them informed of any progress and generally putting the interests of the North British before those of the Gifford & Garvald. It was not, however, Wieland's personal failings which were really at issue, for the problem was that the North British wanted to control (but not own) the new company and to run the railway as a branch line as far as Gifford only, whereas the local interests were more concerned with retaining control and building their line out to Garvald, with a possible future extension eastwards towards Dunbar and the East Coast main line.

The real battle was now about to begin. At 12.30 pm on Thursday 1st September, 1892 Wieland, on his own initiative, called a Half-Yearly Statutory Meeting of the Gifford & Garvald company within the offices of the North British, notwithstanding the fact that the 1891 Act had made no provision for such a meeting. When the Directors arrived they were informed that they had all, in their absence, been deposed and replaced as Directors by three of the existing North British Directors, namely John Jordan (as proxy for the absent Marquis), Henry Grierson and Sir Charles Tennant, Bt. The deposed Directors then repaired immediately to their solicitor's office nearby and at 1.30 pm they held a Directors' Meeting where they resolved to replace Wieland as Secretary and to take Counsel's opinion as to the legality of the appointment of the new Directors. In the interim

Messrs Jordan, Wemyss (an existing NBR and G & GR Director), Grierson and Tennant held their own Directors' Meeting at which they authorised Wieland to enter into a contract with Pauling & Elliot for the construction of the line on the basis of their offer.

Legal opinion was in favour of the original Directors and in the Court of Session they were granted an interdict against Wieland and his associates from acting further, on the grounds that what had transpired at the Half-Yearly meeting and subsequently was *ultra vires* and illegal. The hand of the North British was now felt: when the original Directors approached Pauling & Elliot with a proposal that they should construct the line from Ormiston to Garvald for £88,000 in fully paid-up shares and £22,000 in debenture bonds they were promptly informed that the contractors were unable to accept this offer. The latter, however, stated that 'we are prepared to negotiate with your Directors a contract to construct their Railway upon the lines of the provisional agreement with the late secretary, Mr Wieland, should they be at any time in a position to entertain it.' This was clearly an attempt by the North British to coerce the Gifford & Garvald and only served to inflame matters more.

On 10th December, 1892 the Marquis of Tweeddale resigned from the Board of the Gifford & Garvald stating that his fellow Directors' actions 'had made it impossible for me at any rate to find the capital for [the line's] construction'. In a spirited reply the Marquis was informed that the Board would accept his resignation, but that they would not allow him to escape from his financial responsibilities undertaken in connection with the formation of the company. The Marquis responded saying that,

> I am quite aware that by resigning the post of Director, I do not thereby relieve myself of any financial responsibility which I may have incurred . . . You must know full well that but for the refusal of my co-directors to make way for the North British directors, the Gifford & Garvald Railway would have long ere thus have been in the hands of a responsible contractor.

Mr Fletcher, who now was the Chairman of the Gifford & Garvald in place of the Marquis, informed the Board on 9th February, 1893 that,

> He had only been induced to consent to the railway passing through the most valuable portion of his estate on the footing that the line was to be a proprietors' line and that it was to be taken as far as Garvald for possible extension to the main line thereafter; and that if the arrangements that he had referred to were reconsidered and if the Board were to be reconstructed he considered himself free to review the arrangements made for the route of the line.

Discussions now took place at the instigation of the Marquis with regard to meeting John Fletcher's objections and altering the route of the line away from the Saltoun estates, in return for consenting to the North British nominees being appointed to the Gifford & Garvald Board. At the Directors' meeting of 17th April, 1893 the Gifford & Garvald Board unanimously approved of a proposed deviation of the line away from Fletcher's lands and the siting of the terminus at Gifford. The next item of business was a motion by Mr Gray for the Directors to agree to a Board reconstruction to the satisfaction of the Marquis by, effectively, replacing the present Gifford &

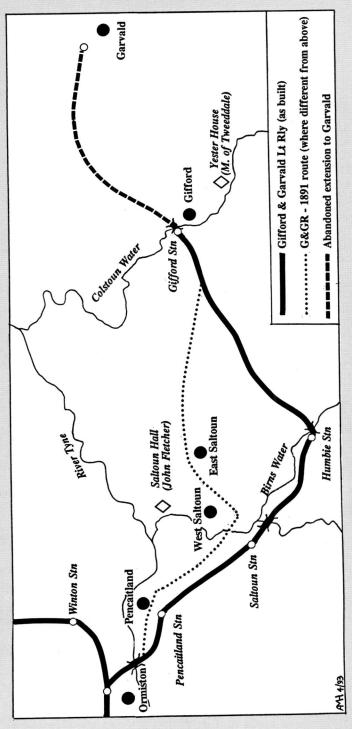

The deviation sought by the 1893 Act.

Garvald Directors by the North British nominees and to provide financial reliefs for the original Board members. This motion was carried, but the dispute between Fletcher and the Marquis did not end here for the latter then tried to force the former into accepting shares, as opposed to cash, in return for the much smaller amount of the Saltoun estate which would now be needed for railway purposes. The Marquis threatened that if he did not do so then the Marquis would withdraw from the whole scheme and the original Directors' financial relief would be nullified. A telegram was sent to Fletcher (who had been absent from the meeting) in the following terms:

> The Railway Directors at a meeting today strongly urge you to accept shares for and on deviated line. Jas. Hope yesterday along with your factor and Agents fixed compulsory conveyances for your land at £1500. If you do not accept this in shares, Tweeddale will withdraw from the whole affair and leave you and your co-directors responsible for all expenditure. Your co-directors will not entertain the idea of an action for damages. Have adjourned meeting till three o'clock to await your reply. Answer Paid.

Despite this strong warning Fletcher did not choose to use the Answer Paid facility and the Gifford & Garvald Directors, realising that their threats were unheeded, reluctantly decided to take up the £1500 of shares themselves if necessary.

Matters now began to move again, and in due course the unreconstructed Gifford & Garvald Board began to attend to the promotion of a deviation Bill which became the Gifford & Garvald Railway Act 1893. This provided for a substantial deviation of the line southwards from the original route, so that it now skirted the Saltoun estates instead of bisecting them and then continued south of the Birns Water to Gilchriston where it swung north towards Gifford. The purpose of this deviation, which defied both economic and geographical realities, was so that the line could run over as much as possible of the Marquis' lands rather than those of Fletcher. It undoubtedly led to the early demise of the line whereas the original route might well have prolonged its life. A summons was now served by Thomas Meik & Sons, the consulting engineers who had drawn up the plans for both the original and the deviated lines, in respect of their unpaid professional fees amounting to £1,446 16s. 11d. and a further £1,£94 12s. 8½d. being claimed by Reid & Guild, W.S. in respect of legal fees to date.

While the outstanding financial matters were being sorted out and shares in the Gifford & Garvald company were being transferred to the North British nominees, little could happen; since the Marquis appeared to be unwilling to construct the line at his own expense and there was no other readily available source of finance (the North British still steadfastly refusing to contribute anything) progress was effectively stalled. Then an approach was made by another contractor, Joseph Phillips of Victoria Street, London, who offered to construct and arrange the financing of the line. Phillips was an experienced railway contractor, having worked on the Forfar & Brechin line and on the immensely prestigous Forth Bridge contract. But the Gifford & Garvald Board had to decline his offer at that time because they were still anxious to put their own house in order first. In the interim the North British sought, and obtained, parliamentary power to extend the compulsory purchase powers needed for the line for a further period.

With the passing of the Light Railways Act in 1896 a new possibility was opened up, in that, if an Order was granted under the Act, the Gifford & Garvald could be constructed at a reduced cost to a lower specification with cheaper facilities and a relaxation in safety standards. The Act had been designed to help to open up the isolated areas of the country where conventional branch lines would have been too costly, and in Scotland a number of these lines were eventually built pursuant to these orders. The Gifford & Garvald Directors considered the matter and eventually resolved to apply for an Light Railway Order; their application was finally sanctioned by the Board of Trade on 14th July, 1898. The Gifford & Garvald Light Railway Order made it quite clear that the nature of the line was to be something rather different from a normal North British branch line. It provided that a standard gauge single track line should be built upon which the maximum axle weight of permitted locomotives was to be 12 tons, that the maximum speed of trains would be 25 mph, that there were to be ungated level crossings, that the company had no obligation to provide shelter or conveniences at their stations, that no turntable had to be provided ('but no tender engine shall be permitted to run tender first at a speed in excess of 15 mph') and that there was to be a fixed fare per mile of 3d. (1p) first class and 1½d. third class. The Gifford & Garvald Railway Company was to have five Directors, three of whom were to be appointed by the North British. The latter company was to work the line pursuant to the original agreement of 1891, which was only modified in respect that the North British was permitted to pay the Gifford & Garvald a fixed sum of £300 per month in lieu of a share of the gross revenue.

Events now gathered pace and in August 1898 the Gifford & Garvald's solicitors served the appropriate notices on landowners whose lands they wished to acquire. The Registered Office of the company was established in Edinburgh and it adopted as its seal a device which incorporated upon it a representation of the old market cross at Gifford. Since the Company was to have few direct dealings with the public the device was destined to remain only on the seal and never to see the light of day on any rolling stock or publicity. Within a short period of time the necessary arrangements were all in hand with the exception of those concerning James Reid of Tyneholm near Ormiston who, for reasons of his own, was proving somewhat difficult. In December of the same year the Marquis returned to the Board of the Gifford & Garvald* and began a series of meetings with Joseph Phillips who was still apparently keen to construct the line. On 8th February, 1899 Phillips agreed to construct the deviated line between Ormiston and Gifford, in return for the whole issued share capital of £100,000 or such other sum as the line might actually cost to construct.

The contract having been signed, construction could now begin and on Saturday 8th April, 1899 Candida Louise, Marchioness of Tweeddale, performed the ceremony of the cutting of the first sod at Red Row, between Ormiston and Pencaitland. She used for the purpose a silver mounted spade

---

*In a bizarre coda to the Boardroom disputes of earlier times, the Marquis was forced to resign from the Boards of the Gifford & Garvald and North British in March 1899, a casualty of Wieland's successful battle for power with the much respected General Manager of the North British, John Conacher. Wieland succeeded to the Chairmanship of the North British in 1901 and, in the words of Dr Adams in his article on the Gifford & Garvald, 'when the first locomotive steamed into Gifford station its victorious whistle must have been heard in Yester House.'

LIGHT RAILWAYS ACT, 1896.

GIFFORD AND GARVALD LIGHT RAILWAY ORDER, 1898.

ORDER

MADE BY THE

LIGHT RAILWAY COMMISSIONERS,

AND MODIFIED AND CONFIRMED BY THE

BOARD OF TRADE,

EMPOWERING THE

GIFFORD AND GARVALD RAILWAY COMPANY

To construct and work their authorized Railway as a Light Railway.

Presented to both Houses of Parliament by Command of Her Majesty.

LONDON:
PRINTED FOR HER MAJESTY'S STATIONERY OFFICE,
By DARLING & SON, LTD., 1–3, GREAT ST. THOMAS APOSTLE, E.C.

And to be purchased, either directly or through any Bookseller, from
EYRE & SPOTTISWOODE, EAST HARDING STREET, FLEET STREET, E.C., and
32, ABINGDON STREET, WESTMINSTER, S.W.; or
JOHN MENZIES & Co., 12, HANOVER STREET, EDINBURGH, and
90, WEST NILE STREET, GLASGOW; or
HODGES, FIGGIS, & Co., LIMITED, 104, GRAFTON STREET, DUBLIN.

1898.

[C.—8956.]   *Price 2d.*

and a special wheelbarrow; a local photographer was commissioned to record the event for posterity and the G&GR accounts show that he was paid the handsome sum of 7 gns [£7.35] for this. A reception was then held at the nearby Ormiston Hall; in his speech to the assembled guests the Marquis stated that the creation of the railway owed much to Major Gray of Nunraw 'who was not only entitled to the credit of having originated the idea, but who had also been indefatigable in his efforts to carry the project to a successful issue.'

A depot for the contractor was established at Broomrig, close to Pencaitland, where a wooden shed was constructed and two sidings laid to accommodate Joseph Phillip's locomotives and stock. The two engines used in the construction of the line were a Hudswell, Clarke 0−6−0T (No. 531 of 1899) which was bought as new for the project and which was given the name *Ormiston*, which it proudly carried on a brass plate fixed to the tank sides, and the more prosaic 'No. 2', a Manning, Wardle 0−4−0 saddle tank which had been acquired second-hand from an English contractor. The latter had been used in connection with the Otterington widening contract on the North Eastern Railway main line. In addition a Hawthorn, Leslie four-coupled locomotive was apparently used although no details of this seem to survive. The *Haddingtonshire Courier* referred to *Ormiston* as 'a particularly good-natured looking little pug dog of an engine'. A variety of open wagons were employed and these included both wagons in Phillip's own strident livery and examples of old North British wagons, which the contractor acquired second-hand but which were still labelled 'N.B.'. Much use of mechanical machinery was made and this included a large mechanical excavator known as a 'steam navvy' but, the petrol engine being but in its infancy, most of the power was still supplied by men and horses.

On 24th April, 1899 the Directors reported that the contractor was 'carrying out his operations vigorously' and the consulting engineers, Thomas Meik & Sons (who had presumably been paid their outstanding fees by then!) reported in the following terms:

Earthworks − the grading of the formation has been finished for the first quarter of a mile and further excavations have been commenced in the cutting at Pencaitland.

Fencing − about 1500 yards of post and wire fencing have been erected.

Culverts and Drains − the first culvert near the junction with the NBR has been completed.

Plant − a considerable amount of plant has already been placed upon the ground and all the preparations made for expediting the work.

A cryptic entry in the Gifford & Garvald Minutes for 27th November, 1899 states that 'the Board see no reason for the appointment of an inspector of the North British Railway on the line.'

The contractor worked on steadily, his resident engineer, F.D. Maw, being on site and within a few months work began on the building of the Tyne and Humbie viaducts, the two main engineering features of the line − indeed the structure over the Humbie Water was a major engineering work in its own right being 150 ft in length and carrying the line 48 ft above the height of the

Candida Louise, Machioness of Tweeddale, performs the ceremony of the cutting of the first sod of the G&GR at Red Row, Pencaitland on Saturday 8th April, 1899; note the silver spade and special wheelbarrow.

J.G. Gordon; David Neilson Collection

The salaried staff of Joseph Phillips pose at the contractor's siding at Broomrig; the man marked with a cross is the timekeeper and cashier, James McKinlay; his daughter preserved for posterity his album of photographs of the line being built. The status of the dog within the organisation is not known!

David Neilson Collection

river. Both viaducts were built using stone quarried at Fountainhall, half a mile from the Gifford & Garvald trackbed near to Ormiston and the contractor built a short temporary line to link the quarry and the main railway. Other important works included the rock cutting at Red Row (close to where the Marchioness had cut the first sod) where some 4,000 cubic yds of rock were blasted out, the huge embankment at the Kinchie Burn and the high embankment leading to the Humbie viaduct which used in excess of 30,000 cubic ft of material. Fortunately for posterity a very literate reporter from the *Haddingtonshire Courier* visited the works while they were in progress and has left us the following vivid account of the building of the Gifford & Garvald Railway.

Deep in a 20-foot cutting, deliberately but with determined energy in every slow mighty bite, is the 'steam navvy', a combination of the modern railway truck, a giant crane, a thing like a steam telescope, a bucket like the underjaw of Giant Despair, with a human being or two thrown in for details. The tremendous brute – for its monstrous mouth and bite give you an ugly impression that it is alive and likely to make a mistake on biting on desperately small provocation – creeps up on rails to its work. It inclines forward its crane-neck, there is a fearsome rattle of chains in its throat, and the jaw with its awful glittering fangs falls to the limit of its gape. Before it is the gory gash of the red bank where it rent out its last mouthful. The ogre gives a greedy chuckling hitch forward to get a better grip, and then the jaws begin to close, the teeth slide into the ground, the steam telescope rams away, up goes the jaw tearing a couple of tons of clay and stones from top to bottom of the cutting. It stops for a breath at the top, jerks the bite, as it were, safely onto its tongue, wheels round about to a truck behind and spits the half-chewed mass on to it, as if it were not quite to its palate. No doubt it is all a question of wheels and steam, but it looks as if it were horribly alive, and knew exactly what it were doing, and took a satisfaction in its work. As we stood it started a bite, and suddenly half way up it stopped with a sore-toothed expression, and took a look at the bank. We expected to see it put up a paw and claw its ear. 'Got a big stone,' said Mr Maw laconically. So it was, but it just went back a little, took a better bite and snapped the obstruction in two as a collie crunches his dinner bone.

We left it grunting and crunching and pitching its mouthfuls behind it. Full wagons run away back with the material to help bank up the Humbie viaduct and valley sides. The 'steam navvy' will eat out 300 cubic yards of ground in a day and fill a hundred wagons. As one looks on the horses here, with trundling wagons, running horses, the slippery ground, the beetling torn banks, and the terrible monster biting and swinging in front, the feeling comes of how easily a slip, a moment's mistake, would mean a human life crushed out of its shell. The responsibility as well as the capability of those in charge of all of this is appreciated as we look on. 'Risky?', we venture. Mr Maw smiles in a way that made us feel we might have used a stronger word. 'Yet', he said, 'we have had comparatively few accidents. We have only had one man killed – and he should not have died so far as one could see from his injuries. We have been very fortunate considering everything, and we have about 350 men employed.'

At the Humbie viaduct the method of gaining access is interesting. The temporary line runs up to the edge of the valley, and then it did on a large scale just what a cautious person would do, it tacked away down to the easiest places on the right, then it tacked away to the left, and so zig-zagged down and across the bottom of the valley, and up the other side. It is curious to see the engines dodging away down this queer stairway, with the fine viaduct growing overhead, where soon the trains will flash across in a few seconds, all unmindful of the ingenuity and toil that lay in the valley below. For of course once the bridge is finished all this lattice work of railway will vanish, and the now sorely disorganised bracken will resume its own. From the Ormiston side the bridge has pushed out like a long legged, very high-stepping caterpillar that has become afraid to go any further. The shed higher up in the trees is the locomotive 'hospital', where injured locomotives and wagons get patched up, and there is always something doing there.

At the Annual General Meeting of the Gifford & Garvald, held on 26th April, 1900; it was reported by the Engineer that,

> . . . rail communication has now been established beyond Humbie Water and the principal bridges have already been erected. The extremely bad weather of the past spring has to some extent retarded work and the contractor has also had some difficulty in finding a sufficient number of workmen but he now has on the works a large staff and everything is proceeding as satisfactorily as could be wished . . . The bridges over The Tyne Water and Birns Water are completed, as also the bridges carrying the roads over the line at Red Row and Lempock Wells have been completed; the piers and abutments of the viaduct over the Humbie Water are practically completed and the centering for the arches is now being erected.

By now Phillips had been issued with 4,315 £10 ordinary paid-up shares in payment to account, 50 per cent of the cuttings had been excavated and the station yards at Saltoun and Humbie had been completed and sidings were being laid there. There was a minor setback, however, in December 1900 when the Engineers reported that a landslip had taken place about a quarter of a mile to the south of the Humbie viaduct. Subsequently additional land had to be acquired from Lord Polwarth to make the gradient of the cutting sides there less steep and therefore less likely to slip.

Passenger stations, each with a distinctive small wooden ticket office, were provided at Pencaitland (on the edge of the Easter village), Saltoun (half a mile from West Saltoun and a mile and a quarter from East Saltoun), Humbie (a good two miles from the village of that name) and Gifford, where the station was described by the *Courier* as being 'a queer little terminus tucked out of sight at the edge of a woodland half a mile from the village'. Goods were handled at all stations and in addition at private sidings at Lempockwells (for the Saltoun estate) and Highlea (for the Polwarth estate). Staff were appointed by the North British and at Gifford the first station master was John Douglas, a native of Meadow Mill, Tranent. The latter, upon his transfer here from the post of station master at Gilnockie on the Langholm branch was presented with 'a handsome marble timepiece, with a suitable inscription, and a purse of gold in thanks for the impartial way in which he had discharged his duties to all classes.' Mr Douglas proved to be a popular and long-standing holder of the post at Gifford until he finally retired in 1919; two memorial seats dedicated to his memory are to be found on either side of the kirk gate at Gifford.

The line was fast approaching completion when, on 15th May, 1901, the North British Inspector wrote to the Gifford & Garvald Board with a list of complaints. These included the absence of any passing places on the line, the fact that level crossing gates (where provided) would normally be left

The 'steam navvy' at work on the Gifford line – 'a combination of the modern railway truck, a giant crane, a thing like a steam telescope, a bucket like the underjaw of Giant Despair, with a human being or two thrown in for detail'.

David Neilson Collection

ORMISTON, a Hudswell Clarke 0–6–0ST of 1899, supplied new to the contractors. 'A particularly good-natured looking little pug dog of an engine.'

David Neilson Collection

The Tyne Bridge at Ormiston, showing the contractor's temporary line crossing the river at a lower level.   *David Neilson Collection*

The bridge carrying the line over the Pencaitland to Fountainhall road, looking towards the village.   *David Neilson Collection*

The bridge at Lempock Wells, looking in the up direction towards the Milton accommodation bridge and vice versa – in the lower view Fletcher's Siding lay a short distance beyond the second bridge on the right hand side of the line.

David Neilson Collection

The Humbie Viaduct under construction showing the temporary wooden trestle built parallel with the rising piers and one of the zig-zag lines which reached the valley floor. The 'steam navvy', 'Ormiston' and the contractor's own wagons are all in evidence.   *David Neilson Collection*

Two views of the Humbie Viaduct shortly after its completion – this was the major engineering feature on the Gifford & Garvald Railway. *David Neilson Collection*

Gifford station under construction with tracklaying and levelling works in progress – this view looks north and the extension to Garvald would have run behind the trees in the centre of the picture.

David Neilson Collection

North British Railway Company.

M
No. 3537.

Notice to Station-masters, Engine-drivers, Guards, Signalmen, and others.

Opening of Gifford Light Railway for General Traffic

ON

SATURDAY, 12th OCTOBER 1901.

This Railway, which connects with the Monktonhall and Ormiston Branch at Ormiston Junction, will be opened for General Traffic, at 12 noon on the above date.

The Line is single throughout, and will be worked in strict accordance with the Regulations for Working Trains over Single Lines of Railways by the Electric Train Staff Block System, as contained in the current Appendix (No. 28), pages 16 to 24 inclusive.

The Electric Train Staff Block Stations will be :—

Ormiston Junction and Saltoun Station.
Saltoun Station and Gifford Station.

There are no Signals at the following Stations and Sidings, but the Points are controlled by Ground Frames, secured by Annett's Locks, the key of which is affixed to the Staff, and cannot be opened without the Electric Staff for the Section on which the Station or Siding is situated, viz.:—

NAME OF STATION OR SIDING.	DISTANCE FROM ORMISTON JUNCTION.	
	Miles.	*Chains.*
Broomrigg Siding (Temporary)...	1	23
Pencaitland Station	1	50
Fletcher's Siding...	2	52
Polworth's Siding	4	49
Humbie Station	5	33

On arriving at the Station or Siding the Driver must hand the Electric Staff to the Guard or other person in charge of the shunting operations, who will open the Points. When the shunting has been completed, and the Points have been placed in their proper position for Trains to pass upon the Main Line, the Guard or other person in charge of the shunting operations, must remove the Electric Staff, and return it to the Driver, and the latter must not proceed on his journey until he has obtained it.

Working of Level Crossing Gates on Gifford Light Railway.

All Trains and Engines must be brought to a complete stand before reaching the Level Crossings at **Saltoun Public Road,** 6 miles 9 chains from Ormiston, and **Gifford Public Road,** 8 miles 36 chains from Ormiston (the gates of which must be kept closed across the Railway night and day), and the Guard or, when there is no Guard, the Fireman, must walk forward, open the gates, and protect the Crossings whilst the Train or Engine is passing over them. No Driver must pass over these Crossings until signalled to do so by the Guard or Fireman. It will be the duty of the Guard or Fireman to shut and relock the gates after the Train or Engine has passed.

NBR Circular giving notice of the opening of the Gifford & Garvald line – the date was subsequently amended to Monday 14th October.

open for road traffic and thus closed against the railway, the sidings were only capable of being worked in the 'up' direction and that consequently 'tail-roping' (the practice of shunting wagons by means of a hooked rope fixed to a locomotive on a parallel line) might have to be used. He also complained that there were no houses built to accommodate staff, and that additional signalling would be required so that more than one train could operate on the line at any one time. The Gifford & Garvald response was that their line was being built in accordance with the Light Railway Order and that the likely traffic would never warrant the operation of more than one engine at a time. They drew a comparison with their line and that of the Great Western Railway's Lambourne Light Railway in Berkshire which, they claimed, was busier than the Gifford & Garvald was ever likely to be but which coped well with similar arrangements. The North British appealed to the Board of Trade who strongly suggested that a passing place was needed. They also insisted that either there be some form of communication from Ormiston to the next station down the line, so that trains would not approach the junction unannounced, or that trap points or other devices be installed there. The Gifford & Garvald reluctantly gave in, agreeing to install signalling, a block post and a passing loop at Saltoun station, the latter involving the construction of a second passenger platform to serve the loop.

On 4th October, 1901 the line was inspected by Major Pringle for the Board of Trade and, no doubt to the Directors' relief, he found that the railway was satisfactory for passenger traffic. The stage was now set for the opening of the line to the public and in Gifford, which was already en fête for the forthcoming marriage of Lady Clementine Hay of Yester and where the two hotels, the Tweeddale Arms and the Goblin Ha', had both been refurbished ready for the expected influx of trippers, excitement was high.

On Saturday 12th October, 1901 the line between Ormiston and Gifford was finally opened and a North British officers' special train was run on that day with public services beginning on Monday the 14th, although they had been advertised as starting at noon on the 12th. The driver of the first train was Thomas Hooton of St Margaret's shed, Edinburgh. Hooton was something of a local hero for his bravery shown in 1897 when he had been in charge of a North Berwick train on which the crank shaft of his locomotive broke, the lever striking him on the chest and knocking him back into the cab. With great presence of mind, and at no inconsiderable danger to himself, he managed to reach the brake handle which he then clung to until he managed to bring the train to a safe stop, thus preventing what might have been a very serious accident to the train which was carrying 200 passengers. In recognition of this he was presented with 'a very handsome sum' by the passengers 'having been confined to bed for some six weeks or so owing to the erratic movements of the liberated lever.'

The *Haddingtonshire Courier* commented thus on the opening:

Of course it has been coming for some time, but until one actually sees these onewhile remote localities, as remote localities are reckoned nowadays, put in a permanent place in a timetable, the fact does not fully get home. The just completed Gifford & Garvald Railway is of course not really completed, because

Garvald is as yet as innocent of the railway whistle as is the man in the moon of bagpipes, but it has completed itself to Gifford, and this quite sufficiently disturbs the rural simplicity of things to give us the shock alluded to . . . East Lothian is not a county at all well served by railway advantages, and probably it never will be, certainly not in memory now living. For this unsatisfactory state of things the good people who waked and slept, principally the latter, in the county town fifty years ago are largely responsible . . . the true line of traffic lay out through the county town with various branches to be arranged in something like the natural sprouting order but, alas, the distortion of the original stem can never be got over. The branches have now consequently to make the best of it, and the best of it will never be the best for Haddington . . . How will the new line develop or help to develop the country and, in short, is it going to pay? Only time will show, but in any case it is to be hoped that a successful career is before this latest addition to the industrial facilities of the county.

Saltoun station shortly before the line opened. *David Neilson Collection*

The contractor's locomotive poses at Gifford while the workmen and two local boys look on.

Chapter Seven
Slow Train to Gifford

THE GIFFORD LINE, 1901–1922

'Is it within your powers to interfere with the railway company or their services? The first train from Edinburgh takes two and a quarter hours to cover 21 miles. The first train from Gifford takes 1 hour and 25 minutes to cover the first ten miles.'

Letter from W. Gray to Board of Trade, April 1902

The initial train service provided by the North British over the Gifford & Garvald line was not impressive. Two trains per day dawdled their way along the line to Ormiston where, after frequent and unexpected delays, they continued at a leisurely pace to Smeaton, Monktonhall Junction and over the main line to Edinburgh – the latter being a unique feature amongst Light Railways which usually terminated their services at inconvenient junction stations and did not run through to a large city station. Trains on the Gifford line usually consisted of five wooden four-wheeled coaches, namely two brake thirds, two thirds and a first class carriage for the more affluent daytrippers and commuters. In charge would be one of Dugald Drummond's diminutive 'R' class 4–4–0 tank engines, which dated back to the 1880s, and presented a quaint and toy-like appearance. These locomotives, which were ideal for light railway use having a maximum axle weight of just over 12 tons but enough power to haul their small trains over the switchback gradients of the Gifford line, had a virtual monopoly on the line for almost 30 years surviving to become members of the LNER 'D51' class. Their only regular rivals, which were more like occasional interlopers, were the Wheatley 'E' class 0–6–0s (LNER class 'J31') – a venerable batch of light tender locomotives suitable for branch line work having a similar axle load to the 'R' class tanks. A familiar sight to be found on the locomotives were the oil-cans slung across and above the front buffer beam – a necessity in the days when stations were oil-lit and supplies had to be sent out from Edinburgh. A peculiarity of the branch was the fact that for many years the trains carried the express passenger headlamp code although the reason for this is unclear.

A number of special operational instructions applied to the line and the North British Working Timetable contained the following:

BETWEEN ORMISTON JUNCTION AND GIFFORD (Light Railway)

(a) There are no gates at the crossings on the branch, but cattle guards are provided, and Drivers must approach the crossings with great caution and be prepared to stop short of any obstruction. Drivers must also sound the engine whistle when nearing the crossings.

(b) No engine, carriage, or truck bringing a greater weight of 14 tons upon the rails by one pair of wheels will be allowed to run upon this railway, except on that part of the line from Ormiston to a point about 250 yards beyond the east end of the loop points at Woodhall Colliery, which is suitable for any class of engine.

(c) 'Double heading' will be allowed on any train between Ormiston and Gifford, provided no engine, carriage or truck bringing a greater weight than 14 tons upon the rails by any one pair of wheels is run.

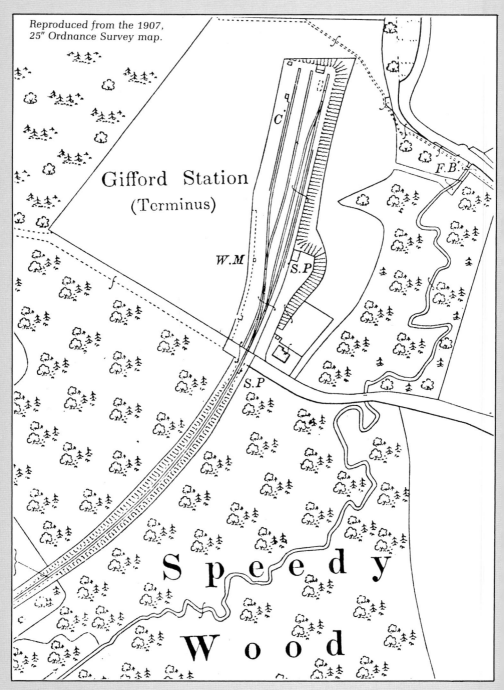

Gifford Station

(Terminus)

W.M

C

S.P

F.B.

S.P

S p e e d y

W o o d

Gifford – the 'queer little terminus tucked out of sight at the edge of a woodland half a mile from the village'.

The average speed of trains on the line was so poor that it caused almost immediate comment and within days of the opening of the line the *Haddingtonshire Courier* printed the following letter from someone who styled himself 'Cuckoo'.

After reading about the charms of the Gifford & Garvald Light Railway, and being a migratory bird, I planned a little journey to the picturesque village of Gifford. On arrival at Waverley station after breakfast, I enquired what trains there were, and was informed that one had left at 7 am, and that there was not another until 5 pm. This was rather a damper, but undaunted I started by the latter train, and we had a fair journey to Ormiston, where all the passengers were pulled out and stranded on the bleak platform there for at least half an hour. During this time the engine and some empty carriages danced the 'Kitchen Lancers' for our benefit up and down the line. Soon after that we entrained again for Gifford, and I discovered that a 'light' railway does not live up to its name, for the only light in the carriage, which was pitch dark, was my cigar. After crawling along for some way, we came to a standstill and I feared that perhaps Botha or DeWet was 'holding up' the train, and I told the guard not to surrender. However he was only opening some gates, which seemed to have very stiff hinges. After two or three more of these stops we eventually arrived at Gifford, having taken nineteen miles in the record time of two hours. Such rapid travelling is not good to a delicate bird like myself, and I returned on Tuesday, via Haddington and Longniddry, to Edinburgh.

The criticism was well-founded but the lack of speed was not entirely the fault of the North British – the Light Railway Order having placed such onerous restrictions on the operating methods of the line, and the severe gradients and low-powered locomotives did not help either. Soon other similar complaints were being made and the speed (or rather lack of it) became a favourite topic for jokes at the meetings of the East Lothian County Council. Alterations were made to the timetable for November 1901 and a new service from Gifford, leaving for Edinburgh at 9.25 am, was provided in response to the repeated requests for such a later departure 'more convenient for the general public'. In April 1902 another frustrated passenger, a Mr W. Gray of Leith, made a formal complaint to the Board of Trade about the slowness of the service and he also brought up another matter.

At Saltoun station there are two platforms, not opposite one another. Going to Edinburgh you walk along one platform, cross the line, mount another platform and get into your train; then the train proceeds to pass the other platform on its way to Edinburgh. Only one carriage at a time is flush with that platform; however if there is any luggage the van is put beside that part of the platform flush with the railway, and the luggage is put into it. This seems a ridiculous arrangement and the railway officials admit it but they blame the Board of Trade and say that it is because of some requirement of yours that this extraordinary inconvenience is necessitated. This irregularity could be remedied by taking up the rails and moving them slightly so as to run flush with the platform on which the station house is built, or the other platform (which has no shelter from wind or rain) might be moved opposite to the other platform.

On 30th October, 1901 a sale of plant and equipment was held at the Broomrig Workshops by an Edinburgh firm of auctioneers on behalf of Joseph Phillips & Son. The locomotives were sold to a dealer, J.H. Riddel, who advertised them for sale in the following week but they appeared to have remained in the shed at Broomrig for another 10 months or so. Ormiston later passed into the hands of Hugh Symington of Coatbridge and was used by them on a number of contracts, including Gretna Ammunition Depot and the construction of the new Edinburgh to Glasgow road at Baillieston in 1925–6. On 8th November, 1901, in terms of an agreement between the North British and Gifford & Garvald companies, the NB took over the maintenance of the Gifford line paying the smaller company £878 in respect of platelayer's materials, £26 for tools and £15 per week in respect of the four weeks during which the Gifford & Garvald had maintained the line following upon the Board of Trade inspection. The North British were paid £1,000 in respect of relief of the contractor's maintenance obligation.

At the Annual General Meeting of the Gifford & Garvald Railway Company held in April 1902, a statement was made as to the final costs incurred in the building of the line. A total of £95,000 in paid-up shares had been issued and £87,495 4s. 10d. had been spent on construction works with a further £9,758 incurred in respect of the incorporation of the Company and £2,076 6s. 2d. paid for 'general expenses', making a total of £99,330 3s. 10d. A 3½ per cent dividend had been declared and the North British had duly paid their £300 per month. The Board of the Gifford & Garvald was now reconstituted according to the requirements of the Light Railway Order. It now consisted of Major Gray of Nunraw and Mr Hamilton Ogilvy of Biel (the two original Directors of the company) and the three nominees of the North British, Messrs Grierson, Carlow and Jackson. Charles Carlow was a well-known figure in the coal and railway industry having been connected with the local Carberry Colliery and was the Chairman of the highly successful Fife Coal Company and Deputy Chairman of the North British while William Fulton Jackson was the General Manager of the North British.

From the point of view of the North British, the Gifford & Garvald was not a great financial success since they were obliged to pay the fixed sum of £300 per month irrespective of actual revenue. The combined passenger receipts from Gifford, Humbie, Saltoun and Pencaitland amounted to just over £1,531, or only £29 per week, and the goods receipts were even less encouraging. It was now obvious to Phillips that his decision to be paid in shares rather than cash for the construction works had not been a wise one. He asked the Gifford & Garvald Board for payment of interim monthly dividends, given that the North British were paying them on a monthly basis. The Gifford & Garvald declined to meet this request, stating that they had taken legal advice and that they were prevented from so doing by the Companies Act 1845 which prohibited the payment of interim dividends. Phillips now attempted to dispose of his majority shareholding in the Gifford & Garvald to the North British but the latter company were not altogether enamoured by this suggestion, stating politely that 'the Directors are not at all anxious to acquire the Gifford Railway and have no proposals to make with regard to it.' Phillips now seems to have lost heart and he then disposed of his shares to Henry Robson of 9 Draper's Gardens, London EC who, through his agent F.D. Maw (the erstwhile resident engineer of the line during its construction) offered the shares to the North British at a discount.

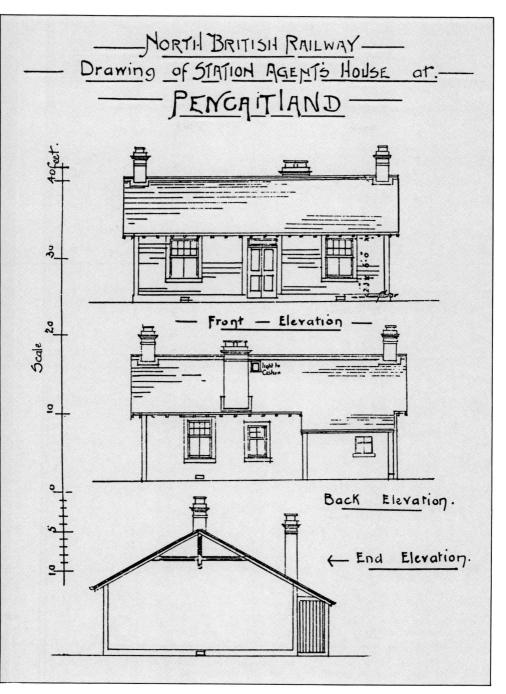

From NBR official plans in the Scottish Record Office.

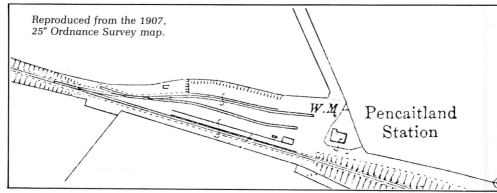

Reproduced from the 1907,
25″ Ordnance Survey map.

Pencaitland
Station

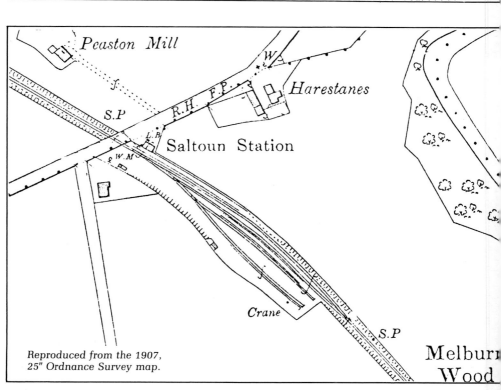

Peaston Mill

Harestanes

Saltoun Station

Crane

Reproduced from the 1907,
25″ Ordnance Survey map.

Melburn
Wood

Saltoun with an un-named 'R' class 4−4−0T, No. 77, entering the up platform, c.1910 and (*lower*) the same locomotive, by now No. 1467, at the very end of the pre-grouping era standing at the small down platform at the station.

R.W. Lynn Collection

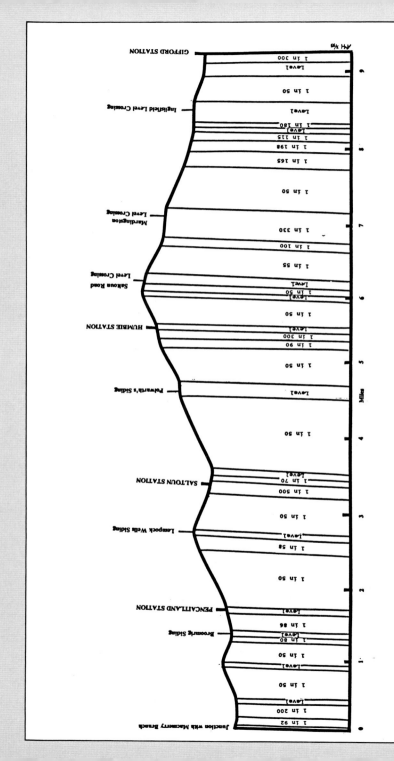

Gradient profile of the Gifford & Garvald Light Railway – it was up this succession of fearsome switchback gradients that the diminutive 'D51s' and, latterly, Great Eastern locomotives were expected to toil with their trains of often ramshackle carriages.

Humbie station – a sylvan scene from the 1920s.   *S.R.O. Collection*

Gifford in NBR days looking north; the train has just arrived and the engine has yet to use the run-round loop.   *R.W. Lynn Collection*

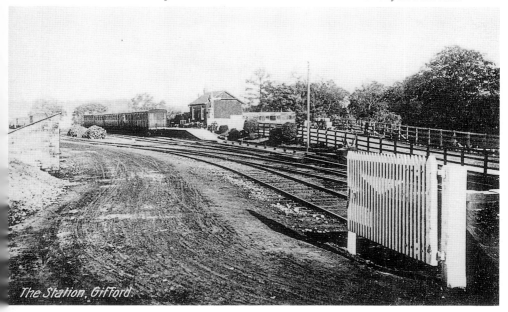

The Station, Gifford.

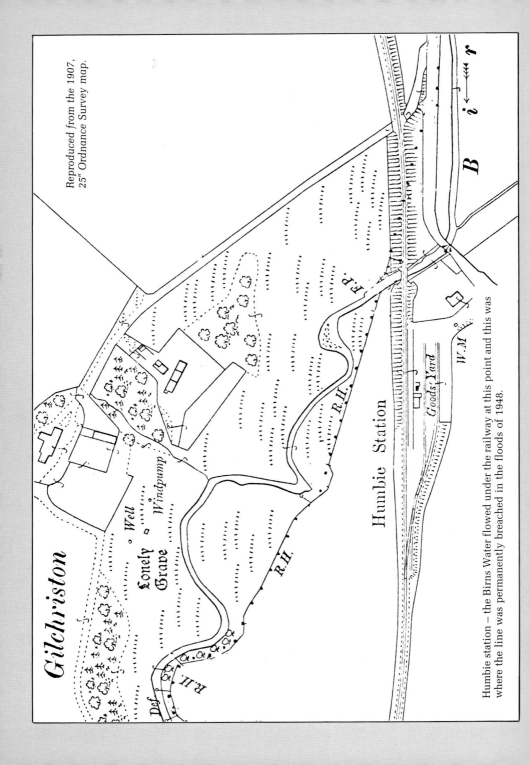

Reproduced from the 1907, 25" Ordnance Survey map.

Gilchriston

Lonely Grave

Well

Windpump

Def

Humbie Station

Goods Yard

W.M.

B i r

Humbie station – the Birns Water flowed under the railway at this point and this was where the line was permanently breached in the floods of 1948.

But the latter company, despite being offered the shares at 91 per cent in return for cash, were not interested.

Although the line might not have been a great success financially it was a success in anothe respect. Within a short period Pencaitland, Humbie, Gifford and Saltoun stations were each handling about 500 booked passengers per week, although the weekly combined gross receipts only amounted to £144. The effect that the line had on the opening up of the lives of the formerly isolated villagers was often dramatic and even at Humbie, where the station was over two miles from the village, nearly 6,700 passengers were booked from here in the year 1910–11. In a history of Humbie parish, written by C.C. Nisbet in 1939, the author summed up the difficulties which had faced travellers in the past.

> The upland districts were never well provided with facilities for railway communication. Until the latter part of the nineteenth century there was no railway station nearer to the eastern and northern boundaries of Humbie parish than Haddington, nine miles distant, but being a branch line from Longniddry there were not many trains and travelling by it sometimes involved a long wait at the junction and in any case a change of trains. The nearest station was at Tynehead, ten miles distant [on the Waverley route] but the express trains did not always stop there to uplift passengers, but in the 1870s the North British opened a branch line to Macmerry, with a station at Winton seven miles distant being used mostly by the people at Humbie.

The author went on to assert that the opening of the Gifford line was a 'great boon' to the inhabitants of Humbie parish. For a time there was additional goods traffic to Humbie station caused by the construction of the Lammerloch water scheme for the Prestonpans Water Supply and the contractors, Messrs Stirling & Kinniburgh, used Humbie as their railhead.

Other matters were considered by the Gifford & Garvald Board – in 1903 they acceded to requests from the North British to provide houses for the station masters at Humbie, Gifford, Saltoun and Pencaitland and these houses were built to the standard NBR pattern. They were sufficiently substantial that they survive to the present day, long after the demise of the railway and its stations.

On 12th December, 1906 the Marquis of Tweeddale wrote to the Gifford & Garvald Board in the following terms:

> With reference to the two level crossings on the Gifford & Garvald Railway, I should be glad if the Directors would consider the propriety of applying to the Board of Trade to rescind the Order requiring the gates to be closed on the two roads during the passage of the train. A motor is entitled to travel the whole of both roads without let or hindrance at 20 miles per hour, yet a train is not permitted to cross a few feet of road at 15 mph. The unreasonableness, or rather the absurdity of such an order is patent to everyone. I cannot but believe that the Board of Trade would give favourable consideration to the matter if the proprietors brought it to the notice of the President. I may add that though I have travelled the line a score of times or more, I have never seen a human being on the road at the first crossing, while the road is visible on both sides for quite a good distance. Again on the Saltoun road the traffic since the line was established has been greatly reduced. There again the road is visible for a considerable distance, rendering an accident almost, if not quite, impossible. Hoping that the Directors will take the matter up.

Gifford, looking south towards the level crossing, c.1910. Note the 'Two No. 7 Platform Seats, 6 ft long, at 27s. 0d. each' provided following a request for the same from the Marchioness of Tweeddale.

A.G. Ellis Collection

The North British superintendent of the line, David Deuchars, was instructed to reply and did so in the following terms:

> It is thought that the Board of Trade would not agree and in any event if they did then the Company would be responsible for accidents caused by the altered mode of working. There is a considerable risk attached to such traffic as a traction engine, janker*, or flock of sheep may cross the line. What is required is that a surfaceman's house should be built at the crossings so that the wives of the men could look after the gates, which would stand open for the railway during traffic hours.

In December 1906 a request was received from the Woodhall Coal Company for a private station to serve their Tyneholm Colliery near Pencaitland and a platform was duly provided at the south side of the Red Row bridge immediately adjacent to the colliery. This station, known somewhat prosaically as the Woodhall Colliery Company Platform, never appeared in the public timetables and it was opened on 1st July, 1907 although no trains apparently called there until after the Board of Trade inspection on the 16th of that month. The delay prompted the coal company to enquire as to when the platform would be opened, since they were 'in pressing need of workmen, having calls upon us for coal greatly in excess of what we are able to provide, and our only means of increasing our output is by the running of these trains.' The Woodhall company contributed £50 towards the cost of the station which was described in the following terms in Major Pringle's Board of Trade Report:

> The platform is intended solely for the use of colliers employed at Tyneholm Colliery. It has a length of 80 feet and a width and height of 7 ft and 3 ft respectively. No nameboard has been provided as the platform will not be advertised in Bradshaw. Lamp posts have been erected and I was informed that, when used after daylight, lamps would be provided.

A new third-class only workmen's service was provided from Macmerry at 6.10 am, calling at Winton, Ormiston and Woodhall Platform and then running empty to Gifford, whence it formed the first train of the day to Edinburgh. The return working left the platform at 3.30 pm and went back to Ormiston, Winton and Macmerry. Special reduced fares were in operation, it being 1s. 6d. (7½p) from Winton and 1s. (5p) from Ormiston for a bundle of six single journey tickets. A request was made to the North British that ordinary trains should be allowed to call at the Platform and David Deuchars replied that

> I have considered this proposal, but for various reasons I do not think that the Company should agree to stop the regular trains at the Platform where there is no staff to deal with the miners alighting or joining there. Besides we have already had complaints as to the length of time taken by trains on this Light Railway and it is not desirable to increase the time taken.

Woodhall Platform was not, apparently, a great success and the special workmen's trains were discontinued as from 18th November, 1907, although the station did see occasional usage thereafter.

In a delightful footnote to the history of the line the solicitors of the Gifford & Garvald received the following letter from the Marchioness of Tweeddale:

*A Scots word meaning a long pole on wheels used for carrying logs, casks or other heavy weights.

> Sir, Do you think that you could intercede with the Directors of the Gifford &
> Garvald Light Railway to bestow on our little station at Gifford two simple wooden
> benches. They are *really* needed. There is much traffic in summer especially. I
> think that ours is the only station without benches now. I do not know who else to
> apply to and hope that you will not mind my writing and asking your support in
> this matter.

The result of this letter was that the North British sent the Gifford & Garvald
an invoice for 'Two No. 7 Platform Seats, 6 feet long, at a cost of 27s. (£1.35)
each.'

Shortly before the outbreak of World War I the Gifford line reached its
zenith with the line carrying over 30,000 passengers annually; Pencaitland
was the busiest station, accounting for one-third of this number. The service
had also been greatly improved and in 1914 there were three weekday trains
from Edinburgh, the 7.33 and 9.32 am and 5.10 pm departures, with an
additional Saturdays Only train leaving the capital at 12.44 pm (this still
being a half-day for office and shop workers). There was also a special late
service on Saturdays leaving Edinburgh at 10.45 pm for the benefit of those
who wished to visit friends or family or the attractions of the theatre or the
new cinematograph. The average speed of trains had also increased somewhat and the 21 mile journey from Gifford to Edinburgh now took a mere
1 hour and 11 minutes. A pony and trap met most trains in order to convey
passengers and their luggage between Gifford station and the village. Even at
this early stage, however, there was a rival for a thrice-daily bus service,
operated by the proprietors of the Goblin Ha' Hotel, connected Gifford with
Haddington station where connections were made to trains; no train connections were, however, provided at Gifford for the return service.

The condition of Woodhall Platform was deteriorating and, following an
inspection by the North British Engineer, the superintendent of the line
wrote a memo to the General Manager on that subject.

> I see no objection to the arrangement which was entered into some years ago being
> continued whereby the 9.38 am train from Gifford to Edinburgh was ordered to
> call at the Wodhall Colliery Platform on previous notice being given to the station
> master at Pencaitland for the accommodation of Mr Reid and his colliery manager,
> Mr McGregor, who both hold trader's tickets. The facility is only taken advantage
> of on average two times weekly and, as the train service is somewhat meagre, it is
> desirable that the two parties named should be accommodated in this way. It is
> understood that Mr Reid states that there is no probability of the platform being
> required in connection with the workmen's trains in the future and he is prepared
> in the event of the existing arrangements being continued, to point out to our
> engineers the extent of the Platform required – about one carriage length.

The coal company paid the £10 necessary for the repairs to the platform
and these were duly carried out in October 1915. For how long Messrs Reid
and McGregor continued to use the facility is not clear, but the last mention
of the station occurs in February 1925 when an internal railway memorandum states that 'This platform is not now used'. However the 1930 working
timetable contains the following entry in connection with the 9.44 am Gifford to Edinburgh passenger train: 'Calls at Woodhall Colliery Platform to
pick up Manager of Woodhall Coal Co., on intimation being made to the
Pencaitland or Ormiston Station-masters.'

Throughout its life the Gifford & Garvald Railway Company was still enjoying the monthly payment of £300 per month from the North British and paid its shareholders a 3½ per cent dividend. William Fulton Jackson continued as Chairman of the Gifford & Garvald until his retirement in 1917 and he was succeeded by William Whitelaw, grandfather of the politician and Chairman of the North British. Mr Whitelaw went on to become the highly respected first Chairman of the London & North Eastern Railway and he had the distinction of having both an A3 and subsequently an A4 pacific locomotive named after him.

The proposed extension of the line from Gifford to Garvald had all but been forgotten* when, in 1920, suggestions were made locally that this part of the line should now be built. The route suggested was that of the original 1891 Act, with an extension southwards from Garvald to Stenton and onwards until it joined up with the East Coast main line 1000 yards south of Eastbarns. Several prominent landowners in the county expressed the view that the proposed line would lead to a considerable increase in agricultural output in the area, but the proposals fell on stony ground for already the internal combustion engine was making itself felt on the highways and byways of East Lothian and the railway age was drawing to a close.

---

*According to an eye-witness, however, the wooden pegs used to survey the line in 1891 survived for many years *in situ* on the section between Gifford and Tanderlane Farm until they were eventually removed and used as firewood in the 1930s.

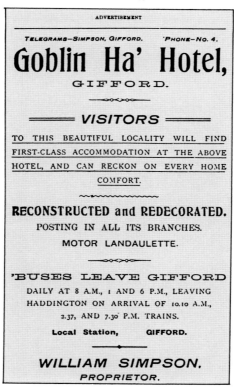

The pretty lines of a Drummond 'R' class ('D51'), No. 10458 (the former NBR No. 99 Roxburgh) at Ormiston, c.1928.

G.N. Heathcote

Chapter Eight
The LNER takes over
THE POST-GROUPING YEARS

'There being no legal objection to the withdrawal of the passenger trains, and as the district is already well served by the buses of the Scottish Motor Traction Co. Ltd., it is not anticipated that any serious complaints will arise from the public.'

LNER Memorandum, 27th February, 1933.

On 1st January, 1923 the three branch lines became part of the London & North Eastern Railway, one of the four amalgams created by the government by the passing of the Railways Act 1921. In the case of the North British, the passing of control to London had met with some spirited opposition, but with the Gifford & Garvald Railway the desire to continue as an independent concern was rather less marked. The shareholders of both companies were given LNER stock in substitution for their shares and the affairs of the Gifford & Garvald company as a legal entity were finally brought to an end in August 1923 when it was formally absorbed with retrospective effect, £90,000 of 4 per cent second guarantee LNER stock being given in exchange for the £100,000 of G&GR ordinary stock; Alexander Guild, W.S. was given £135 as compensation for his loss of office as Company Secretary and a cash surplus of £63 15s. 2d. was declared. At that time, the Gifford & Garvald company had 24 separate shareholders, both private and institutional and their holdings ranged from 2,100 shares held by the North British & Mercantile Insurance Company of Edinburgh down to the 15 shares held by a Mr Robert Gracey of Exeter. Several of the shareholders had acquired their shares as a result of legacies and this included the London Metropolitan Hospital Sunday Fund, but it was particularly appropriate that some of the early shareholders had still retained their holdings.

At first changes were few, although the LNER name rapidly appeared on rolling stock, locomotives and publicity. Minor changes were made to the pattern of services on the branch lines, but it was rapidly becoming clear that the post-war expansion of rural bus services in southern Scotland was beginning to affect the viability of the local train services. The Macmerry branch, never the most profitable of lines, was particularly hard hit by the rival Scottish Motor Traction Company services which started in February 1921 and first became daily in May of that year. The buses, Lothian single-deckers on the Haddington to Edinburgh route, ran along the newly designated A1 road via Macmerry, Tranent and Musselburgh, and, from the bus stop outside Macmerry station, a modern and fashionable bus would take passengers direct to Edinburgh in 40 minutes at a cheaper rate than the train and at a frequency of three buses per hour, as opposed to the railway's two daily services. Many years later the Minister of Gladsmuir parish (in which Macmerry was situated) wrote in *The Third Statistical Account of Scotland* that:

> The great advantages that have accrued through the development of bus services in the parish can be realised when they are compared to the slender opportunities provided to the inhabitants thirty years ago, when considerable distances had to be

walked before most of the people could avail themselves of the scanty rail arrangements.

The evidence of this competition was clear – at Macmerry 2,257 passengers had booked there in 1920 but by 1922, when the bus services had been properly established, bookings had fallen to only 409, or less than 10 passengers per week, while the gross receipts there had plummeted to a mere £1 per week! Winton was less affected directly by bus competition, but even here there was a slight fall. The passengers did not return to the railway and it could therefore have taken few by surprise to have read the following discreet notice which appeared in the *Haddingtonshire Courier*, sandwiched between advertisements for lost walking sticks and 'The Further Adventures of Dr Fumanchu' at the Prestonpans Picture House.

L.N.E.R.

CLOSING
of
WINTON & MACMERRY STATIONS
for
PASSENGER TRAIN TRAFFIC

THE PUBLIC are Respectfully informated that *on or after 1st July, 1925* WINTON and MACMERRY stations will be CLOSED for PASSENGER TRAIN TRAFFIC.

Goods and Mineral Traffic will continue to be dealt with at these stations.

The closure of the Macmerry branch to passengers seems to have caused little interest locally, although a crowd of Macmerry folk did turn out to witness the arrival of the last train and there was some merrymaking which ended in a slight disturbance. Following the cessation of passenger services the LNER brought into effect other economies on the line, such as the closure of the signal box at the terminus and the simplifying of the operating arrangements there, the withdrawal of crossing keepers at Penston and Winton East Mains, and the appointment of a single station master to cover both Winton and Macmerry stations.

The General Strike of May 1926 did little to promote the appeal of the branch lines of the county and the timing of it was something of a disaster since it helped to demonstrate the power of the deadly combination of the car, bus and motor lorry locally. In 1926 the number of private motor cars licensed in East Lothian amounted to 808; by 1930 they had increased to 1,155 and by 1938 1,958. Goods vehicles licensed in the county increased from 326 in 1926 to 691 in 1938 and 766 after World War II, by which time they were used widely by farmers, tradesmen and local industry. Between 1931 and 1935 there was a 53 per cent increase in motor traffic in the county, compared to a Scottish average of 69 per cent but on the county B roads the percentage increase in East Lothian in the seven year period from 1929 was 81 per cent for buses and cars, 65 per cent for lorries and, remarkably 181 per cent for pedal cycles, while the county's horse drawn traffic decreased by 43 per cent. In respect of lorries this was equal to the Scottish average, while for buses and cars it was double the average and constituted the second highest increase in the whole of Scotland. A measure of the effectiveness of bus competition was the fact that in July 1930 some 291,000 journeys were made on SMT bus services, while nine years later this figure had increased to some 419,000.

Every rural branch line had its own tales and stories, some of them true and some not and apart from the familiar stories of crews stopping their trains to poach rabbits and gather mushrooms, and the use of the locomotive coal in a form of local bartering for chickens, eggs and dairy produce there were a few more original anecdotes. One of the best concerned the senior partner of a prestigous firm of Edinburgh solicitors who lived in the area and who was, for many years, a regular commuter from Humbie. Each morning his Rolls-Royce would take him to the station at Humbie so that he could travel up to town in a first class compartment while his chauffeur would take the car to Edinburgh, meet his master off the train at Waverley Station and then take him to his office in Charlotte Square! Another reputedly true tale concerned a loaded coal train which ran out of control down the falling gradient from the Bog Siding between Ormiston and Crossgatehall before smashing through the level crossing gates at Smeaton Shaw – the driver, nonplussed, is supposed to have written in the official accident report that 'the gates were in need of paint'.

A more serious accident occurred on 23rd July, 1924 when the evening passenger train from Gifford collided with a fish salesman's lorry at the Woodhall open level crossing near Pencaitland. Thomas Lancelot Nicholson of Seton Sands, Longniddry, who was the owner and driver of the lorry, was killed and in the words of the London *Times* newspaper, 'the engine driver had sounded his whistle as usual on approaching the level crossing. Evidently Nicholson expected to effect a safe passage before the train reached the roadway, but the engine caught the motor lorry on its buffers and smashed it.'

Staff mobility seems to have been a feature of this time. At Gifford John Laing, who had held the position of station master since 1919, was replaced by William Hogg, who stayed there until his retirement in 1936. His son, Robert Hogg, was latterly the head of the BR Historical Records Office situated at the old NBR offices in Waterloo Place, Edinburgh and whose collection was later transferred to the safe keeping of the Scottish Record Office, to whom the present author owes a debt of gratitude. A long serving railway employee began his career at Gifford, namely John Logan, whose first engagement was that of junior clerk at the station in 1924 and who only finally retired from BR in 1974 having been successively station master at Cockburnspath, Peebles and Broughty Ferry. At Pencaitland the station master, David Broatch, was transferred to Humbie in 1927 and from there to Saltoun in 1930. John Gold, whom he replaced at Humbie, was promoted to the post of Inspector at Thornton Junction in Fife. At Winton and Macmerry (where, in 1921, the respective station masters had been George Wood and Arthur Kettles) R. Purves was in charge until he was transferred to Gartsherrie in 1927. He was succeeded by W. Peacock from Bowland who, after four years, was transferred to Dirleton while Mr Purves eventually returned to Humbie. Some idea of the respective importance of the branch line stations when they were all still fully staffed can be gained from their NBR classification – Edinburgh Waverley was a Class 1 station while Haddington and Longniddry were Class 2, Smeaton (under whose jurisdiction also came Crossgatehall Halt) and Ormiston were Class 3, Gifford was Class 4 and in the least important category, Class 5, were placed Winton, Macmerry, Pencaitland, Saltoun and Humbie. Wages had risen substantially since the War and local station masters were now (1925) paid between 65s. (£3.25) and £5 15s. (£5.75) per week; other local weekly wages included signalmen at between 65s. (£3.25) and 85s. (£4.25), porters at between 40s. (£2) and 46s. (£2.30) and girl junior clerks at 13s. 6d. (67½p). The branch engine drivers received between 12s. (60p) and 15s. (75p) per day plus overtime. In comparison the average East Lothian farm labourer received about 30s. (£1.50) per week although this was in effect supplemented by free housing and other benefits in kind whereas railwaymen had to contribute to the rent and rates of their company-owned houses.

By the mid-1920s the small Drummond 4–4–0 tanks, by now LNER class 'D51', were reaching the end of their working lives and the Wheatley 'E' class ('J31') 0–6–0s which were occasionally seen on Gifford passenger turns were also somewhat elderly. Of the 'D51's two were particular favourites on the line namely LNER No. 10458 (formerly NBR No. 99 *Roxburgh*) and No. 10467 (the unnamed NBR No. 77). These faithful little engines festooned with oil cans to provide station lighting could put on a surprising turn of speed especially on the run to Portobello. The most common 'J31' was the former NBR No. 1178, which was finally withdrawn in August 1925. The LNER were now obliged to try and find replacements for the 'D51's but it was not easy to find small but powerful locomotives whose axle weight did not exceed the limit imposed by the Light Railway Order. Eventually, a replacement was found and in July 1931 an 'F4' class 2–4–2 tank was transferred from London to St Margarets for evaluation. This was No. 7176, one of a large number of 'M15' small suburban passenger engines built by S.D. Holden for the Great Eastern Railway in 1908 to a design of T.W. Worsdell that dated back to the 1880s. No. 7176 was followed by two of her sisters and three locomotives of a basically similar class of Great Eastern 2–4–2Ts – Holden 'F7's (GER 'Y65' class), of which No. 8301 became a regular performer on the Gifford line. The 'F7' class had disproportionately large cabs with glazed windows and accordingly they were known to London crews as the 'Crystal Palaces' while at St Margarets they were dubbed the 'Tomato Houses'. The remaining 'D51', No. 10458, was banished to the remote Fraserburgh and St Combs line and the Great Eastern locomotives were destined to see out the passenger service to Gifford. Coaching stock now tended to be the regular branch set of four- and six-wheeled carriages but from 1930 onwards bogie stock became much more common on the line – appropriately enough some of this stock came from the Southern Area of the LNER and was of Great Eastern origin, while other carriages came from the North Eastern and North British.

The new motive power did nothing to stay the decline in passenger usage

A down goods train passes Ormiston in the charge of class 'D51' No. 10458 in 1928.
G.N. Heathcote

'D51s' at Gifford — (*top*) a curiously 'touched-up' postcard view *c.*1910; (*middle*) a 1926 picture showing Brownlie's sawmills in the background and (*bottom*) ready for departure to Edinburgh, *c.*1928.
Author's Collection;
W. Muir, SRO Collection;
W. Lynn Collection

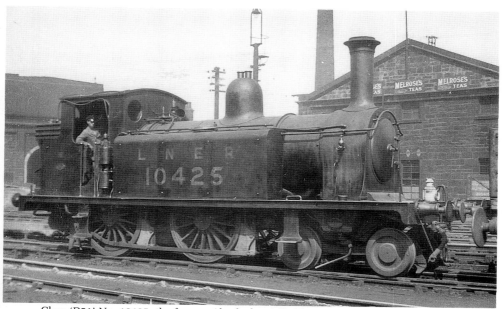

Class 'D51' No. 10425, the former *Aberfoyle*, at St. Margarets, c.1926.
R.W. Lynn Collection

A class 'D51' approaches Portobello with a Gifford to Edinburgh train, c.1924.
R.W. Lynn Collection

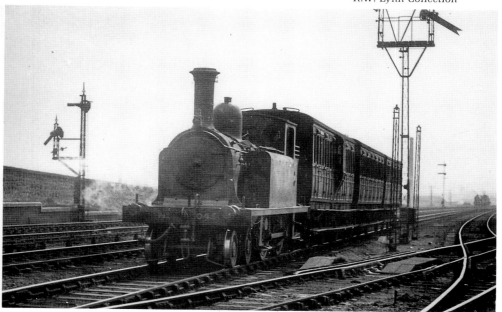

Two 'Londoners' in exile which worked the Gifford branch between 1931 and 1933; (*upper*) a Great Eastern Holden 'M15' (LNER 'F4'), transferred to St Margarets in July 1931 and (*lower*) the first of the GER 'Y65s' (LNER 'F7s') sent to Scotland; their large cabs earned them the soubriquet 'Crystal Palaces' at Stratford and 'Tomato Houses' in Edinburgh. *A.G. Ellis Collection*

and spectacular losses were made to the buses of the SMT Company, in which the LNER was to acquire a shareholding. By 1921 Ormiston had a regular bus service to Edinburgh via Tranent and in February 1928 an Edinburgh to Gifford and Haddington service via Ormiston, Pencaitland and East Saltoun (with occasional diversions to West Saltoun) was started up which, along with other local services, effectively proved to be the death knell of the Gifford passenger trains. The first casualties of this competition were the stations at Smeaton, where the number of passengers booked had dropped from over 3,000 in 1920 to just over 500 by 1930, and Crossgatehall Halt, where there were 1,500 bookings in that year; the combined passenger receipts from Smeaton and Crossgatehall in the three months prior to closure averaged 25s. [£1.25] per week. With effect from 22nd September, 1930 (i.e. the last trains calling on Saturday 20th September) these two stations were closed* to passengers (and, in the case of Crossgatehall, entirely since it did not handle goods) leaving Ormiston as the first station on the branch. Goods traffic showed a less marked decline and the coal traffic continued almost unabated – almost all of the small mines of East Lothian remained in production and there was less unemployment amongst the miners there than in many of the more 'traditional' mining areas like Lanarkshire. For a time there was some additional traffic to Gifford in connection with the construction of the Hopes Reservoir close by.

As the economic situation continued to deteriorate nationally LNER staff wages were cut consequent upon a Wages Board Award and further staffing cuts were made in the area. The one bright note, however, was provided by the fact that since the closure of Smeaton and Crossgatehall Halt the journey time from Gifford to Edinburgh had been cut to a mere 57 minutes, the best ever and the basic weekday service now consisted of three return trains with an additional three Saturdays Only trains.

On 2nd January, 1933 further economies were brought into effect on the Gifford line when 'one engine in steam' working was introduced between Saltoun and the terminus. The branch engine was transferred from Gifford to St Margarets and the train service was recast so that annual estimated savings of £499 in the traffic department, £10 in the engineering department and £190 in the locomotive department could all be made, while a further £57 was saved by signalling alterations. The pattern of services was now as follows: on the Macmerry branch there was a single daily goods working in each direction while on the Gifford branch the service was more complicated in that there were three daily passenger trains to Edinburgh, one of which was a mixed train between Gifford and Ormiston, and there were two additional Saturday services. Goods workings consisted of a daily train in each direction between Portobello and Gifford, a Tuesdays only livestock train from Gifford to the Edinburgh markets at Gorgie and four mineral trains daily in each direction from or to Portobello or South Leith which commenced or terminated at intermediate points. Passenger services were worked by the two GER 'F4s' which also worked some of the goods services, while others were worked by two double-shifted engines from St Margarets.

An investigation was now carried out by the LNER into the economic

---

*On the same day the GWR, LMS and LNER closed a large number of stations throughout Britain making it reputedly the biggest single spate of closures prior to Beeching. On the former North British system alone 24 stations were closed and another East Lothian casualty was Seton Mains Halt on the main line between Prestonpans and Longniddry.

viability of the Macmerry and Gifford lines and in a report dated 20th January, 1933, it was stated that the lines produced an annual operating surplus of £41,079 but that this sum was almost entirely due to the heavy mineral traffic. It was considered that the introduction of one of the Sentinel Cammell steam railcars, used elsewhere on the LNER including the North Leith and North Berwick branches, was not a viable proposition and thus the 'Chippies' (a local name derived from a supposed similarity between the units and a mobile fish-and-chip shop) never appeared on the line; no other economies could be suggested. By the closing of the Gifford line to passengers, however, adjustments could be made to goods services which would result in the saving of one crew's wages, while the passenger train locomotives could be withdrawn and 827 passenger miles per week could be saved (less those incurred by an additional Edinburgh to Musselburgh train to give additional services to main line stations at which the Gifford trains called). Furthermore three six-wheel brake thirds, three thirds and two firsts could all be cut out of the next LNER carriage building programme. The case for closure appeared to the company to be overwhelming and on 27th February, 1933 the following memorandum was issued to the Traffic, Locomotive and Works Committee by the Southern Scottish Area Manager:

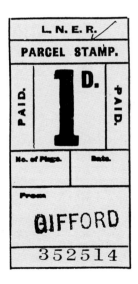

A selection of LNER Gifford branch tickets: (left) two parcels stamps issued after nationalisation; (below) two tickets issued on the last day of passenger services, Saturday 1st April, 1933.

Closing of Branch Lines – Gifford Light Railway
SCOTTISH AREA

The passenger traffic on the Gifford Light Railway, which has been falling away for a number of years as a result of road competition, can no longer justify the present passenger train service, and in view of the geographical position of the line, it is not anticipated that, by increasing the number of trains it will be possible to recover the traffic to rail.

The goods traffic, principally coal, has been well maintained and continues to show satisfactory results, but for the twelve months ended 30th June, 1932 the Gifford Branch passenger receipts, including through traffic to and from Edinburgh, only amounted to £2,565, while the gross contributory revenue was £696. An intensive passenger service on this branch, even if it were desirable, would have a retarding effect on the working of the mineral traffic. . .

The cost of working has already been reduced to a minimum consistent with requirements, and no further economies which would increase the net revenue can be effected in the working of the passenger trains, short of their complete withdrawal. If this were done, it is estimated that, by utilising the goods train service for the parcels and miscellaneous traffic, receipts amounting to £477 per annum therefrom could be retained, and the loss in revenue would be considerably more than offset by reductions in expenditure. Two Class F.4 engines could be withdrawn from service, and the estimated net saving, allowing for an almost complete disappearance of branch and contributory passenger revenue is £515 as under:

Savings	£	£
Maintenance of Way & Works	75	
Maintenance and renewal of carriages	485	
Locomotive Department	2,040	
Traffic Department	452	
Miscellaneous	14	3,066
Loss in Revenue		
Passengers	2,060	
Parcels	384	
Miscellaneous	28	
Payment for conveyance of Mails	77	2,551
Net saving		£515

There is no legal objection to the withdrawal of the Passenger trains, and as the district is already well served by the buses of the Scottish Motor Traction Co. Ltd., it is not anticipated that any serious complaints will arise from the public. It is accordingly RECOMMENDED that, in order to effect economy, the Passenger train service on the Gifford Branch may be withdrawn on or after 3rd April, 1933.

(signed) J. CALDER

The only caveat entered by the company was in respect of the people living in the vicinity of Saltoun and Humbie stations, since these were areas which were not directly served by buses and because the SMT had 'indicated their unwillingness to give a service to these places on economic grounds without a guarantee from the Railway company' the LNER resolved to deal with all such objections 'on their merits'. The figures spoke for

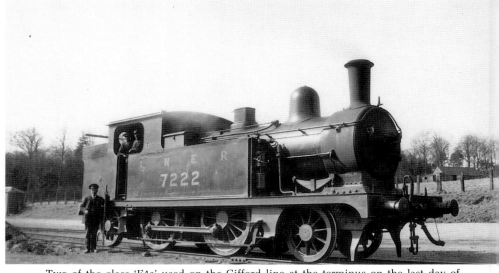

Two of the class 'F4s' used on the Gifford line at the terminus on the last day of passenger services (Saturday 1st April, 1933) – note the bogie stock on the Edinburgh train shown in the lower photograph. (*The negative of this view is unfortunately damaged*).   *G.N. Heathcote*

themselves – Ormiston, Pencaitland, Saltoun and Gifford stations were each handling less than 50 per cent of the passengers that they had handled previously and even Humbie, with no bus opposition, was one-third down on its 1920 figure. There was little likelihood of any substantial housing or industrial developments near any of these stations which would lead to an upturn in usage.

In the event protests appear to have been muted and the passenger service over the branch was discontinued as from 3rd April, the stations at Ormiston, Pencaitland, Saltoun, Humbie and Gifford all being closed to passengers after the passage of the last train on Saturday 1st April. Many locals, and a handful of railway enthusiasts, turned out to see Nos. 7222 and 7236 at work on the final day and they included several people who had witnessed the opening of the line only 32 years before. The two 'F4' tank engines were duly dispatched to the Fraserburgh to St Combs line, where in turn they replaced the previously transferred 'D51s', which were then scrapped. Further staff economies on the branch were now made and the post of station master at Gifford and Humbie was abolished in 1936, control of these stations being transferred to Saltoun.

One casualty of closure of the branch to passengers was, however, the Gifford Games. These had originally been held in the village for many years prior to World War I as a form of local games confined to the parishes of Yester, Saltoun and Garvald but after the war they were revived and metamorphosed into a much bigger gathering where piping, highland dancing, tossing the caber and other more obviously Scottish events took place, attracting both sportsmen and spectators from a wide area. The peak years of the games were 1927–8 when it was estimated that 2,000 persons attended, a special train being run from Edinburgh to accommodate them. On the closure of the railway to passengers promises were given by the SMT and local bus operators that sufficient coaches would be made available to service the games, but in the way that these undertakings were often given when lines were closed the bus companies failed to live up to their promises, and an immediate and sustained fall in attendances at the Games was experienced. The organisers struggled on until 1938, when the Games were finally abandoned, an early example of the all too-common empty promises given by bus companies when railway lines were closed.

During the early 1930s, the final chapter in the history of the ill-fated Smeaton to Hardengreen line was unfolding. Since the closure of the line to through traffic at the end of the First War the branch had been used for wagon storage. As the LNER found its economic position deteriorating all maintenance of the line (including the Victoria Viaduct) ceased and the end finally came on Armistice Day, 11th November, 1934, when Thorneybank depot was closed and the line was then severed leaving two isolated sections, namely a stub at the Hardengreen Junction end and a half-mile siding at the Smeaton end. The siding, known as the 'Thorneybank branch' continued in use for the storage of crippled wagons until the early 1950s when new colliery developments brought out its resurrection while the Hardengreen stub, known to railwaymen as 'the Hole' was used as a siding for the setting back of pilot and banking engines for the Penicuik and Peebles lines so that the engines involved did not foul the running lines; this usage continued until the summer of 1961. The fate of the Victoria Viaduct was a sad one for, after remaining as a rusting hulk for several years the girders were removed in 1940 and contributed some 300 tons of scrap to the war effort. The masonry piers were left until the summer of 1964 when, after fears that they were becoming unsafe and that in any event they were considered an eyesore, they were demolished, the whole area thereafter being landscaped beyond recognition. Some of the demolition work was carried out by Cistercian monks who were engaged in building a new Abbey at Nunraw near Garvald and next to the former home of Walter Wingate Gray, erstwhile director of the G&GR. The monks hoped particularly to be able to use the granite blocks which footed the masonry piers but although some material was removed by them to Nunraw it proved, in the event, to be of little use and was later discarded.

In the mid 1930s the usual motive power on the Haddington, Macmerry and Gifford branch lines was still mainly ex-North British, but there were a few interlopers. The usual locomotive to work the 10.50 am Gifford Goods was an NBR Holmes 'D' class ('J33') 0−6−0, No. 9169, one of the examples which had a curiously antiquated open cab. This engine, together with an equally venerable sister, No. 9249, were the last surviving members of their class; No. 9169 worked the Gifford Goods with such regularity that the booked times of this daily run were scratched out on her cab paintwork. When this locomotive was not available, and after her withdrawal from service in December 1938, another English exile was used, this time in the form of one of the three class 'J24' 0−6−0 tender locomotives transferred to St Margarets between 1928 and 1932. The 'J24s' originated on the North Eastern Railway as Thomas Wordsell's 'P' class, built in the 1890s as short-haul mineral engines. Ten 'J24s' were sent to Scotland for use on lightly-laid branch lines where their 14 ton 6 cwt axle load proved to be useful when many of the older Scottish light engines were reaching the end of their lives. Although not popular with the St Margarets' crews (who sarcastically dubbed them 'Coffee Pots'), they served the line faithfully for more than 20 years. Presumably the cab of these locomotives was capacious for, on one occasion when the pick-up goods service arrived at Ormiston, it was found that there was a calf to be taken from there to Pencaitland. As no cattle wagon was available on the train, the crew hoisted the terrified beast into the cab of the 'J24' with them and gave it a footplate ride to its destination!

The Gifford Goods was normally worked by the St Margarets' coal train link; the locomotive crews were rotated so that on average each crew would only work the train one week per year. The usual guard of that time was Will Henderson of Portobello, who was said to have ruled the service with a rod of iron and who was widely known as 'The Duke of Gifford'. Among his eccentricities was the substitution of his uniform cap with a battered old trilby once the train had cleared Monktonhall Junction, his insistence on strict timekeeping, whatever the circumstances, and his visits for 'refreshment purposes' to, alternatively, the Tweeddale Arms and the Goblin Ha', once the train had reached Gifford. Other regular turns worked

NBR Holmes class 'J33' No. 9169 at Craigentinny – this veteran locomotive was for many years the mainstay of motive power for the 10.50 am Gifford Goods in the 1930s and the booked times of this run were scratched by the crew into her cab paintwork.   *A.G. Ellis Collection*

The cab of No. 9169 a well laid out design.   *G.N. Heathcote*

North Eastern Railway 'P' class (LNER class 'J24') No. 1897 at Craigentinny – one of a number of these small goods engines sent up to work, *inter alia*, the Gifford Goods in the war years and after. *G.N. Heathcote*

GER 'R24' (LNER class 'J67') transferred to Scotland to work lightly laid lines – this example was seen on the Gifford line but normally worked the Lauder branch complete with a tender. *G.N. Heathcote*

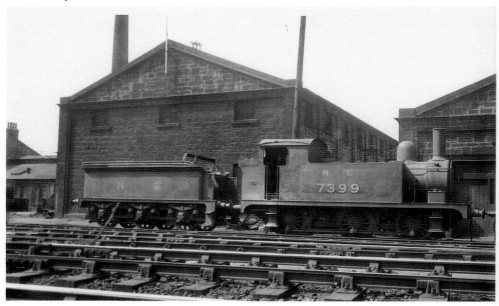

by 'The Duke' included the weekly cattle train from Gifford to Gorgie and the 'Fordell', alias the 11.28 am Portobello to Macmerry coal train which also worked to the Fordell Mains Colliery near Cousland.

Another regular goods service was the 'Widha' (Woodhall) or, more prosaically, the 4.55 am Portobello to Pencaitland Colliery Class D mineral train which was also worked by the St Margarets coal train link. This was not a popular run as it involved crews signing on at 4.18 am and, being the first train of the day to run beyond Smeaton, often involved a struggle to climb the 1 in 50 gradient past there in damp or frosty weather. Another working was known as the 'Back Shift Widha', being the 1.50 pm Portobello to Pencaitland Colliery. The return workings left the colliery at, respectively, 7.20 am and 3.13 pm.

What was probably the last ever passenger train run over the whole length of the Gifford & Garvald line was a train chartered by the Gifford Women's Rural Institute to take people from Gifford to see the 1938 Empire Exhibition held at Bellahouston Park, Glasgow. The return fare was a bargain at 6s. 9d. [34p] and this jaunt was apparently greatly enjoyed, although the WRI Minutes record that 'several members managed to lose the train for the return journey but got back safely to Gifford eventually' – one wonders how!

On the Haddington branch, bus competiton had intensified to the extent that buses ran from there to Edinburgh directly every fifteen minutes, the journey being helped in no small way by the reconstruction of the A1, the London trunk road. A new by-pass was built to the north of the town and this crossed the railway close to St Lawrence on a large concrete and steel bridge – somewhat optimistically, in view of the fact that the line had been singled in the 1850s, double-line clearances were provided. An even more worrying factor was the effect of competition from the motor lorry and private car, and traffic began to fall off to the extent that traders were deserting the railway and local people no longer regarded it as indispensible. With the exception of the Friday market train, there were now no through passenger services to Edinburgh and although the four- and six-wheeled passenger stock was beginning to be supplanted by new or cascaded bogie stock, the rather shabby trains were not seen to have the same style and panache of the buses, and once farmers and the better-off town dwellers acquired a motor car they were proud to use it on every available occasion.

An unusual incident occurred at Haddington station on Friday 10th December, 1937 when the market train from Edinburgh, drawn as usual by 'C16' tank No. 9449 and due in the terminus at 11.19 am, failed to stop at the passenger platform, ploughed through the buffer stops and ended up hanging over the retaining wall at the station forecourt, providing a great object of interest to local children returning from school for their lunch. The cause of this accident, in which no one was hurt apart from the driver, who suffered shock, was found to have been ice on the rails which resulted in the brakes failing to grip as they were applied on the short 1 in 220 decline into the station. The incident caused much amusement locally but, unfortunately, was overshadowed by the far more serious accident which occurred later that same afternoon at Castlecary, between Edinburgh and Glasgow, when two LNER trains collided and 35 passengers were killed.

As war approached, and preparations were made, the government once more assumed responsibility for the railways, and this meant that three days before hostilities officially commenced the LNER came under state control. After a false start, in which children were evacuated by train from Edinburgh, little happened locally under March 1941 when a German plane dropped a stick of bombs on Haddington, killing two people. Passenger journeys on the branch line increased due to the presence locally of allied troops stationed at Amisfield, the RAF presence at the Lennoxlove airfield and by the fuel rationing which affected both private cars and the SMT buses. The strangest cargo carried during this period, when there were many unusual items carried by train, consisted of the tanks of the First Polish Armoured Division unit from Amisfield – on one memorable day in late 1943 these tanks trundled through the town *en route* for the station where they were put onto low-loaders and taken to the south as part of the preliminaries to D-Day. Thus, in a small way, did the Haddington branch contribute to the liberation of Europe! Another activity involving the army engineers was the coastal defence works and anti-tank blockade on the East Lothian beaches and the materials for this were carried by train to Longniddry and Aberlady; at the former station a coastal defence special train was kept in the charge of an ex-GER 'F4' $2-4-2T$ locomotive fitted with War Department armour plating and full camouflage. Originally No. 7573, built at Stratford in 1907, the Longniddry locomotive emerged in its new guise with grey, green and khaki paint and bore the letter 'K' reflecting the WD identification of the unit with which it and its artillery train served. After the war the locomotive reverted to civilian use but carried a special brass plate with the following inscription: 'LNER. During the war of 1939/45 this locomotive was armoured and hauled defence trains on the coast lines.' It was finally withdrawn and scrapped in 1951.

On the Macmerry and Gifford branches there was some extra traffic in coal but towards the end of the War, this was beginning to decline and the closure of the Tyneholm and Fordell Mains Collieries was only partly off-set by the development of the existing pits. Timber for use as pit-props, always an occasional traffic from Humbie and Saltoun, showed a modest increase at this time. Much of the labour used in its production came from Axis prisoners-of-war billeted in the area. An unusual wartime freight was the traffic in rose hips from Gifford – sacks of these were gathered by local children for a small reward and sent by rail to a factory near Newcastle. Here they were processed into rose-hip syrup for the nation's babies when other sources of Vitamin C were hard to come by. Another wartime treat was provided by the crews of the 'J24': when it arrived at the terminus footplate rides were often given to the children who had turned out to watch and even, on occasions, 'shots' at driving the engine up and down the sidings were provided. All this extra traffic was not, however, enough to prevent the daily booked Gifford goods from being reduced to a thrice-weekly working for at least part of the war years, and the branch continued its slow but inexorable decline.

Haddington station in the 1930s. (*Top*) a porter holds a door open for a third class passenger on a wet and windy afternoon; (*bottom*) the 'C16' on the Friday market train fails to stop and ploughs through the buffers, perhaps as a result of a surfeit of Bovril! 10th December, 1937. *Author's Collection; George Angus Collection*

Three views taken on a dull July afternoon in 1943. (*Top*) class 'C16' No. 9451 ready to depart with the 5.50 pm to Longniddry; (*middle*) the shunter and crew of a class 'D32' No. 9893 pose for the photographer, (*bottom*) a view showing the grain and goods shed – the small brick building on the platform survives to this day.

A.G. Ellis

The First Polish Armoured Division load their tanks at Haddington station in 1943 *en route* to the South of England and (eventually) D-day; judging by the fact that a number of local children and their mothers are seen looking on security seems to have been somewhat lax here. *George Angus Collection*

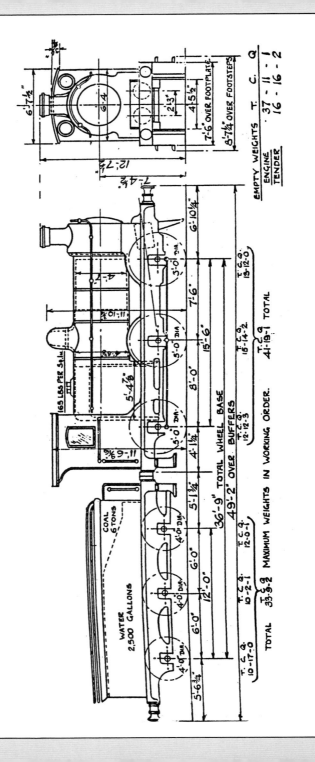

North British Railway 'C' class (J36) 0–6–0: these versatile locomotives were often seen on the branch lines of East Lothian and lasted until the very end of steam in Scotland; No. 65243 *Maude* survives into preservation.

LNER drawing – SRO Collection

Motive power seen east of Smeaton at this time became varied and unpredictable, owing to the exigencies of war, and although the 'J24s' were the only locomotives officially permitted to work the light railway section beyond Pencaitland Colliery, a large variety of other locomotives worked the remainder of the line. According to an article by W. Hennigan during one week in December 1941 the 'Widha' was worked in turn on Monday by No. 9777, a 'J36' normally shedded at Polmont, on Tuesday by No. 9458, a Carlisle 'J37', cancelled on Wednesday, on Thursday by a 'J24' No. 1900 (this day the trip including a run to Winton, Saltoun and Humbie with cattle wagons), on Friday by No. 1405, a Gresley 'J38' from Dundee and on Saturday by No. 9758, a St Margarets 'J36', described as 'a wreck'.

Locomotives noted on the Haddington branch during the war years, apart from the regular 'J36' allocated to Prestonpans Pilot duties and Haddington branch turns, included Reid 'C15' and 'C16' 4–4–2T Nos. 9012 and 9448 – this latter engine, which became No. 7492 under the LNER 1946 renumbering scheme, was for many years the booked branch engine stationed at the Longniddry sub-shed; her regular driver Willie Griffin lived next to the main line at Blawearie level crossing. On the 'opposite' shift to Mr Griffin was a newly qualified driver, Andrew Riddell, who started his railway career as a fireman at Haymarket during the war and was transferred to Longniddry shed. Mr Riddell still remembers with affection the 'C16s' and described them to the author as 'grand wee engines which did everything expected of them' and that they ran very smoothly on the well maintained trackwork. At this time Wattie Bell, who had been a driver on the branch in the 1920s and 1930s, became the caretaker of the shed at Longniddry. Other engines seen on the branch included Reid 'J' class intermediate 4–4–0s (LNER class 'D29', but known as the 'Scotts' because of their names) Nos. 9895 *Rob Roy* and 9897 *Redgauntlet* on cattle and goods trains; the latter required the assistance of a 'D30' (superheated Scott), No. 9411 *Dominie Sampson* when it came to grief after running away with the Haddington goods on 6th February, 1945. Another 'D29', No. 9900 *The Fair Maid*, was occasionally seen on branch passenger workings. The elderly Holmes and Reid NBR 0–6–0s were often seen on the branch and, under the LNER Route Availability for locomotives the Haddington line was classified as '6' with, additionally, 'J37' and 'J38' engines being permitted. Off-peak passenger services were often reduced to a single composite brake coach, and, for some time this was a particularly fine example that had originated on the Hull & Barnsley Railway.

The coming of peace was to bring little respite to the three branch lines and the new Labour government, determined to bring transport undertakings into public ownership, announced that the LNER would, from 1st January, 1948, be subsumed into the Railway Executive of the British Transport Commission. In the same way that the NBR had fought hard to prevent the loss of its independence, the LNER mounted a reasoned but hopeless campaign against nationalisation. This did not prevail, and from the due date, the branch lines of East Lothian became part of the Scottish Region of British Railways.

Haddington in the last phase of passenger services — the floods have resulted in the disuse of the station building and the loss of its canopy. Note the temporary ticket office in the old coach in this view of 18th July, 1949.   *A.G. Ellis*

The well-filled goods sidings at Haddington, on the same day.   *A.G. Ellis*

Chapter Nine

Decline and Fall

FROM NATIONALISATION TO CLOSURE

'For those of us who travelled frequently by the branch line trains or conducted business at the station, Haddington's railway services will always be remembered with affection.'

R.M. Hogg, 'East Lothian Courier', 29th September, 1949

The take-over by the new concern was at first little felt and the trains still worked according to the practices and timetables of the LNER and still remained in the livery of that company. Changes were, however, in the offing and by the first summer of nationalisation, the new name and totem symbol had begun to appear locally. But, before any radical steps could be taken, nature intervened in such a spectacular manner that the chain of events which followed have become part of the folklore of the county, and are still the subject of numerous school projects and reminiscences.

On 6th August, 1948, rain began to fall in East Lothian and the neighbouring counties of Berwickshire and Northumberland and for six days this deluge continued in a steady and relentless manner. Disaster would have been averted, however, had it not been for the fact that for almost the whole 24 hours of a markedly unglorious 12th of August an unprecedented downpour took place. This caused an almost immediate run-off from the sodden hills into the burns and rivers which drained the area. As a consequence, widespread flooding, damage, death and disruption was caused over a wide area. By that evening the East Coast main line had been breached in several places; the down 'Flying Scotsman' was marooned, the Waverley line blocked, trains were stranded and, everywhere, bridges and telegraph poles were down, cuttings had slipped and embankments were washed away. In the landward areas of East Lothian the Tyne and its tributaries had become so swollen that much of Haddington was under water and boats became the only means of travel.* At the station at Haddington a cascade poured down the embankment and seriously undermined the main passenger building and at Coatyburn the waters rose up the side of the embankment and reached rail level but the greatest disaster in the area was at Humbie station where the normally puny Birns Water had become a raging torrent. Much of the day was spent here in a vain attempt to prevent the hen coop at the station house from being swept away but this had to be abandoned. Shortly afterwards the Gilchriston bridge carrying the line over the Birns Water at the east end of the station collapsed due to the swift current and the mass of trees and debris, leaving a length of track suspended in mid-air over a heap of rapidly diminishing rubble. When the floods finally subsided the services over all three branch lines were still suspended, and there was much minor damage in the form of landslips at Limeylands and Winton, and blocked and broken drains everywhere.

Within days the service between Longniddry and Haddington had been restored, although the main station buildings at the terminus were boarded up and the canopy, which had partially collapsed, was demolished. A

---

*The level that the flood water rose to at Haddington is still commemorated, along with that of an earlier occasion, by a plaque on the wall of a building in the Sidegate.

temporary waiting room and ticket office, situated in an old carriage body placed alongside the platform, was brought into use. The goods services over the Macmerry and Gifford branches were also re-instated but, in the case of the latter trains, ran as far as Humbie only where sleepers were placed across the line 30 yards to the east of the platform to act as a temporary stop block while the service between Humbie and Gifford was temporarily suspended, pending a decision on the rebuilding of the Gilchriston bridge.

Another blow was to follow. As the austerity of the immediate post-war period began to diminish, the private car and bus began a renewed assault upon the already precarious position of the Haddington branch passenger service. As the *Third Statistical Account* put it:

> The burgh is well provided with regular bus services by the SMT. On the direct route to Edinburgh via Tranent, there is a thrice-hourly service throughout most of the day. One of the three buses runs only between Haddington and Edinburgh, another calls at Haddington on its journey between Edinburgh and Dunbar and the third connects with Berwick and Newcastle . . .
>
> The convenience, frequency and cheapness of the buses has vastly reduced the use of the railway for passenger traffic, a change specially marked in Haddington, owing to the position of the station half a mile from the centre of the town. A number of trains, mostly in the morning and evening, give connections at Longniddry for Edinburgh and the south but generally these are small and poorly filled.

Various attempts were made by British Railways to shore up the dwindling passenger figures and these included greater publicity and the introduction of cheap day return tickets designed to match the much cheaper SMT bus fares, e.g. the prevailing ordinary single fares from Edinburgh by bus being 1s. 4d. [6½p] and by rail 2s. 0d. [10p]. These changes were, however, too little and too late and the travelling public had all too obviously voted with its feet and abandoned the railway, no longer savouring the characteristically sooty and musty compartments of the branch train when the bus could take them from the centre of Haddington to St Andrew Square in Edinburgh. Closure proposals were inevitable therefore and in September 1949 the Railway Executive announced that passenger services on the line were to be withdrawn as soon as possible.

Surprisingly there was a great outcry in Haddington and a meeting was convened immediately in the Assembly Rooms in the town where J.J. Robertson, the Member of Parliament for Berwickshire and Haddington, told those present that he would be willing to pursue the matter further if a good case could be put forward for the retention of the service. He continued by saying that:

> The Railway executive had supplied me with the reasons why they found it necessary to consider the closing of the branch line between Longniddry and Haddington. They stated that, in spite of all their efforts, they could not continue to operate the branch line for passenger traffic without incurring considerable loss. They also informed me that each day few passengers took advantage of the service. The transport service of the country was undergoing great change, and considerable expenditure had been incurred in taking over the railways, in view of the tremendous amount of work which they had had to do during the war. Moreover, the increased cost of wages had shown, in many cases, a deficit in the trading

account, but the principal reason for the closing of branch railway lines, which were not serving a large number of people in the community, was mainly with regard to the conservation of coal. The railway system of the country had a certain allocation of coal, and in order to keep the main lines running consistently, they had to economise with the supply.

In some ways this was an indictment of state planning and the failure of the Transport Act of 1947 to set up a properly integrated transport system instead of the fragmented Executives of the British Transport Commission. No subsequent British government, of whatever hue, has even attempted to address this issue, despite the clearly expressed views of the electorate. In the case of the Haddington branch, mirrored in the case of the Macmerry and Gifford lines, no real case on economic grounds for the retention of the passenger service could have been put forward, and road congestion and new housing development in the area could not have been reasonably foreseen in the dying days of Attlee's administration. The chairman of the meeting, Mr A.P. Robertson of Haddington, in replying to the MP's remarks added in something of a *non sequitur* and with strict disregard for historical accuracy, that 'the time to have protested would have been when the Gullane branch was closed in 1924 [sic] and not when three buses per hour were leaving Haddington for Edinburgh'. The most valuable contribution however, was probably from the Haddington Town Clerk who said that:

He had been informed that the Railway Executive had fully considered all of the representations which they had received on the subject but it seemed that despite the added inducement to use the trains caused by the reinstatement of cheap day tickets, the introduction of which was fully advertised locally, there was an approximate increase of only eight daily passenger bookings from Haddington and this, of course, had little effect upon the operating loss incurred on the branch. In fact the daily average of passengers worked out at little more than three per train,and there seemed little doubt that the majority of the public found the bus services more convenient. In these circumstances, the Railway Executive had no option but to recommend that the passenger train service from Haddington should be permanently withdrawn.

The Haddington Town Council reluctantly concurred with this view and the Town Treasurer, after stating that he often saw virtually empty trains passing by his house, moved that the Council take no further action in the matter, although the Baillie who seconded that motion added that she wished to see whether BR 'would be willing to provide a special coach . . . when a body of people wished to travel by rail to Haddington.'

The formal closure notice, was now issued and it indicated that on or after Monday 5th December, 1949, Haddington station would be closed and that passengers for the town would be booked to Dunbar or Edinburgh 'from which places bus services are available'. It is perhaps noteworthy that no provision was made then, or afterwards, for the few local passengers who wished to travel between Longniddry and Haddington in the same way that no direct alternative bus had been provided on the closure of the Macmerry or Gifford lines. For a few more weeks the branch trains continued to run with most services, fittingly, still in the hands of the ex-NBR 'C16' No. 67496, until that engine was put in for repairs. Then, on 12th November,

Class 'C16' No. 67496 at Haddington on 18th July, 1949; note the early BR livery and absence of shed plate: to the right is the original 1846 station building.   *A.E. Ellis*

The crew of the Gresley class J39 look on as the photographer catches the last day of passenger services at Haddington, Saturday 3rd December, 1949.   *George Angus*

1949, a class 'D32' 4–4–0 No. 2445, originally built as a mixed traffic locomotive at Cowlairs in 1906 and the second last survivor of her class, was put in as a temporary replacement. Unfortunately, this locomotive, which had been booked as 'unfit for main line traffic' was not up to the task and had to be withdrawn – this proved to be its last turn in service for it was condemned the following month and scrapped soon afterwards. The 'D32' was succeeded, in turn, by a Reid 'B' class 0–6–0 ('J35'), No. 64492, which covered the branch for a mere two weeks before beint sent away for attention. Thus it was in the last week of services, when a handful of enthusiasts and local people were to make their final journeys, that a Gresley 'J39' 0–6–0 No. 64946 in lined black livery and sporting the legend 'BRITISH RAILWAYS' on its tender, took over to provide an unusual finale. On the evening of Saturday 3rd December, 1949 this LNER locomotive and a single bogie carriage made the last regular passenger run on this, the first branch line of the North British. As it steamed off into the night there were those who felt nostalgic as they witnessed the end of an era in the town's history.

At the end of the year the *East Lothian Courier*, in its annual review of the affairs of the county, commented that

> Even more disconcerting to the public of Haddington than the discontinuance of the passenger trains has been the disappearance of the station clock from its prominent position. Few people passed the station without giving a glance at the clock to see if they were early or late for the business that they had in hand. If Haddington cannot have passenger trains, then it would be a generous gesture on the part of the Railway Executive to return the station clock to its old position.

Alas, not only the station clock but the building itself was doomed to disappear and, within a short period, demolition of the red-brick station took place although the original 1846 station building was spared.

By the beginning of 1950, therefore, all three branch lines were solely dependent upon revenue from goods and mineral traffic and the government was following a policy whereby the railways had to earn their keep with no cross-subsidy available from any other element of the British Transport Commission. Competition was now rapidly increasing and this was especially felt in the non-coal short haul traffic to Edinburgh and the Leith docks where the railway could now neither compete on grounds of cost or convenience. One such notable loss was that of the flour and grain traffic of Messrs Montgomerie & Co – this company owned the Bermaline Mills in Haddington producing the famous loaf of the same name which, for many years, was the town's most noted export. In post-war days the company imported mainly Canadian wheat via Leith docks which was taken by rail to Haddington, but now the whole of this traffic went by road rather than rail, something which would have been unthinkable 20 years before. Another threat was that of the long-distance road haulier and the *Third Statistical Account* commented that:

> The largest road transport contractors in the district are centred in the town. Until 16th February, 1949 this firm was known as George Paterson & Sons. On this date it became nationalised and became the British Road Services Unit B44. The firm was founded in 1874 by George Paterson, a farmer from Beanston. Mr Paterson

began with one horse and one van plying between Haddington and Edinburgh as a carrier. He went three times a week to Edinburgh returning to Haddington on alternate days. When the firm was handed over to the government in 1949, 32 horses were still employed and 43 motor vehicles of all kinds. These included nine 12–15 ton AEC lorries with trailers. Journeys as far afield as London are undertaken. The firm carries out the largest amount of stock-transport in the south-east of Scotland.

On the Haddington branch the principal source of revenue was coal and the chief customers were the hospital, the mills and the gas works – the latter, at the time of the nationalisation of the gas industry, still requiring some 100–150 tons per week and supplying gas to some 1,344 individual customers. Coal merchants at the yard kept the public supplied for domestic use but all forms of coal usage were beginning to decline as a result of coal rationing and shortages and the advance of electricity, which had been available in the town from the Lothian Power Company since the 1920s. Other traffic handled included lime, building materials, corn, artificial inorganic fertilisers, linseed oil and cattle feed – the latter being handled by the establishment at Haddington station of a depot by the British Oil & Cake Mills Ltd (later BOCM-Silcocks). Live stock by rail was becoming far less common than formerly and, by the end of the 1950s an average of only eight cattle wagons per week were being handled at Haddington. All in all, however, the branch was still profitable and this was helped by certain economies such as the simplification of signalling and infrastructure at Haddington and Longniddry and the closure of the Longniddry West sidings, the 'dung lye' having gone out of use with the virtual eclipse of the horse.

If the Haddington branch was still profitable the same could not be said of the Macmerry and Gifford branches, at least at their extremities. On the Macmerry branch the terminus handled a variety of products including potatoes, fertilisers and beet (this being destined for the sugar factory at Cupar), together with other agricultural traffic, some minerals and miscellaneous traffic for an RAF depot and the works of the Lothian Structural Development Company who, at that time, built electricity pylons. At Winton, a small amount of agricultural and general goods traffic was handled but this had been diminishing over the years and barely justified the keeping on of the station here. At Gifford, traffic was still handled, but not by rail, and everything was received and despatched via Haddington and the BR carrier service, at the same rates as if the railway had still been open. The track east of the vanished Gilchriston bridge remained until about 1953, when the Railway Executive seemed to have decided finally to abandon this part of the line. The rusting rails were then prised up from the encroaching flora and despatched for scrap. Humbie and Saltoun stations were still relatively busy with timber, coal, whisky and potatoes and two private sidings on this section continued to contribute occasional traffic, but Pencaitland station was extremely quiet and some concern was being expressed as to the loss of the agricultural and strawberry traffic from here.

In contrast, the line west of Ormiston was still busy, mainly due to the coal traffic from the pits at Fleets, Carberry, Limeylands, Tynemount, Oxenford and Dalkeith Colliery, all of which had survived nationalisation to become part of the National Coal Board Lothians Area. It was this coal traffic which helped to stave off any immediate closure plans, notwithstanding a recommendation made in 1953 that the lines should be closed beyond Winton and Saltoun. The *Third Statistical Account* stated that

> Goods traffic is still considerable, and two goods trains run in both directions every week-day, carrying chiefly agriculture on the northward journey. There is a big coal traffic on the line below the junction of the mineral railway from Limeylands and Tynemount pits. Three coal trains run daily, carrying about a hundred wagons of coal and dross to destinations in Edinburgh and Glasgow.

On the section of the Gifford line east of the former Woodhall Colliery the LNER Route Availability '2' applied – this put a severe restriction upon the types of locomotive which could work the line. By the end of the era of private ownership the company had only two types of locomotive with which it could operate the rather meagre service – the 'J24's and the 'J67's. This latter class of engine was another class of ex-Great Eastern tank, this time Holden 0–6–0Ts which were seen from time to time on the Gifford line, but more often on the Lauder line for which service, by reason of their higher axle loadings, they were fitted with auxiliary tenders for water. Then, in one of the first manifestations of the integration of the services provided by the rival LNER and London Midland & Scottish Railway in the Edinburgh area, train workings on the Gifford branch were, from 14th June, 1950, placed in the hands of three members of a class of 2–6–0 class '2MT' light locomotives designed for the LMS by H.G. Ivatt and introduced in the last two years before nationalisation. These engines, allocated to St Margarets and known there as 'doodle bugs' (although this name might have been better suited to the Gresley 2–6–2 tanks), replaced the 'J24', No. 65617, which had virtually single-handedly provided the service since 1949. The '2MTs' were ideally suited to the Gifford line being light enough to comply with the weight restrictions and yet powerful enough to cope with the gradients and Nos. 46461 and 46462 were to operate the line until closure while a sister engine, No. 46460, occasionally operated both the Gifford line and the Haddington branch goods service until her eventual transfer north to Fraserburgh. Other interlopers from the LMS in the form of 4–6–0 class '5MT' locomotives ('Black Fives') were seen on coal trains run from former LMS (Caledonian) locations to the new NCB Central Coal Preparation Plant at Dalkeith Colliery. Other locomotives which worked to the colliery included the LNER Thompson 'B1' class 4–6–0s and a wide variety of ex-NBR 0–6–0s such as the 'J35s', 'J36s' and 'J37s'; the NBR engines were often used as the Smeaton pilot on a weekday single daytime shift, the night shift having been discontinued during the war and also to provide banking assistance between Smeaton and Dalkeith Colliery signal box. Following the introduction of the '2MTs', the Gifford goods engine eventually ended up serving Macmerry, Winton Mine, Fleets and the other remaining sidings east of Dalkeith Colliery. In the mid 1950s, the Ivatt '2MTs' were joined by two BR Standard class '2' 2–6–0 locomotives, Nos. 78048 and 78049, designed at Derby on strongly LMS lines and shedded at St Margarets and for many years these locomotives shared the duties with the Ivatt engines.

Haddington, showing the station building immediately after closure; note the detail changes from the earlier picture on page 47.   *George Angus Collection*

May 1961 and the piers of the Victoria Viaduct stand forlorn and awaiting demolition; in the background is the inter-war Shadepark housing scheme of the Dalkeith Burgh Council.   *W.S. Sellar*

The ill-fated Gilchriston Bridge, shortly after completion. It was this bridge which was swept away in the floods of 1948 and caused the abandonment of the Gifford to Humbie section of the line. *David Neilson Collection*

The aftermath of the floods – the tracks at Gifford station stand forlorn and rusty on 9th July, 1952, four years after the passage of the last train but the station remains open for goods, albeit now served by BR lorries from Haddington. *A.G. Ellis*

Two press photographs showing the wreckage of the 12.41 am up special parcels train at Longniddry station on 17th December, 1953. The locomotive was 'A2' Pacific No. 60530 *Sayajirao* and the only casualty was her fireman, Robert McKenzie of St Margarets. Behind the steam crane is the Garden City Stores shown on *page 41*.

Rae Montgomery Collection

On the Haddington branch the motive power was still mainly ex-NBR and included a 'Glen', Reid 'K' class 4−4−0 ('D34') No. 62487 *Glen Arklet* (a sister of the now preserved *Glen Douglas*) and 'J35' 0−6−0 No. 64486, which was for some time the Prestonpans Pilot.

On the whole the 1950s were uneventful times for the branches, but at Longniddry station a spectacular accident occurred on 17th December, 1953. At about 1.18 am on a cold, clear night the 12.41 am up special Christmas parcels train from Edinburgh to Kings Cross ran into an obstruction as it was passing through the station at about 60 mph. As a result, the engine, a relatively new Peppercorn 'A2' class 4−6−2, No. 60530 *Sayajirao*, was thrown over the up platform and came to rest with its wheels uppermost at the bottom of the embankment next to the road, having turned through an angle of 180 degrees. Damage was considerable and the engine, tender and a number of wagons all received a battering while six wagons were completely written off. The driver and fireman received extensive injuries and the fireman, Robert McKenzie of St Margarets, died as a result, while the driver spent many hours trapped until the fire brigade managed to cut through the side of the cab. The obstruction was found to have been a prefabricated 2 ft gauge 'decauville' turn-out which had been made by Robert Hudsons and loaded at their private siding at Gildersome West on top of seven others. The truck with this load then formed part of the 9.25 pm down goods from Heaton to Niddrie. The next day many of the older children of Longniddry Primary School could not be persuaded into their classrooms because of their fascination with the fearful sight of the wrecked train near their school. In the official accident report, Colonel McMullen concluded that the load had fallen from the wagon because it had been secured in such a way that the rope holding it in place had become frayed. He concluded that:

> This accident, which might have been still more serious if a passenger train had been involved, was the result of a failure of a responsible member of staff to obey instructions . . . Experience has showed that serious accidents can result from the movement of loads in goods vehicles and it is important that everyone concerned should be meticulous in the examination of loads that are liable to become displaced.

A permanent record of the accident can still be seen in the form of the small blue brick retaining wall at the bus stop next to the station – this was built to stabilise the embankment afterwards.

Throughout the decade, staff costs were continuing to escalate and further economies were carried out. Only one station master, William Rhind, based at Ormiston, was now in charge of the Macmerry and Gifford branches and he was provided with a motor cycle to enable him to cover all of the stations in his area; staff who worked here at that time included George Aitkenhead, Alexander Macdonald, Peter Smith, Bill Fairgrieve, James Clydesdale and William Bell, who was the last signalman at Ormiston. Winton and Pencaitland were both reduced to unstaffed public sidings at which no staff were normally in attendance, and further cut-backs in signalling were introduced and a number of redundant assets, including Ormiston Junction signal box, were removed. The one encouraging note in the face of this retrenchment was the implementation of various recommendations made in a 1944 report on the Scottish coal industry. The NCB continued to develop the Lothian coalfield and, as a result, Dalkeith Colliery was greatly expanded and modernised in the early 1950s. New sidings and a washery were provided next to the old Hardengreen line, south of Smeaton Junction. At Limeylands, where the colliery had closed, a washery and coal preparation plant was opened. A new mine was opened at Cowdenfoot, near to Thorneybank, and a half mile or so of the Hardengreen line was relaid to serve this. Other new mines included Winton, near Ormiston station, Tynemount No. 3 and Bellyford and all of these were rail-served; for a time it must have seemed that the coal industry in the Lothians had a rosy future.

In 1956 sufficient concern was being felt by BR over the state of traffic east of Ormiston, that they ordered their District Commercial Manager to produce a report on the Macmerry and Gifford Lines. This report, dated 30th July, gives a valuable insight into the present and future position of the branches. Starting with Macmerry it was noted that traffic had decreased considerably since 1951 and that the only outward traffic now consisted of grain, potatoes and sugar beet. This was confined to the winter months only, while inward traffic consisted of beet pulp from Cupar, potatoes and (in winter) fertilisers. There were also small and irregular consignments of steelwork for the Harelaw Synthetic Stone Company but the traffic for the Lothians Structural Development Co. had ceased, being now handled through Haddington. However, there was still some sundries traffic (totalling 4 tons per annum), two-thirds of which was handled in the winter months. The originating parcels traffic averaged one parcel per week, being mainly mail order traffic being returned to the sender in Liverpool. Winton station, now unstaffed, dealt with only four wagons of received fertilisers for local farmers during the year 1955–6 and staff were sent from Ormiston to handle this traffic when necessary. There was, however, considerable traffic from the NCB Winton Mine and this averaged 16 full wagon loads of coal daily.

Turning to the Gifford Branch, the 1956 report noted that it was served by one train per day, the 8.23 am goods from Portobello to Humbie which worked 'as required' on the orders of the station master at Ormiston, and the same train also worked Macmerry, Winton and the Winton Mine. At Pencaitland, traffic was negligible, in the past having consisted of one wagon of seed oats and two of grain being forwarded and five general wagons of farm traffic received; staff attended from Ormiston if needed. Saltoun, under the control of George Fenton, was now the most important station on the line, bringing in an annual revenue of £10,000 consisting mainly of livestock, agricultural produce and requisites and the traffic from the Glenkinchie Distillery. There was a great reluctance to lose this latter source of revenue, without which the line would not be a viable concern. At Humbie, the forwarded full load goods traffic consisted entirely of seed potatoes and pit wood and the mineral traffic of stockfeed potatoes, while the received full load traffic was made up of beet pulp, fertilisers and miscellaneous farm traffic. The decrease in traffic since 1951 was attributed to a fall in forwarded seed potato traffic and 'it is understood that one of the largest seed potato growers in the area now owns two heavy lorries with which he conveys his traffic to the south of England and this probably accounts for a large part of the decrease'. The pit wood traffic was forwarded by Messrs Jones of Larbert and Messrs Morganof Crieff from the Co-operative Forestry Society who ran a local felling operation.

Gifford station was still busy although all traffic was, of course, sent by BR vans from Haddington and despatched in the same way, or by the trader's own lorries. Full load traffic consisted of seed potatoes and grain in the outward direction and fertilisers, grain, clay, beet pulp and agricultural machinery. A small amount of parcels and sundries traffic was handled including miscellaneous farm traffic such as empty bags and sacks, seed and sheep-dip for the out-lying farms, cases of pottery from the Castle Wynd Pottery and timber from Brownlie's sawmills; other similar traffic included ice cream, perishables and livestock. It was acknowledged that much of this traffic would be lost if Gifford station was closed and traders were charged for the extra mileage of the delivery vans from Haddington. In the words of the report

It is extremely difficult to assess the results of the application of Haddington mileages to the Gifford traffic. The traffic is almost entirely to and from English destinations and rail carriage charges are therefore unaffected. Traders would have the choice of providing their own cartage or paying the higher rural cartage charges. It might be thought that the latter would influence the traffic to through-out road transport, in which case the loss of carriage revenues would be greatly in excess of the cost in wages of the Gifford porter. While the volume of parcels and sundry traffic handled at Gifford is not very heavy, we believe that a marginal case would exist for the establishment of a parcels, etc. agency in Gifford village should the staff be withdrawn from the station.

The conclusion of the report was that, with a few minor changes (including the reduction of the Macmerry porter's job to a winter-only appointment), the status quo should be maintained, provided that the present circumstances were unaltered and pending further considerations of the position at Gifford.

Two years later, BR commissioned a similar report into the state of the Haddington branch and it was revealed that further economies would have to be made.

The branch is served by the undernoted goods train trips:

E.56 Class K	SX	E.140	daily	SO
Longniddry dep.	2.45 pm	Longniddry dep.	7.40 am	2.30 pm
Haddington arr.	3.00 pm	Haddington arr.	8.10 am	2.50 pm
" dep.	5.20 pm	" dep.	9.10 am	3.30 pm
Longniddry arr.	5.35 pm	Longniddry arr.	9.30 am	3.45 pm

There are no other stations on the branch nor are there any manned level crossings. Coatyburn unstaffed public siding is situated midway between Haddington and Longniddry and is worked by any of the above trains as required.

The passenger rated parcels traffic consists of hosiery for Messrs Kilspindie, game in season from Mr J. McLean, and general town traffic. The goods traffic is principally agricultural in nature and, during the early spring, two local firms despatch many small consignments of agricultural seeds. Haddington acts as the railhead for the undernoted stations: Macmerry, Winton (unstaffed), Ormiston, Pencaitland (unstaffed), Saltoun, Humbie and Gifford (scheduled for closure). The cartage units based at Haddington deliver and uplift passenger-rated parcels and sundry goods consignments in and around the above villages and also deliver TCF ['To be Called For'] parcels to manned stations. One vehicle runs cross-trips to and from Longniddry uplifting and delivering passenger-rated parcels and mails from and to the passenger trains. Goods sundries are received and forwarded by sundries vans on the goods trains.

Figures were given for traffic and staff and economies were proposed including the reduction of staff numbers, the relocation of the goods office and other matters which, it was felt, would effect an annual saving of £1,561 17s. 11d. 'plus the cost of coal and light in the present goods office'. It was also recommended that the post of station master at Haddington be abolished since,

> The station master's duties operating duties under the 'one engine in steam' signalling arrangements are negligible and can be adequately overtaken by the Grade 2 station master at Longniddry. There is no 'bus service in operation between Longniddry and Haddington, but visitations could be made by making use of the BTC cartage motors and freight services. In the event of an emergency, a taxi service is available at Haddington.

The Haddington proposals were implemented and, following upon a reassessment of cartage charges, it was decided that there was no longer any justification for retaining the facilities at Gifford. In the event it was a convenient time to close this station since the last remaining member of staff, Tom Smith, the Gifford goods porter, would reach retirement age within a few months and there would accordingly be no need for redundancies. With effect from 1st January, 1959 Gifford station was closed to all traffic, thus ending the possibly unique situation of a railway station which handled traffic for more than ten years after the passage of the last train. The same year saw the beginning of the retraction of local coalmining operations when the Fleets and Oxenford pits were closed, and it was becoming increasingly obvious that the future of the Gifford and Macmerry lines was now at stake.

The fate of these branch lines were once more in the balance. A second BR report, made in 1958, recommended the complete closure of all the lines east of Ormiston and the concentration there of all remaining traffic, namely coal from Winton Mine and whisky and other traffic for the Glenkinchie distillery. The coal traffic was already in doubt, since the NCB were transporting much of the coal by lorry and the future of the pit was now uncertain, but the Glenkinchie traffic was not. This amounted to about 10 tons of coal daily and 5 tons of whisky, grain, empty barrels and miscellaneous goods. If Saltoun, the railhead for Glenkinchie, was closed it was estimated that an additional 6-ton cartage unit, 2 hydraulic tipper trailers and two flat bed trailers would be needed at Ormiston. Although consent was given to closing the Macmerry line, the branch to the Winton Mine and to Saltoun were given a reprieve, for the time being.

In April 1960, the Carberry Colliery ceased production and, largely as a result of a spiralling wages bill and falling traffic, Winton and Macmerry

stations were closed to all traffic as from 2nd May of that year. The Macmerry branch was now abandoned in its entirety, except for the short length
from Ormiston Junction which served the Winton pit. On the same day,
Humbie station was also closed, and the Gifford branch now terminated at a
temporary stop block a couple of hundred yards east of Saltoun station.
Redundant assets were quickly recovered and the trackbeds were rapidly
sold off so that a potential right of way was lost. Station buildings were
demolished and the former station masters' houses at Gifford, Pencaitland
and Humbie were all sold. Beyond Saltoun nature began to take its course in
places where it was not being used for new access roads, and, at Humbie the
great viaduct began to decay once regular maintenance ceased.

The year 1961 saw the extinction of the new Bellyford mine and in April
of the following year, the Winton mine also ceased production, so that soon
afterwards this remaining vestige of the Macmerry branch was lifted. In
November of that year the Bog Siding and its signal box were closed and, in a
strange turnround, there was now no originating coal traffic east of Smeaton.
In an effort to cut costs weekend working beyond Smeaton was discontinued
as from 21st December, 1963 when the goods stations at Smeaton, Ormiston
and Saltoun were all closed on Saturdays. Further rationalisation was to
take place and at Longniddry, where the small shed had seen little use after
1958 the goods yard was finally closed at the end of 1964, the Coatyburn
siding having closed some nine months earlier outlasting Pencaitland unstaffed siding by six weeks. Concomitant with this decline, however, was a
rise in interest in what remained and between 1957 and 1968 several enthusiasts' specials visited the line. These trips included one to the now quiet
and virtually moribund Macmerry line, when on 6th September, 1958 class
'C16' No. 67492 brought an unprecedented number of passengers to the
terminus on a Stephenson Locomotive Society special.

In August 1963 another SLS special visited Saltoun, hauled throughout by
an ex-NBR Reid class 'J37', No. 64624. This was an unusual occasion for
such heavy locomotives were not normally permitted to work on the light
railway section east of Tyneholm Colliery – by this time closure was immi-
nent and the weight restrictions were waived for the occasion. This was,
however, by no means the only time that 'overweight' locomotives had
worked the line – on one memorable occasion in 1961 two BR Standard
2–6–4 tank engines had been seen east of Ormiston when one worked the
daily Saltoun goods and the other hauled the District Engineer's saloon – a
venerable ex-Great Central vehicle known as 'Watkin's saloon' (after the
famed Sir Edward) and which was frequently to be seen in its special lye at
Waverley station. On the Haddington branch several specials were run
including an SLS special in June 1960, hauled by a class 'J35', No. 64489. In
August 1964 the peculiar combination of a Holmes class 'J36', No. 65234,
with the stock of the 'Talisman' express was seen on the branch. Such
luxurious stock as these BR Mark I carriages (which had themselves been
displaced from the 'Talisman' by the experimental XP64 stock), being un-
heard of at Haddington previously.

By the spring of 1965 the only remaining train serving the Gifford line was
the daily pick-up freight to Saltoun, still in the capable hands of the two

Two views of Macmerry on 6th September, 1958, showing the last passenger train, an SLS special hauled by class 'C16' No. 67492, which probably brought more passengers than had ever been seen here before. The bungalow seen in the upper picture behind the locomotive survives as a reference point.   *W.S. Sellar*

Pencaitland station in later days – (*top*) looking east towards Saltoun; the chimneys of the station master's house can be seen in this view of 9th July, 1952; (*bottom*) the Ivatt '2MT' in charge of the Humbie goods calls at the now unstaff station on 4th March, 1960; note that the platform has been demolished.   *A.G. Ellis; W.S. Sellar*

Ormiston station looking eastwards on 17th April 1955. *C.J.B. Sanderson*

The truncated terminus at Humbie on 9th July, 195— the sleeper acts as a temporary stop block to protect the gap where Gilchriston bridge once stood. *A.G. Elli*

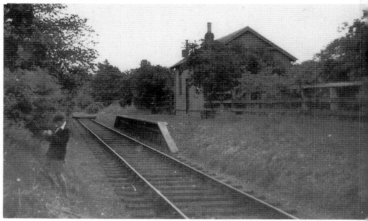

A group posed at Humbie in the month before closure. From left to right are the fireman, Driver Joe Cairns of St Margarets, Guard Charlie Dodds, Rae Montgomery and the surfaceman. The locomotive is BR Standard No. 78048. Note the LNER sacks still in use for the potato traffic.

George Murray

End of the line – the daily pick-up goods in the hands of the Ivatt '2MT' reaches Humbie, 4th March, 1960. (*Top*) the former passenger platform looking towards Saltoun; (*lower*) a view of the goods yard with the station master's house behind the loading bank.

W.S. Sellar

Scenes at Saltoun – (*top*) the Humbie goods arrives on 4th March, 1960; (*middle*) casks of Glenkinchie whisky are secured in an open wagon in the last week of the service; George Aitken, the regular goods guard, stands to the left in the wagon; (*bottom*) the Ivatt '2MT' shunts the station yard on the same day.

W.S. Sellar (top); G.N. Turnbull (others)

Two post-closure views. (*Upper*) Humbie station awaiting the demolition train, 25th September, 1961 (note the proper buffer stop provided at the end of the branch); (*lower*) Saltoun in October 1965 – five months after the cessation of all services.

Harold D. Bowtell; G.N. Turnbull

The view from Hardengreen Junction signal box on a wintry day in February 1960; the Waverley Route main line to Edinburgh is in the foreground with the platform at Esbank & Dalkeith station visible beyond the Bonnyrigg Road bridge and the truncated Smeaton branch can be seen diverging to the right.

J. Inglis; Rae Montgomery Collection

The severed remains of the Smeaton branch at Hardengreen on 30th September, 1961, shortly after the final abandonment of 'the hole'. *Rae Montgomery*

Two views of the afternoon Penicuik goods being banked by an NBR 'S' class (LNER class 'J37') No. 64594 on the Smeaton branch stub at Hardengreen – the only photographs the author has ever seen of a train on this most mysterious of lines. The wagons contain esparto grass for the Penicuik paper mills and the date of the pictures is 6th February, 1961.   *Rae Montgomery*

An Ivatt '2MT' running tender first passes under the Lempockwells bridge with the goods train from Saltoun to Edinburgh in April 1964; the Lammermuirs form an impressive backdrop. *G.N. Turnbull*

An AEC Monocoach bound for Edinburgh crosses the Red Row bridge, beyond which, on the right hand side, Woodhall Colliery Platform used to stand. This view was taken from the brake van of the Saltoun goods train on 17th May, 1965. *G.N. Turnbull*

An unusual view taken from the brake van as the '2MT', tender first, approaches Smeaton Shaw on 17th May, 1965 with the woods of Carberry Tower on the right. In the open wagon sit three casks of Glenkinchie whisky. *G.N. Turnbull*

The Saltoun goods engine shunts at Smeaton, 17th May, 1965. *G.N. Turnbull*

Ormiston station in its dying days.

G.N. Turnbull

Ivatt class '2MTs' or the two BR standard 2–6–0s. These locomotives had seen off an interlope in the form of Hunslet diesel No. D2585, which had been temporarily transferred from Thornton depot for this duty in 1963 but which was ignominiously sent back home after a week largely due to the fact that St Margarets was still a steam shed and that insufficient trained diesel crews were available. There was, however, no future for even this small remaining part of the Gifford & Garvald Light Railway, although for several months the diminutive Saltoun goods trains, usually under the control of goods guard Charlie Dodds, continued to plod their way along this sylvan backwater. But such was the traffic that all freight east of Smeaton could now be handled by a single train crew on one daytime shift. The end was inevitable, and, on 25th May, 1965, Smeaton, Ormiston and Saltoun stations were closed and the whole line between Smeaton Junction and Saltoun was abandoned, the last commercial load carried being said to have been, appropriately, casks of Glenkinchie whisky. The Smeaton station master, who had by now been put in charge of the whole line, was John Bond and he was transferred to Leith Walk where he was relief supervisor before being made station master of another station in a colliery area – Shepherds Well in Kent! The only traffic now remaining was on the rump of the line from Monktonhall Junction was coal traffic to the Dalkeith Colliery and prepara-tion plant at Smeaton. On 19th July, 1965 the section east of Smeaton was officially declared 'out of use' and demolition commenced. Ironically a huge new maltings which could have provided new traffic on the line, was being completed next to the site of Pencaitland station – it was said that its siting here was at the insistence of the County Planning Officer who had envisaged that the railway would be used to transport the grain and malt, but no proper attempt seems to have been made to liaise either with BR or the owners of the maltings.

The Haddington branch continued to soldier on but here too the writing was on the wall, BR in the Beeching era being no longer interested in short workings, pick-up goods trains and mixed traffic flows, and there was a determination to centralise and concentrate what traffic did remain. The Haddington branch did not fit any of these criteria but, surprisingly, it survived the demise of the steam locomotive in 1966 when the faithful NBR 0–6–0s were despatched to the scrap heap and Clayton Type 1 diesels (known later as class '17s' and to railwaymen as 'the room and kitchens') appeared on the Millerhill to Haddington trip workings. These were popular with crews on account of their comfortable cabs and facilities such as a heating ring on which tea could be prepared. These were not the first diesels to appear, for in the 1950s both the Haddington and Gullane branches had seen Metro-Cammell and Gloucester diesel multiple units on training runs from Leith Central diesel depot and these journeys, for some reason, seem to be well remembered by local people to this day. Another diesel, in the form of a BRCW Type 2 (class '26') locomotive, No. D5317, appeared on the branch on an enthusiasts' special called the 'Scottish Rambler No. 6 railtour' in March 1967. By this time the station area was looking decidedly run-down and the weeds were advancing; the same train also visited Smeaton.

The end of services to Haddington came in two stages. On 5th March, 1968 all goods facilities with the exception of coal traffic were withdrawn from Haddington and three weeks later, on 30th March, the branch line was closed entirely. The *East Lothian Courier* had a brief report of the event:

> The end of an era passed almost unnoticed on Friday when the signals [sic] at Haddington Railway Station clattered up and a train rumbled over the rusty rails for the last time. Pulling five freight wagons, three of which were empty, the massive 900 horse power engine crawled out of the station. A lone camera enthusiast recorded the departure on film, but otherwise the event went almost unnoticed. Since the early 1960s Haddington station has run on a skeleton staff with only six goods trains running each week. As more and more people began to use road transport the once busy county town station ground to an unspectacular halt. Following an enquiry into the efficiency of the station and the traffic handled, it was decided last June to close the depot. News of the closure received little attention and only the men who worked at the station were really affected. One man who came to bid farewell to the last train was Mr Alexander Preston, 4 Davidson Terrace, Haddington who worked at Haddington station for 30 years. 'For me this is a sad occasion. Thirty years is a long time – and to see the last train go in such a quiet unspectacular way is really rather sad', he said.

Within a short period, track-lifting had commenced and it seemed as though the branch line was destined for oblivion. What ought to have been the end of the line's history was not, however, reached. At this time the railway preservation movement was gaining momentum and both the cessation of steam on BR and the closing of many branch lines had brought about several grandiose (and a few practical) schemes to re-open lines. In 1970 the Scottish Railway Preservation Society, which had been collecting locomotives and stock at their Falkirk depot for a number of years with a view to running its own line, became interested in buying the Haddington line. It appeared to be an ideal choice with main line connections at Longniddry, pleasant scenery, a terminus town that was worth visiting in its own right and a workable length. The SRPS issued a prospectus and entered into negotiations with BR, but there was opposition from some of the inhabitants of Haddington who feared that there would be noise, smoke pollution and a danger to children. Some members of the Society had their own reservations about the viability and location of the plan and a breakaway group had already gone to found the Strathspey Railway. Some preliminary work as undertaken and in May 1972 the SRPS issued a leaflet entitled 'A new attraction for Haddington and East Lothian' which dealt with the benefits which local businesses could expect while, at the same time trying to allay residents' fears. Part of the leaflet read as follows

> HOW WILL IT BE DONE? First of all, the track will be relaid at Haddington station, and a number of the Society's smaller engines will be brought in by road. Then the line will be extended to the bridge carrying the A1 by-pass road over the line about a mile from Haddington. At the A1 an engine shed with maintenance facilities will be provided, unobtrusively and away from residential areas. Finally, the line will be relaid in stages across to Longniddry on the East Coast main-line. Terminal facilities will be located at the junction, though the precise nature of the link-up with the main-line is still to be determined. The terminus at Haddington will be set aside as a passenger station and railway museum. During each stage, trains will be run on summer weekends from Haddington to the end of the line so far laid.

Unfortunately, the plans did not come to fruition and the Society moved on to consider other proposals, before settling on the reconstruction of the Bo'ness & Kinneil Railway. In retrospect it is a pity that matters were not handled better locally but it is easy to blame enthusiasts, the townspeople and the county planning officers who withdrew their support at a crucial stage when, in the early 1970s, few people had much experience of the setting up and effects of such a project.

The trackbed of the Haddington line was left intact for another 15 years at the insistence of the planning authorities and vague thoughts were harboured of it forming part of a proposed Edinburgh area rapid transport system; a central goods distribution depot at or near to Haddington was also considered. In 1978 the East Lothian District Council purchased the route, which was, despite encroaching vegetation, a popular unofficial pathway, in an effort to keep it as a right of way. During 1986–7 it was cleared and new footbridges reinstated so that it is now possible to walk or cycle from Haddington to Longniddry along the 'Railway Walk' and park or have a picnic at the site of Coatyburn Siding.

This was not the only example of such a use, for in the late 1960s, East Lothian County Council started to formulate plans for a series of additional bridleways and recreational paths in the county. In January 1969 the County Planning Officer was instructed to approach BR and indicate the Council's interest in purchasing the trackbed from the county boundary near Cousland up to Saltoun (beyond which the land was no longer in the ownership of BR). Negotiations proceeded and these culminated in the Council buying, for £3,860, the 47.5 acres of trackbed between these points, thus making it the first old railway line to be acquired for recreational purposes in Scotland. A grant was then obtained from the Scottish Development Department, under the provisions of the Countryside Development (Scotland) Act 1967 to cover the estimated £4,500 capital expenditure needed to bring it up to standard and a pioneer study entitled the 'Pencaitland Railway Walk Management Plan' was drawn up. Within a few years the walk was a reality and further negotiations took place with the Midlothian authorities to extend the walk back to Smeaton (although not wholly on the trackbed) and with private landowners with regard to an extension to Gifford. Whilst the former has had a successful outcome, the latter has still to be effected, a major drawback to the same being the fact that the Humbie Viaduct was, as a result of allegedly becoming unsafe, blown up in 1986; perhaps by this act John Fletcher finally obtained his posthumous revenge on his fellow directors!

In 1973 the line between Monktonhall Junction and Dalkeith Colliery was once more reduced to single track and the old up line removed, the volume of traffic now no longer requiring double track. Coal trains, by now mainly in the hands of class '20' and '26' diesels, continued to use the line for a few years more. Then the final stage in the history of the branch was about to unfold. In December 1978, when the Dalkeith Colliery finally ceased production, the traffic began to fall as the only remaining installation served by what was by now known as the 'Smeaton branch' was the NCB coal washing plant next to the pit. Trains continued for a further two years and a number of enthusiasts' specials, including two diesel multiple units, visited

Then, at the end of 1980 and as part of the continuing rundown of the local coal industry, the coal washing plant was abandoned. The line was left with no other remunerative traffic and, after lying derelict for a time lifting commenced at the Smeaton end. Within a short period of time, the last surviving remnant of the Haddington, Gifford and Macmerry branch lines was no more. Part of the massive embankment adjacent to the housing scheme at Whitecraig was subsequently removed for roadworks, and the colliery buildings and washery at Smeaton were subsequently demolished and the area landscaped.

The remaining railway buildings which survive on the three branch lines are nearly all used as private houses but the distinctive station building at Saltoun, so typical not only of the Gifford & Garvald but of light railways everywhere, was left to rot until the District Council, wishing to clear the site and make it a car park for the Pencaitland Railway Walk, offered the building to the SRPS, together with the old grounded carriage body alongside. Volunteers from the Society subsequently removed these two trophies to Bo'ness in December 1990 and it is hoped that, one day, the Saltoun building will be rebuilt on its new site and form a lasting memorial to the little line that once served this beautiful part of East Lothian.

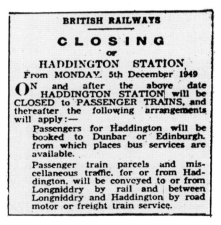

The closure notice from the *East Lothian Courier*.

A last day ticket.

Reid 'B' class (LNER class 'J35') No. 64489, waits at Smeaton station with a railtour in September 1958.

R.W. Lynn Collection

A 1978 railtour brings a Metro-Cammell dmu to Smeaton for the first time.

Forbes Alexander

Haddington shortly before closure, (upper) a Clayton Type 1 shunts the yard and (below) a forlorn view showing the signal box and disused Slaughter House Siding; in the background is Traprain Law. *G.N. Turnbull*

Clayton Type 1 locomotives worked the Haddington goods trip working in its final years – No. D8583 passes the site of Laverocklaw Siding in 1967.

G.N. Turnbull

Diesels at Smeaton – No. D5317, a BRCW Type 2, stands at the platform with a railtour on 27th March, 1967. The Dalkeith Colliery and Washery can be seen in the background and the bed of the lifted Gifford and Macmerry line diverges to the left behind the locomotive. *Harold D. Bowtell*

A Clayton Type 1 runs down the Haddington branch towards Longniddry in 1967 – the main line can be seen in the background. *G.N. Turnbull*

The 'Scottish Rambler No. 6' railtour brings a BRCW Type 2 to Haddington on 27th March, 1967; another view of this train is seen opposite.   *G.N. Turnbull*

Looking towards Longniddry from Haddington showing the signal box and over-bridges built to double track clearances, 1964.   *George Angus*

Railtours at Haddington. (*Top*) NBR class 'J35' on an SLS railtour, 11th June, 1960 with the original 1846 station building in the background; (*bottom*) a veteran class 'J36' dating from 1891 stands at the platform with a special train of BR Mark I stock from the 'Talisman' express displaced by the XP64 experimental train. The date is 29th August, 1964 and the locomotive still has 32 months of active service left.

W.S. Sellar; John Edgington

Chapter Ten

A Journey into the Past

THE THREE BRANCH LINES DESCRIBED

'The line runs through a country in the finest condition and cultivation, rich in corn and cattle.'

Thompson's Guide to the North British Railway, 1846.

The Haddington Branch

The branch passenger trains left from the outer face of the down island platform at Longniddry and ran eastwards parallel to the main line for ¼ mile or so through the lands formerly owned by the Marquis of Lorn. The locomotive shed, signal box and down sidings were all passed and, close to the point where the main line and branch diverged, a siding leading to the Harelaw Lime Kilns left by a facing junction to the south. By now the branch line had begun its climb at 1 in 66 – the ruling gradient for the next two miles and a good illustration of why the main line did not follow the proposed southern route. As it swung to the south-east the Redhouse to Setonhill by-road was crossed and a glimpse obtained of the tiny Blawearie accommodation crossing on the main line. A wide panorama now opened up to the north and in the foreground were the ruins of Redhouse castle while in the distance, across the fields, could be seen the Gullane branch meandering its leisurely way towards Aberlady. Providing a spectacular backdrop lay the Firth of Forth and the coastline of Fife and several clearly discernible landmarks were all visible on a clear day, including the North Berwick Law, the Isle of May and the Bass Rock.

By now the line had entered the Wemyss Estate and, after a cutting, the gradient eased until Coatyburn was reached. Here a small siding and loading bank were situated on the up side of the line, 1¾ miles from the junction. The line was now virtually on the level and a wide vista of farmland opened up until, by a clump of Scots Pines, Laverocklaw siding was reached. This was a short single siding facing south, close to the farm of that name. After passing the site of the accident in which a train ended up in a turnip field, the railway passed beneath another sandstone bridge near to the quaintly-named Merryhatton; with the Garleton Hills and the Hopetoun Memorial clearly visible to the east a new panorama opened up as the line began its descent on a ruling gradient of 1 in 80 towards the Haddington as the Tyne Valley, backed by the rising Lammermuirs, unfolded to the south and west.

After passing under the Huntington road the branch line now entered a cutting and turned due east, paralleling the London road close to the point where the original route diverged from the 1930s by-pass; the latter then crossed the railway on a massive steel and concrete skew bridge. Two original overbridges now followed before the terminus was reached, the gradient having eased out to 1 in 220. Here the main passenger platform was on the right, alongside the goods and grain sheds, and at the station yard throat was situated the signal box and Slaughter House siding. Leaving the platform by the covered stairs, the 'dusty little omnibus' was waiting in the station forecourt, ready to take passengers right in to the wide streets of what was described by one writer as 'this most delightsome of county towns.'

Monktonhall to Smeaton

From the down East Coast main line at Monktonhall Junction the branch line swung south-eastwards and began a steady climb away from the Esk at a ruling gradient of 1 in 75, passing by on a high embankment the settlements at Cowpits and the now-vanished Deanstown. On the right the Carberry branch, serving Carberry Colliery and the Deans Pit, joined at a trailing junction ¼ mile north of Smeaton. The station here, one and a half miles from Monktonhall Junction, consisted of an island platform, although latterly only the eastern face was used by passenger trains. On the up side was the tall signal box with its impressive tangle of rodding and wires and, virtually surrounding the station, were the extensive west and east sidings where lines of coal wagons bound to and from the Dalkeith and Carberry Colleries were stabled. At the south end of the station platform was Smeaton Junction where the Hardengreen and Macmerry lines diverged.

Smeaton to Hardengreen

This line left Smeaton Junction and ran south towards Smeaton Head where the Dalkeith Colliery was situated and where the Brick & Tile Works had formerly been and where, at a later stage, the new NCB sidings and washery were constructed. Just before the bridge which carried the Cousland to Dalkeith road (B6614) over the line a short branch to the new Cowdenfoot mine came in on the east side at a trailing junction. At Thorneybank, one and a quarter miles south of Smeaton, were the sidings originally owned by the Duke of Buccleuch and later made public and here was a passing loop and, until 1896, a small signal box. From Thorneybank the line swung westwards and crossed the South Esk on the massive Victoria viaduct – a slender structure from the deck of which good views of the, as yet, undeveloped valley and the wooded demesne of Newbattle Abbey could be obtained. The line now turned south-west behind the Burgh of Dalkeith and passed the site of Mushet's siding and the Dalkeith gas works before entering a cutting and joining the Waverley and Peebles line at Hardengreen Junction, a little to the south of Eskbank station.

Smeaton to Ormiston

From Smeaton Junction the Ormiston line swung through a wide arc before crossing a by-road at the manned Smeaton Shaw level crossing, known locally as Calder's Crossing, after the family who manned it for many years and close to the collier's houses and football pitch and the huge bing which was to later engulf them. The line was now running in a generally eastwards direction on a ruling gradient of 1 in 50 and entered a deep cutting as it passed through the Cousland Gap at Crossgatehall. On the south or up side the Dalkeith Colliery branch joined at a trailing junction controlled by the small signal box of that name. Almost immediately opposite was the small wooden platform of Crossgatehall Halt, with its diminutive wooden building, and path leading up to the Musselburgh to Pathead (A6124) road which crossed the line here. To the north were the woods surrounding Carberry Tower and Queen Mary's Mount, where Mary Queen of Scots surrendered to the Confederated Lords on 15th June, 1567. The line now gained the shallow valley of the Bellyford Burn north of Cousland village, which it then followed as far as Ormiston.

The scene was now a curious mixture of rural and industrial and several sidings were passed in rapid succession. The first of these, on the south side and joining by a trailing junction, was the Cousland Siding serving the lime and cement works and the Fordel Mains Colliery branch. Three-quarters of a mile further on there were two sidings, one on each side of the line. To the north was a trailing siding named Billyford Farm Siding, which had originally been built to serve the first Bellyford Pit, while on the south side with a facing connection was the old Cousland Siding, abandoned in 1895, while 25 chains further on and to the same side was the Oxenford Siding, which served the colliery situated there. To the north, and served by a facing siding on the up side, was the Bellyford Siding, serving the Deans & Moore colliery of that name and linked to the Elphinstone Chapel Pit by a horse tramway.

Half a mile from here the extensive complex around Bog Siding was reached. The signal box of that name was situated on the down side at the point where the Bog Siding and Fleets Branch diverged on the up side and began their steady climb up past the Bog, Howden and Elphinstone collieries towards the Fleets Pit; in later years the NCB built yet another mine named Bellyford close to this junction. On the south side lay Limeylands Colliery with its ramshackle surface buildings adjacent to the line and served by a facing junction leading to the Tynemouth branch. Passing under a by-road the 'main' line now swung south-west and the sidings leading to Ormiston Station Colliery diverged on the up side before the single-platformed and rather modest junction station at Ormiston was reached. To the north lay the goods sidings and colliery while to the south was a passing loop and the small signal box. The platform was on the up side and ended at the Puddle Bridge, a narrow structure which, despite being strengthened by iron bands because of subsidence, still survives to carry the Tranent to Ormiston (B6371) road across the track. Beside the bridge was one of the curious cylindrical water tanks used by the NBR and this was a regular watering place for locomotives working the line.

Ormiston to Macmerry

From the junction with the Gifford line, just beyond the Puddle Bridge, the Macmerry line ran generally eastwards and, almost immediately, the connection with the NCB Winton Mine joined it on the up side by a facing junction. The line now bridged the insignificant Puddle Burn and then reached the manned East Mains level crossing, where a by-road was crossed. At West Mains Cottage, close to where the original Pencaitland Siding had been situated, the line then swung in a north-easterly arc to reach the Pencaitland to Tranent (B6355) road which dipped through a cutting here so that the line could cross over it. Winton station then followed and here there was a small level crossing, a platform and station building on the up side, and a series of sidings facing north on the down side. The line continued north for a mile until Penston Colliery Junction was reached and the mineral line diverged on the down side. The terminus at Macmerry was now entered and this consisted of a single platform with a modest building on the up side and a loop and two goods sidings all situated on the south side of the main London road.

Ormiston to Gifford

From Ormiston Junction the line turned south and passed the Meadow Colliery, served by facing sidings on the down side of the line. The branch now crossed the Tyne on a three-arched viaduct before entering a cutting and passing under the Haddington to Dalkeith (A6093) road at Red Row, the site where the Marchioness of Tweeddale cut the first sod in 1899. Immediately after the bridge and on the down side was the Woodhall Colliery Company Platform, a short wooden platform provided with lights but no nameboard or shelter. As the line swung east the sidings serving the Woodhall (or Tyneholm or Pencaitland) Colliery were passed on the down side. From here the restrictions of the Light Railway Order applied and the first of the ungated level crossings, Woodhall, where the unfortunate fish salesman came to grief when his lorry was hit by a train in 1924, was crossed. On the up side the original contractor's siding, named at various times Workshop, Broomrig and Brander's Siding, was passed before Pencaitland station was reached. This had a single platform on the up side with a small building and adjacent to it was the station master's house, while to the north lay the two facing sidings and loading bank which comprised the whole of the goods facilities here. Then followed a long climb at 1 in 50, partially in a cutting, to Lempockwells where a trailing siding on the up side was situated. The line now continued in a cutting, falling at 1 in 50, and passed under both a by-road from West Saltoun and a path at Milton – the latter being carried over the line by a curious wooden accommodation bridge. A massive embankment marked the place where the Kinchie Burn was crossed and to the west the buildings of the Glenkinchie Distillery could be seen; the name 'Glenkinchie' being thought, by the Victorian distillers, to sound more authentically Scottish than Kinchie Burn!

Saltoun station was now reached immediately after the West Saltoun to Peaston Bank road was crossed on the level – this was the most important intermediate station on the Gifford & Garvald and boasted a passing loop, signalling (controlled by a ground frame) and a two-siding goods yard on the south side. The main passenger platform was on the up side and a standard wooden building in typical light railway style was provided for the booking office. On the down side loop was a short wooden platform, devoid of shelter, at which the Edinburgh trains called. Following the closure of the line to passengers the down platform was removed and the up platform, in common with those at Pencaitland and Humbie, was shortened and made to serve as a goods loading bank. The station master's house was next to the level crossing.

From Saltoun the line began a stiff two mile climb at a ruling gradient of 1 in 50 and crossed the Humbie Water on a tall stone viaduct high above the river. Passing through a cutting, and then woodlands and the river to the north and farmland to the south, Highlea Siding was reached on the up side – this was connected by a track to Lord Polwarth's estate at Humbie House and marked the point where the line turned east before reaching Humbie station. Here the platform was on the down side together with a goods yard of two sidings and a house for the station master; any passengers for Humbie village would be faced with a long walk to their intended destination from here! The railway now crossed the Birns Water by the ill-fated Gilchriston bridge and an accommodation crossing leading to the farm at Gilchriston was reached. This had gates which were normally kept locked against the road; there was some correspondence in the early years of the century regarding the provision of additional keys for the driver of a bread van making regular calls to the farm. By now the line had turned north-eastwards and reached its summit close to Saltoun Road level crossing, which carried the Haddington to Soutra (A6137) road across the railway. A steep descent at a ruling gradient of 1 in 50 now followed and there were two more ungated level crossings – Marvingston and Inglefield, the former carrying a by-road and the latter the B6355 Gifford to East Saltoun road. The last stretch was through the inappropriately named Speedy Wood, and the terminus was reached when the road crossed the old Gifford to Edinburgh road half a mile from the village. Here there were two sidings, a loop and a sawmills on the up side and the passenger platform and building on the down side all perched on a shelf of land above the Gifford Water. From here the narrow Station Road crossed an ancient (and weight restricted) bridge into the village.

The Lines Today

The Haddington branch has, for virtually its entire length, been converted into a path known as 'The Railway Walk' and this commences at Longniddry station, behind the down side platform and reached via a gate in the platform fence next to the new footbridge. The station itself is unrecognisable, having been completely rebuilt and realigned to the east in the 1980s; curiously the village itself has expanded in the opposite direction! The site of the Dung Lye is a private house which was formerly the local telephone exchange. Along the route of the Haddington branch a couple of under-bridges have been rebuilt but most of the other railway civil engineering features remain. Among the sites of interest are Coatyburn Siding, now a car park and picnic area (the latter being situated on the loading bank), and Haddington station where part of the platform complete with a brick-built shed, the original but much altered 1846 booking office, and the brick retaining wall of the later station building all survive. The line forms an easy walk or cycle ride on a Saturday afternoon and can easily be reached by public transport, Longniddry being served by the hourly Edinburgh to North Berwick electric trains and Haddington being served by frequent buses along the A1 back to Edinburgh. For cars the best access point is at Coatyburn, reached via the B1377 Longniddry to Drem road at Spittal.

Tracing the other lines is more difficult although the major portion, from Crossgatehall to Saltoun station, forms the well-signposted 'Pencaitland Railway Walk'. The junction at Monktonhall can be seen from passing trains on the main line although the trackbed has been ploughed over nearby. Much of the high embankment past Whitehall has gone but Smeaton station site is still recognisable, being reached by a minor road off the A6094 Dalkeith to Inveresk road. There are few colliery remains although the massive bings at Smeaton Shaw survive as a mute reminder of the once busy Dalkeith Colliery, but the disappearance of other mining remains will come as a shock to any reader standing beside the markers provided by the East Lothian council and trying to identify many of the sites known in the photographs in this book. Of the Hardengreen line, there is nothing left of the Victoria viaduct and such is the landscaping around this point that it is almost impossible to imagine that such a mighty monument once existed. Thorneybank is covered by an industrial estate but at Ancrum Road, close to the old A7 at Eskbank, a cutting and overbridge can be found and these are the most substantial, if almost the only, surviving mementoes of this most mysterious of lines.

The platform at Ormiston remains as do the majority of the bridges, most notably the Tyne viaduct. The Macmerry line survives in places and the site of both Winton and Macmerry stations can be traced. At Woodhall the colliery site is now a pleasant wooden picnic area but of the Red Row bridge no trace remains, the road here having to be realigned in 1969. Pencaitland retains the station master's house and a gradient post and from here to Saltoun the most pleasant stretch of the surviving trackbed remains; a worthwhile diversion can be made to the nearby Glenkinchie Distillery at its pretty location where conducted tours can be had on weekdays during working hours (no prior booking is necessary). Saltoun still boasts a station house and the station building here also survives, albeit at present in a dismantled stated at Bo'ness. The Humbie viaduct site can be seen from a farm road running north-east from Old Duncrahill, and Humbie station site can be easily reached from the A6137 and the sinister gap, where Gilchriston bridge once stood, can be examined. The trackbed between Humbie and Gifford has been adapted for farm roads in places and elsewhere is now disappearing under the encroaching flora, but Inglefield level crossing is still discernible. The Gifford station site can be seen although only the station master's house is clearly visible, the rest now being private property. From Gifford station one can still follow the route of the 'Duke of Gifford' and visit the 'Goblin Ha' and the 'Tweeddale Arms' and then enjoy the beauties of this village with its cross, town hall, avenue and 18th century parish kirk, by the gates of which are the memorial seats to John Douglas, the first station master at Gifford.

The Gifford and Macmerry lines are best followed by car or cycle since with the exception of Ormiston and Pencaitland, served by the hourly SMT bus No. 113 from Edinburgh, and Dalkeith, the provision of public transport is scant. Car parks at Crossgatehall, Pencaitland and Saltoun stations enable the Walk to be followed on foot or cycle and, rather curiously, painted wooden signposts still direct travellers to the latter station from the Humbie road, despite the fact that there is no community of this name and the station has been closed to passengers for over sixty years and to goods for nearly thirty. This is, however, a land of anachronistric signs for on a by-road in the locality there are even examples of pre-1930 Ministry of Transport road signs still in use, as well as a selection of road signs from the 1950s. Both the Crossgatehall to Saltoun section (particularly that to the east of Pencaitland), and the whole of the Haddington line, make ideal family walks for children and dogs and one can very effectively disguise the real nature of the field-work in industrial archeology being undertaken!

The end point of the Pencaitland Railway Walk–Saltoun station with Ivatt '2MT' No. 46462 ready to depart for Ormiston and Portobello in April 1964.

C.N. Turnbull

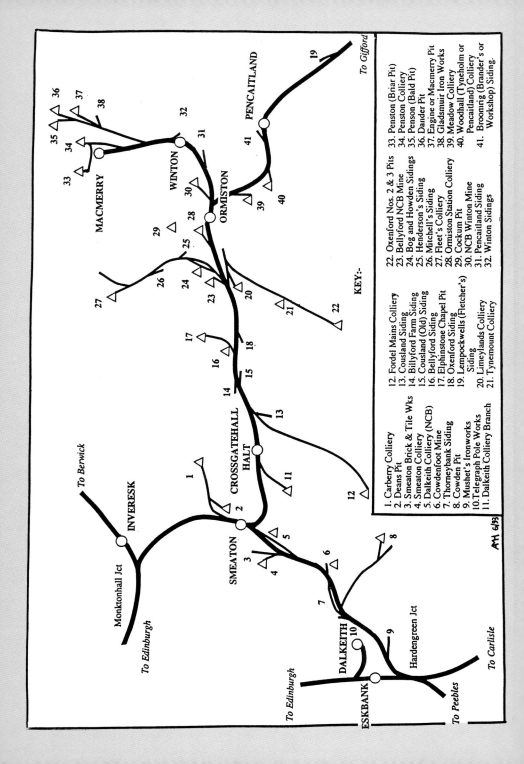

KEY:-

1. Carberry Colliery
2. Deans Pit
3. Smeaton Brick & Tile Wks
4. Smeaton Colliery
5. Dalkeith Colliery (NCB)
6. Cowdenfoot Mine
7. Thorneybank Siding
8. Cowden Pit
9. Mushet's Ironworks
10. Telegraph Pole Works
11. Dalkeith Colliery Branch

12. Fordel Mains Colliery
13. Cousland Siding
14. Billyford Farm Siding
15. Cousland (Old) Siding
16. Bellyford Siding
17. Elphinstone Chapel Pit
18. Oxenford Siding
19. Lempockwells (Fletcher's) Siding
20. Limeylands Colliery
21. Tynemount Colliery

22. Oxenford Nos. 2 & 3 Pits
23. Bellyford NCB Mine
24. Bog and Howden Sidings
25. Henderson's Siding
26. Mitchell's Siding
27. Fleet's Colliery
28. Ormiston Station Colliery
29. Cockum Pit
30. NCB Winton Mine
31. Pencaitland Siding
32. Winton Sidings

33. Penston (Briar Pit)
34. Penston Colliery
35. Penston (Bald Pit)
36. Dander Pit
37. Engine or Macmerry Pit
38. Gladsmuir Iron Works
39. Meadow Colliery
40. Woodhall (Tyneholm or Pencaitland) Colliery
41. Broonrig (Brander's or Workshop) Siding.

AH 6/93

Chapter Eleven
Mines, Minerals and Merchandise

GOODS YARDS, PRIVATE SIDINGS AND FREIGHT FACILITIES

'The Company shall make and maintain in all time coming . . . a suitable siding at a point to be fixed by the owner in or as near as conveniently may be to the field numbered 60 on the deposited plan [and] a station for passengers, animals and goods.'

Gifford & Garvald Railway Act 1891, s.30(1).

Much of the traffic carried on the Haddington, Macmerry and Gifford branch lines consisted of goods, minerals and coal and, in this chapter, more detailed descriptions of the various facilities provided by the railway for the handling of these commodities are given; the map printed on the page opposite gives the location of the yards, sidings and mines in the most complicated stretch, i.e. the lines between Monktonhall and Hardengreen, Macmerry and Pencaitland.

Goods Yards and Public Sidings

With the exception of Crossgatehall, all the passenger stations on the three branch lines handled public goods traffic. At Haddington the goods yard was fairly extensive and handled general goods, livestock and minerals. A goods shed and a separate dedicated grain shed were provided, the latter emphasising the heavy traffic in wheat, barley and oats particularly in connection with the Friday market. Haddington also dealt with large quantities of coal, cattle, agricultural machinery, animal foodstuffs and a considerable amount of general merchandise. Depots were established here by a number of coal merchants and also by BOCM-Silcocks. The goods yard was closed to traffic, excluding coal, on 5th March, 1968 and entirely as from 30th March, 1968. Travelling towards Longniddry there was a siding at Laverocklaw which had a chequered history and for part of its life handled public goods traffic until finally going out of use in about 1950. Half a mile to the north was Coatyburn, an unstaffed public siding opened in 1846 and consisting of a single siding and loading bank; it was closed on 23rd March, 1964. After alterations carried out in 1892 both Laverocklaw and Coatybank sidings were worked by down trains only, the locomotive used in shunting operations being at the Longniddry end of the wagons due to the gradients at these points.

Longniddry had a goods yard with a shed, wagon turntables and a loading bank on the up side of the main line immediately to the east of the passenger station and a wagon weighing machine. Formerly a busy yard, it closed on 28th December, 1964. To the west and on the up-side was Longniddry West or Manure Siding ('the dung lye') which handled horse manure from Edinburgh and Leith; it was closed in 1952.

On the Macmerry line there were public goods facilities at Smeaton, handled at the passenger platform (on the west face of the island) and in the adjacent east and west sidings; the former were also used for Carberry coal traffic and the latter for Dalkeith Colliery wagons. Weighing facilities were provided here and all Carberry traffic and originating goods from the Mac-

Coatyburn siding from the road in 1962 — the loading bank and PW shed can both be seen and in the foreground a gap in the hedge marks the site of a land mine explosion during the war. The siding site is now a car park for the Railway Walk.

George Angus

In 1885 a local coal merchant advertises coal from all over Scotland (but curiously, not East Lothian!).

Bermaline bread was once Haddington's most famous export: the Bermaline mills generated much rail traffic to and from the town until the motor lorry took over.

merry, Gifford and Hardengreen lines were weighed here; the only exception being coal from Dalkeith Colliery, which was travelling south, since this was weighed at Hardengreen. In later years, the BR weighing machine contractor's travelling vans, converted from old coaching stock, were stabled here. Smeaton was closed to the public on 5th May, 1965. On the Hardengreen line, the only public siding was at Thorneybank which had formerly been used as a private siding for the Duke of Buccleuch, but which became public about 1890; the siding here was closed in 1933.

Travelling east from Smeaton, the first public goods facilities were those at Ormiston, where the sidings were situated to the north of the passenger platform and passing loop. They were opened in 1869 and closed in May 1965. On the Macmerry branch, there were public facilities at Winton, where there were three sidings and a loading bank on the down side east of the passenger platform and at Macmerry, where there were two sidings, a loading bank and an engine release loop on the up side to the west of the station. These two stations were closed entirely on 2nd May, 1960.

On the Gifford & Garvald Railway, public facilities were provided only at the stations and not elsewhere. At Pencaitland, two sidings were laid on the up side immediately to the north of the platform; formerly busy in season with strawberries and other fruits grown in the area, the station was reduced to the status of unstaffed public siding in 1954, by which time one of the sidings had vanished, and closed entirely on 23rd March, 1964. At Saltoun, there were two sidings and a passing loop on the down side and, after the passenger service was abandoned in 1933, the passenger platform was used as the principal goods loading bay; a 1-ton crane was provided here. The station was closed completely in 1965. At Humbie, there were two sidings to the south of the passenger station and these continued in use until 2nd May, 1960; the Ormiston Coal Company formerly had a small depot at the station. Gifford had two sidings on the west side of the station and a 2-ton crane; services here continued (from August 1948 by road motor only from Haddington) until 1st January, 1959. There were two small coal depots here belonging, respectively, to James Beattie of Haddington and to A. White & Company, who ran the Oxenford Colliery.

Lime Works and Quarries

East Lothian was for many centuries a notable producer of lime, both for agricultural and building purposes and, accordingly, the county is littered with numerous abandoned lime kilns, quarries and pits. Only two installations were directly served by the relevant branch lines. Close to Longniddry Junction and situated on the down side of the Haddington branch line was the Harelaw Lime Siding, serving the limeworks of the same name. Harelaw had been in operation for many years prior to the coming of the railway and in 1836 seven men and five horses were employed in the burning and production of lime for agricultural use and building mortar; the lime from this quarry was also used for gas purification. Originally not rail-served, a short siding was installed running south-east from the Longniddry engine shed road. The works were taken over by the Charlestown Lime Company of Fife and finally abandoned about 1918; there was an extensive internal system of horse-worked tramways here between about 1895 and 1914. The siding was usually worked by the 8.20 am down goods from North Berwick to Portobello.

Cousland Lime Works were situated on the south side of the line between Smeaton and Ormiston and close to the village of that name on the East Lothian–Midlothian border. These dated from the 16th century and produced a good quality lime particularly suited to building purposes, providing much of the plaster used in the elegant buildings of the New Town of Edinburgh. Concurrent with the opening of the line in 1867, the Cousland Siding was opened at a point 2.5 miles east of Smeaton Junction, and this was connected to the lime works by a horse tramway which ran across the fields in a south-westerly direction for about 1 mile; the lessee of the siding was the firm of Gibson & Mercer. In 1895, a new siding of the same name was built for Messrs Crombie & Fletcher, who now operated the works. This was a short line some 300 yards in length, leaving the NBR line on the down side at a point ¾ mile to the west of the original Cousland Siding which, along with the horse tramway, was then abandoned. In 1903 the Caledonian Portland Cement Works Ltd acquired the works and set about building a new cement factory on high ground close to the railway and the Bellyford burn. A new quarry was opened at Windmill and a system of internal horse tramways, which included a lengthy tunnel, was built to link the quarry with the factory. The factory initially produced 300 tons of cement a week and this was loaded into railway wagons in a large covered shed so that operations were not disrupted by the weather; at one time 20,000 bricks per week were also produced here. Cement production ceased in 1930, (when the works were owned by the British Portland Cement Co) due to competition from England and Belgium, but lime production continued and the siding was still used. In 1960 the tenants of the siding were the Dalkeith Transport & Storage Company. The Cousland Lime Works are still in operation and a modern crushing plant has been built; at the entrance to the works three quarry trucks on a raised piece of track are displayed.

One other lime works is worthy of note, although it was not directly connected to the North British line. This was the East Saltoun Quarry, opened in 1943, which had a 2 ft gauge internal railway system operated by a 4-wheeled Ruston & Hornsby diesel locomotive bought second-hand from Borough Green Quarry in Kent. Loco haulage ceased in about 1970 and by 1975 the works had gone out of use.

Coal Mines

The most important source of traffic in the area was coal and the line south of Monktonhall Junction served the edge of the vast Midlothian coalfield, where a strata of the Limestone Coal group formed a westwards dipping basin with a rich potential. The Camps Ridge, at the county boundary with East Lothian, formed a natural division and to the east the strata reappeared, although now it only formed a shallow undulating basin with

LMS 'Black Five' No. 45183 passes Smeaton station on a train from the NCB Central Coal Preparation Plant at Dalkeith Colliery in June 1964. *J.E. Hay*

The same train approaching Carberry Colliery Junction — note the Clayton Type 1 in the background. *J.E. Hay*

numerous faults. The area had been worked for coal since medieval times and by the mid-19th century the mines at Smeaton, Cowden and Pencaitland were all in production, the latter in the 1830s employing 90 men, 90 women and between 30 and 40 children. Originally supplying mainly local needs, a great expansion in production took place after 1850 when export markets and the increasing pace of industrialisation in Scotland increased demand significantly. In the period up to World War I new pits were opened and existing mines developed. The industry locally was dominated by two large firms, the Edinburgh Collieries Company (founded in 1900 and acquiring the interests of Deans & Moore and, later, R. & J. Durie of Tranent) and the Ormiston Coal Company, founded in 1882. Other local concerns included A. & G. Moore, the Woodhall Coal Company, the Fordel Mains Company and the various companies having an interest in the Macmerry and Penston pits. A feature of this era was the large number of private owner wagons operated by each company and these provided a colourful and varied spectacle right up to nationalisation. According to the NBR Traders' Wagon Register the Ormiston Coal Co. had some 200 wagons, the Oxenford Coal Co. (A. White & Co.) had 25 10-ton spring buffer wagons built by the Lancashire & Yorkshire Wagon Co. and the Woodhall company had 100 12-ton wagons of which 80 were built by Hurst Nelson, 15 by the Motherwell Wagon Co and 5 by R.Y. Pickering. Amongst the liveries were those of the Ormiston company ('Great Eastern' blue with white lettering shaded in red and black iron work), the Woodhall Company ('Medium' green with yellow lettering shaded in red and black iron work), A. & G. Moore (brown oxide with white lettering and black shading), R. & J. Durie (grey with white lettering) and the Edinburgh Collieries Co. (mid-grey with white lettering shaded in black superseded by black with white lettering). Wagons still bearing some of these liveries can be seen today on the SRPS line at Bo'ness.

After 1920 the industry began to undergo a steady decline and the economic depression led to retrenchment in local mining operations, although East and Mid Lothian suffered less than many of the more traditional coalfields such as Lanarkshire and Cumberland, and some development continued. The 1944 Report into the Scottish Coal Industry recommended that further investment in the area be made and on 1st January, 1947, when the mines were nationalised, Carberry, Dalkeith, Fleets and Limeylands all passed into public ownership as part of the Lothians Area of the National Coal Board. Further exploitation of untapped resources resulted in there being several new NCB pits in the area but within a few years the final run-down of East Lothian and Midlothian mining had begun, triggered off by a 25 per cent fall in Scottish coal consumption between 1955 and 1965; by the early 1960s only Dalkeith Colliery remained in production. As this book is written the British coal industry is but a shadow of its past and only one deep level pit is still in production in the Lothians, that of Monktonhall Colliery run by a miners' cooperative and served by sidings off the BR line to Millerhill.

The Macmerry and Gifford lines served the vast majority of the colleries in the area and those not rail-connected (such as the tiny Penkaet mine) were insignificant. Little evidence now remains of this once powerful industry –

surface buildings have been demolished, bings landscaped and even the distinctive rows of miners' cottages in settlements such as Deanstown, Cowpit and Smeaton have gone, the latter engulfed by the giant bings of the Dalkeith Colliery which form the one tangible reminder of a vanished industrial past. This, and the fact that many of the individual pits were designed to have a working life of only some 15–20 years before becoming exhausted or uneconomic, makes any attempt to trace their dates of operation difficult. This is compounded by the fact that there is no comprehensive history of coal mining in the Lothians. The facts given are, therefore, as accurate as the author's researches can establish; it should be remembered that the various sidings mentioned often remained open for several years after the closure of the pits which they served, and were used to transport infilling materials or for storage before being eventually lifted. It should be remembered that not all of the traffic was one-way – inward traffic consisted of pit props, machinery and other supplies and also coal brought in from other pits to the washeries and screening plants at Limeylands and Dalkeith Colliery while in the outwards direction there was also a fair traffic in 'redd' (the colliery waste) which was taken from local colleries to outlying bings.

On the Monktonhall to Smeaton section the Carberry Colliery Branch left the NBR line on the up side some ¾ mile north of Smeaton station and ran ¾ mile E.N.E. to Carberry Colliery Nos. 2 and 3 pits, serving *en route* Deans Pit to the south by a short sub-branch with a trailing junction immediately to the east of the level crossing over the Musselburgh–Pathead road (A6124). The steeply graded branch, which included gradients of 1 in 37 for 154 yards and 1 in 33 for 223 yards, was ¾ mile in length and ran in an E.N.E. direction as far as Carberry Old Mains, was owned by Deans & Moore and dated from the opening of the Smeaton line in 1866, although the junction of the line was extensively altered at the behest of the Board of Trade in 1894. In May 1900 the branch became the property of the Edinburgh Colleries Co., by which time the connection to the Deans Pit had been removed. In 1906 half a million tons of coal per year were being produced at Carberry and 750 men were employed here but by 1948 this had declined to 550 men producing only 130,000 tons of coal. Additional siding accommodation was provided at Carberry in 1903, 1905 and 1912. A number of Barclay 0–4–0 saddle tanks were employed here and one of them, No. 2 which had been supplied new to the Colliery in 1902, bore the name *Carberry*. Gravity shunting was in use here until the 1920s when it was modified following difficulties caused in frosty weather; latterly the branch was served by trip workings by the Smeaton pilot engine. The Carberry Colliery ceased production on 16th March, 1960, although a landsale depot remained in use there until 1963, when the branch finally went out of use. The branch was subsequently lifted but for some time the rails on the level crossing over the A6124 were left *in situ*.

To the south of Smeaton Junction and adjacent to the Hardengreen line were situated Dalkeith Colliery Sidings. These dated from after World War II and served the Nos. 8 and 9 pits and a post-war shaft (described as 'one of the most up-to-date in the Lothians') and eventually replaced the Dalkeith Colliery branch when alterations were made to the siding accommodation

An early line drawing showing the method used to transport coal underground in the East Lothian colleries – a government report highlighting the use of girls and women in the haulage roads of the county's mines led to widespread condemnation of the practice and its speedy cessation.

here, and a new half-mile tramway was built to connect up with the older workings near to Smeaton Shaw; an aerial ropeway connected the mine with the bing there. In 1954 a large washery and central coal preparation plant was established next to the Hardengreen line, half a mile south of Smeaton Junction. All shunting at the sidings was carried out by BR locomotives and in the 1950s 420 men were employed here, 330 of them underground. A Mitchell wagon-marshalling system was installed at the sidings.* The Colliery continued in production until December 1978, and the washery until 1980, thus having the distinction of providing the last traffic of all on any of the lines featured in this book.

Travelling southwards on the Hardengreen line there were three further coal sidings namely Smeaton Colliery, an early mine at Smeaton Head (close to the site of the later NCB Washery) operated by the Marquis of Lothian and originally served by the horse tramway; workings were merged with the later Dalkeith Colliery and the sidings, on the down side, were lifted about 1900. Half a mile to the south, and served by a trailing connection on the up side, was the Cowdenfoot Mine Siding, serving a mine opened by the NCB in 1958 and which resulted in the relaying of over one mile of the former NBR line to serve it; despite the recent nature of the pit it was closed in August 1965. As an Dalkeith Colliery all shunting was done by BR locomotives. The Cowden Pit, opened by the Duke of Buccleuch in 1838, was served by a ¾ mile branch of the original Buccleuch Tramway south-eastwards from Thorneybank and was operated by A.&G. Moore, it was later connected to NBR line by a private siding on the same route.

Returning to Smeaton, and travelling towards Ormiston, the Dalkeith Colliery Branch was a short line, ⅜ mile in length, which left the NBR at Crossgatehall by a trailing junction on the down side and was controlled by the Dalkeith Colliery signal box. The branch was opened in September 1904 and was owned by A.&G. Moore. Internal shunting at the colliery was carried out by a sole Barclay 0−4−0 saddle tank; in 1923, 665 people were employed at the mine. In 1956 the branch was fitted, having been superseded by the new sidings at Smeaton (see above). A headshunt at the end of the branch crossed the by-road from Smeaton, and a long siding extended southwards from the branch.

A mile due south of the Dalkeith Colliery Branch was the terminus of the Fordel Mains Colliery Branch owned by the eponymous Fordel Mains (Midlothian) Colliery Co. and opened in about 1910. The branch left the 1895 Cousland Siding and was almost two miles in length; following the 400 ft contour line in a generally south-westerly direction it ran up to the Jedburgh road (A68) and was worked by North British and LNER locomotives and crew. The colliery was situated on rising ground near to the A68 main road and an electrically worked hutch haulage road took the coal to a sorting point near to the branch railway; 265 persons were employed here and the mine closed in about 1945.

Half a mile east of the new Cousland siding and situated on the up side was Bellyford Siding, a short siding provided on the opening of the line to

---

*A description of this installation appears in the October 1954 issue of *The Locomotive Railway Carriage and Wagon Review.*

serve a small pit of that name. When the pit closed a short time afterwards the siding was renamed Billyford Farm Siding. Half a mile to the east and situated on the down side were the Oxenford Sidings serving the Oxenford Colliery of Messrs A. White & Co of Ormiston and the Oxenford Colliery Company. A new shaft was sunk by James Clark in 1907 and this became Oxenford No. 1 Pit of the Ormiston Coal Company in about 1915. The sidings themselves were sanctioned in 1907 and opened in 1910. The pit closed in July 1932 and the sidings, which had an unusual layout and relied upon a system of gravity shunting, were closed shortly thereafter. Two hundred yards to the east of Oxenford Siding, and situated on the up side, was Bellyford Siding (not to be confused with the earlier Bellyford siding) owned by Deans & Moore and serving the Bellyford Bank Pit and, by means of a half mile horse-drawn tramway running northwards, the Chapel Pit or Elphinstone Tower Colliery. These workings were finally abandoned c.1900, but the Bellyford Pit continued in operation under the auspices of the Edinburgh Colleries Co. until about 1928.

Next came the Bog Sidings, half a mile to the east. These were on the up side and served a number of colleries the first of which was the Elphinstone Colleries of Messrs Davie & Nisbet (later R. & J. Durie and, from 1907, the Edinburgh Colleries Company), 200 yards from the junction. These consisted of two pits, the Howden, sunk c.1850 and served, from 1877, by the Howden Colliery Siding, and the Bog, sunk in 1879 when the Bog Siding was opened. Eighty-three men were employed here in 1884 and a new siding, named Elphinstone Colliery Siding was opened here in 1905. Two years later the Bog Pit was closed and the Edinburgh Colleries Co took over; the Howden Pit was finally abandoned in 1929 which the Bog Siding was latterly used for storage purposes. Between the junction of the Bog Siding with the NBR line and the Elphinstone Colleries a new mine was opened on the north side in 1953 called the Bellyford Mine served by a siding on the up side. BR locomotives did all the shunting here except for a brief period in 1961 when an NCB loco was used. The Bellyford Mine was closed in November 1961 and the sidings lifted c.1963.

The northwards continuation of the Bog Siding was known as the Fleets Branch which ran to the Fleets Colliery, a large concern employing over 800 men upon nationalisation and producing 750 tons of coal per day and situated 1¼ miles north of the junction with the NBR line. Opened in the 1880s, the Fleets Branch saw much traffic apart from a short period in 1928 when, owing to the trade depression, the colliery was temporarily closed. The branch was extended in the 1920s in a northerly direction to join up with a mineral line which ran southwards from the NBR main line at Prestonpans and had originally served the Caerlaverock pit. Coal from Fleets which required washing was sent north over this line to Meadowmill while the remainder was sent south over the branch. Fleets was operated by R. & J. Durie (later Edinburgh Colleries Co.) and a number of tank locomotives were employed on duties here, the most interesting of which was No. 8, a Hudswell, Clarke 4–4–0T which had been built for the Lynn & Fakenhan Railway in 1878 and which was purchased by the Edinburgh Colleries Co. in 1925. After withdrawal in 1935 its replacement was a new Barclay 0–4

–0ST, No. 9, which became NCB Lothians Area No. 29 and survived for many years in a Midlothian children's playground. The Fleets pit finally closed in 1959 and the branch was abandoned two years later.

On the south side of the NBR branch line and opposite the Bellyford NCB mine were the Limeylands Sidings. The sidings dated from 1907 and were shunted by the company's own saddle tank locomotive. After a temporary cessation of production in the late 1920s, the colliery produced 130 tons of coal per day. It employed 295 men in 1948 when the mine was badly flooded in the great storm of that summer. By 1953 the pit had ceased but coal preparation plant was opened on its site and this continued in production until October 1958. Leading off the Limeylands Sidings by a trailing junction was the Ormiston Coal Company's Tynemount Branch which crossed the Ormiston–Cousland road on the level and ran ¾ mile south-west to Tynemount Colliery, opened in 1924. A half-mile extension led to Oxenford Nos. 2 and 3 pits, the latter being opened as late as 1953. The branch was operated by the Ormiston Company's own locomotive – originally this was a Barclay 0–4–0ST of 1924 vintage which was sold to Alexander Stephens & Sons for use in their Govan shipyard in 1942 and replaced by No. 2, a similar but new engine. No. 2, which was kept at Tynemount and, latterly, at Limeylands was in the charge of an ex-NBR driver and the vulnerability of having just one engine to operate the line is demonstrated by the entry in the LNER Sectional Appendix which stated that 'LNER locos are permitted to work the Tynemount Branch in the event of a breakdown of the Company's engine.' There was also a 2 ft gauge system here operated by two Ruston & Hornsby 4-wheeled locomotives; this had closed by 1954. In 1948 Oxenford No. 2 and Tynemount pits produced 111,000 tons of coal and employed 140 men but the run-down was rapid and Oxenford No. 2 closed in 1951, Tynemount in January 1952 and the new Oxenford No. 3 in January 1959.

At Ormiston itself, immediately to the north of the station, was situated the Ormiston Coal Company's Ormiston Station Colliery Sidings, serving the Ormiston station Nos. 1, 2 and 3 pits, opened in 1886. At one time 100 men were employed here and at the No. 4 or Cockum pit, situated to the north and joined to the main complex by a tramway over a mile in length. The Nos. 1, 2 and 3 pits were closed in 1901 and the Cockum Pit in 1909 although the sidings were retained for storage purposes. Subsequently, coal disposal point was situated at these sidings; operated by the Ministry of Fuel & Power, Directorate of Opencast Production, the facility was open until 1960; in about 1951 a shunting engine was kept here for a brief period.

Following the Macmerry branch from Ormiston, the first colliery past the junction was the NCB mine served by the Winton Mine Siding, which left by a facing junction on the up side 400 yards from the station. Opened in 1950, and in its time highly productive, the mine was worked by the Gifford branch class '2MT' locomotive. In 1952 an average of 16 wagonloads of coal were being despatched from the colliery daily. When Winton Mine was closed in April 1962, the siding and the last surviving remnant of the Macmerry branch went with it. In the same area were various small pits such as the Sebastapol and New Winton pits, which were not rail connected, and the original Pencaitland Colliery worked by Deans & Moore and served by the misleadingly named Pencaitland Siding. This was 51 chains east of

View from the brakevan of a coal train, hauled by Gresley class 'J38' No. 65911, rounding the curve past Whitecraif between Smeaton and Monktonhall Junction in June 1961 – in the background are the main line and the spite of Inveresk Church.

M.B. Smith

A loaded coal train pulls out of the NCB mine at Winton, hauled by the Saltoun branch locomotive on 23rd February, 1962, two months before the mine ceased production.

W.S. Sellar

Looking westwards from the Crossgatehall bridge, 16th April, 1956. A west-bound coal train makes its way along the sweeping curve towards Smeaton Shaw farm and level crossing while in the foreground the signalbox at Dalkeith Colliery marks the start of the colliery branch which has just been lifted; note the coal bing. On the right is the site of the halt.   *D.L.G. Hunter*

A westwards looking view taken from the carriage window on a railtour on 6th September, 1958 – the Bog Sidings signal box and Limeylands Colliery sidings are both in evidence.   *D.L.G. Hunter*

Private owner wagons used on the Macmerry line — (*top*) a 12 ton wagon used by the Edinburgh Colleries Company at Carberry and Fleets pits; (*bottom*) an early 10 ton dumb-buffered wagon used at the Howden and Bog Pits by R&J Durie at the turn of the century.   *HMRS Collection*

Two private owner coal wagons used on the Gifford & Garvald – (top) an Ormiston Coal Company 12-ton wagon used at the Meadow Colliery; (bottom) a Woodhall 12-ton wagon used at the Pencaitland Colliery – an example of a Woodhall wagon in green livery with yellow lettering is preserved at Bo'ness.   HMRS Collection

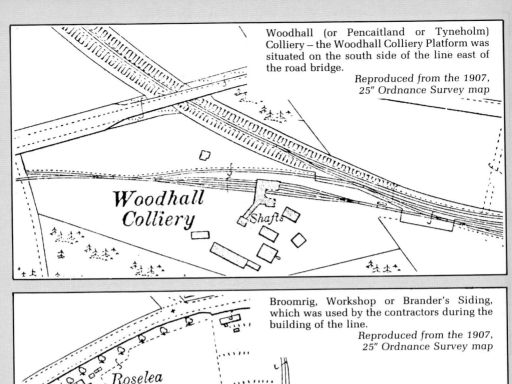

Woodhall (or Pencaitland or Tyneholm) Colliery – the Woodhall Colliery Platform was situated on the south side of the line east of the road bridge.

Reproduced from the 1907, 25" Ordnance Survey map

Woodhall Colliery

Shafts

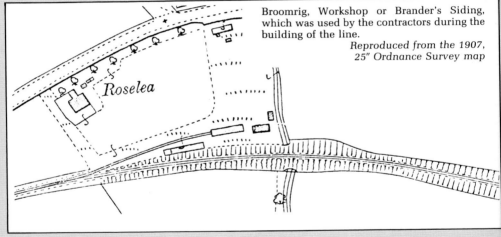

Broomrig, Workshop or Brander's Siding, which was used by the contractors during the building of the line.

Reproduced from the 1907, 25" Ordnance Survey map

Roselea

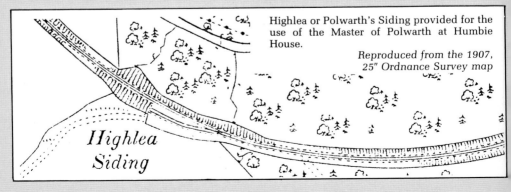

Highlea or Polwarth's Siding provided for the use of the Master of Polwarth at Humbie House.

Reproduced from the 1907, 25" Ordnance Survey map

Highlea Siding

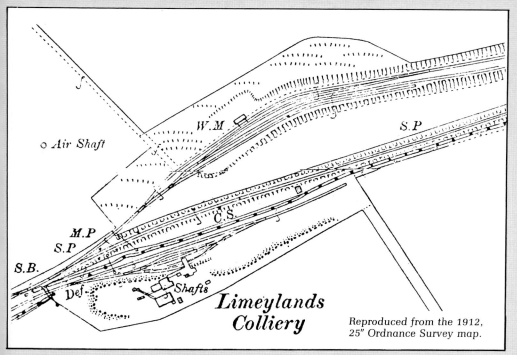

Reproduced from the 1912, 25" Ordnance Survey map.

Limeylands Colliery and the Bog Siding.

The Ormiston Coal Company's Meadow Colliery.

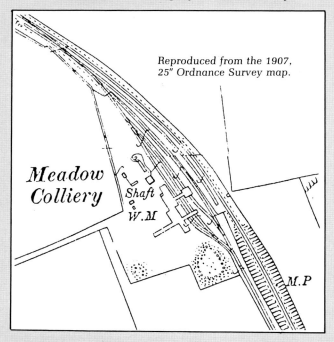

Reproduced from the 1907, 25" Ordnance Survey map.

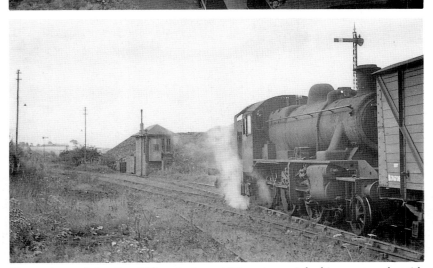

Three views of the Bog Siding in June 1961 — (*upper*) looking eastwards with Bellyford Mine on the left and Limeylands on the right; (*middle*) looking west from the signal box and (*lower*) Ivatt '2MT' No. 46461 ready to depart with the Saltoun goods.

M.B. Smith

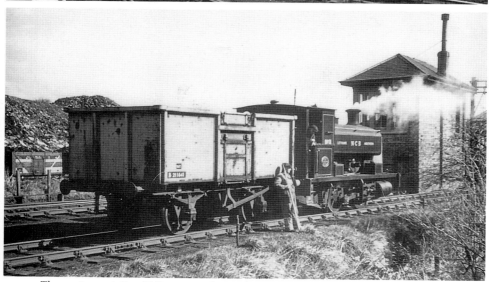

Three views at Bog Siding on 15th April, 1960 – (upper) BR Standard No. 78048 passes the signal box while a Barclay 0−4−0ST (the former Ormiston Coal Company No. 2) waits in the Limeylands siding; (middle and lower) the pug fusses around with a handful of wagons.

Rae Montgomery

Carberry Colliery in the 1920s – this newspaper picture shows the Barclay saddle tanks employed there. *Author's Collection*

The Fleet's Colliery, looking north, in the 1950s. *East Lothian District Libraries*

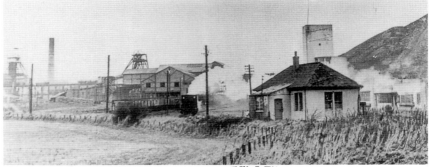

The Pencaitland Colliery, c.1940 – the Woodhall Coal Company's Platform once stood in the immediate foreground of this picture. *East Lothian District Libraries*

Ormiston Junction on the down side close to Winton West Mains and opened in 1869, the colliery having been previously served by the horse tramway from the north. Enjoying a relatively brief life, the siding was out of use by about 1900. Other smaller pits, used intermittently, were served by the Winton public sidings.

To the north were the various colleries known by the generic names of Macmerry and Penston and served by the Penston Colliery Sidings, situated on the east side of Macmerry station and opened in 1885; these were extended in 1907. From west to east the workings comprised the Briar and Penston No. 2 Pits, served by a ¼ mile siding from the No. 1 or Mont Fair Pit, which itself was 200 yards WNW of the station at Macmerry and served by a line from there which crossed the main London road on the level. There two pits were finally abandoned about 1914. To the east was a collection of four pits, namely the Penston No. 3, Bald, Dander and Engine (or Macmerry or Merryfield) Pits; the latter was abandoned in 1908. Penston Colliery Sidings had a variety of lessees, including Deans & Moore from 1879 (who established their main wagon repair facilities here), the Edinburgh Colleries Co. in 1900, the Riggonhead Coal Co. of Tranent in 1905, the Udston Colliery Co. of Glasgow in 1910 and the Penston Colliery Co. in 1912. Some 126 miners were employed in the Penston Pits by Deans & Moore in 1889 and 332 by the Udston Colliery Co. here in 1923 but all production ceased in 1926; the workings were formally abandoned in March 1928.

On the Gifford & Garvald line there were two colleries the first of which was the Meadow Colliery, opened in 1903 by the Ormiston Coal Company and served by sidings 300 yards from Ormiston Junction on the down side. The pit was abandoned in September 1914, but the sidings remained in use for storing wagons until their eventual removal about 1930. To the south of the Red Row bridge, which carried the Dalkeith to Haddington (A6093) road over the line was the Woodhall Coal Company Siding, on the down side again and serving the Tyneholm Colliery (also referred to as the Woodhall Colliery and the Pencaitland Colliery). This was sunk in 1903 by John Reid of Tyneholm and was said initially to have a life expectancy of some 15–20 years. Due to a geological freak the Woodhall Coal Company continued to produce coal here until the abandonment of the pit and the winding up of the company in 1944, when 198 men were still employed there. A private station was provided for the colliers (see Chapter 7) but a more permanent legacy of the Company was the building of the miners' houses by Reid in Wester Pencaitland, which have long outlived the mine.

Other Industrial Sidings

On the Smeaton to Hardengreen line there were a number of private sidings namely the Smeaton Brick & Tile Works Siding, a quarter mile long northwards extension from Smeaton Colliery on the line of the original tramway and abandoned in about 1900, Mushet's Siding, serving the Elmfield Iron Foundry of William Mushet which closed in 1894 and the Telegraph Pole Siding, serving the North British Railway telegraph pole works at Gibraltar close to the Victoria Viaduct, this siding was opened in

An old GNoSR five-compartment coach does duty as Pooley's mobile weighing machine van at Haddington in 1967 – these vans were a common site at locations where no permanent weighing machine for wagon loads was provided and another newer example was often found at Ormiston.

G.N. Turnbull

about 1910. At Macmerry, the Gladsmuir Iron Works had a private siding to the east of the station. This was opened in 1868 and extended in 1870 when it was recorded that a new slag siding was opened and that 'there are no signals, choke blocks or safety points, but the guard of any train using it is responsible for leaving the choke blocks at the entrance to the Iron siding shut and locked.' Gladmuir Iron Works ceased production in about 1882 and the siding was closed. On the Gifford & Garvald line the only industrial siding was that which was situated on the up side near to Roselea, a little to the west of Pencaitland station. This was originally built by the contractor Joseph Phillips to house his locomotives and plant and was known as Workshop Siding. It was rebuilt in 1902 at a cost of £13 to serve a Mr Jones trading as the Larbert Saw Mills, who had applied to the NBR for a 'temporary facility' there. Timber was also handled at Humbie and Gifford yards, the latter having Brownlie's sawmills adjacent, and Workshop siding became known as Broomrig Siding, suffering a third change of name to Brander's Siding before going out of use about 1914; the siding survived unused for several years thereafter.

Miscellaneous Private Sidings and Works

There were a number of other private sidings mainly connected with local farms and agricultural enterprises and, although these were busiest in the days before the motor lorry began to pose a serious threat, several of these survived into BR days. On the Haddington branch there were two such sidings namely Haddington Slaughter House Siding, at the station and in existence from about 1904 until 1960 (its purpose was clearly shown from its title) and Laverocklaw Siding, which, although tenanted by the Ainslie family from time to time, had a chequered career and was listed as 'vacant' for much of its existence; in 1917 the siding was assessed as being worth £100 for local rates valuation purposes, while the neighbouring Coatyburn was given a value of £200. Used mainly for sugar beet and potatoes Laverocklaw Siding was in use right up until 1960. Although not strictly in the same category, the Blawearie Sidings (also known as Longniddry Down Sidings) at Longniddry (situated between the main line and Haddington branch) was private in the sense of not being for public use – this was used for railway purposes, one use being for the cleaning out of cattle wagons with water pumped from the water tower at the east end of the up passenger platform while in the 1950s for the storage of steam locomotives which were laid up until required for use on seasonal traffic. The total number held here was usually five or six and particular examples included a 'Y9' 0–4–0T from St Margarets and a number of LNER class 'D11', 4–4–0s which had been made redundant from Haymarket shed. These sidings were disconnected and lifted in January 1963.

On the Macmerry line the first private siding to be encountered was Billyford Farm Siding, which had been opened in 1869 to serve the original Bellyford Pit. In 1902 it was tenanted by a local farmer, J.B. Young, and thereafter by C. Beveridge of the Tower Farm, Tranent. The siding continued in use here until the 1950s and, in common with most of the similar sidings on the branch, handled sugar beet and pulp (processed at the British Sugar

Corporation's beet factory at Cupar), potatoes, fertilisers and other agricultural goods, albeit latterly in small quantities only. On the Bog Siding and Fleets Branch there were two farm sidings namely Henderson's Siding (also known as Prentice's Siding and Walker's Lye) which served South Elphinstone Farm and was situated on the east side of the line south of the old by-road from Elphinstone to Buxley and close to the Cockum Colliery, and Brook's Siding, subsequently known as Mitchell's Siding, which served the farm at North Elphinstone and which was situated on the up side north of the by-road between Cinderhall and Fleet's House.

On the Gifford & Garvald line there were two private sidings apart from the Broomrig Siding already mentioned. The first of these was Lempockwells Siding, on the up side between Pencaitland and Saltoun and close to and serving the farm of that name. Originally known as Fletcher's Siding, this had been originally provided for the use of the Saltoun Estate but it was later tenanted by the Inch family. The other siding was Polwarth's Siding, better known as Highlea Siding, which served the laird of Humbie House, who rejoiced in the splendidly archaic title of the Master of Polwarth; this faced east and was on the down side of the line and served by a track from the farm at Highlea. Both Lempockwells and Highlea sidings survived into the 1950s. Also on the G&GR, but not connected to it, was Glenkinchie Distillery which provided a fair amount of traffic to the line via Saltoun station. The question of a direct rail siding was discussed several times but rejected on the grounds of cost, the short distance between line and distillery being difficult and expensive terrain in which to build a siding. Horse-drawn drays were used between distillery and station right up until 1949, and thereafter motor lorries took over. Inward traffic handled for the distillery consisted of coal, peat, anthracite, malt and barley while the principal outward traffic was whisky in barrels, usually destined for blending and bottling plants in the Leith area; this latter traffic was particularly heavy in the weeks leading up to Christmas. According to Barnard's classic *Distilleries of the United Kingdom*, Glenkinchie had a fairly extensive internal overhead rail system which carried barley in wicker baskets between the hoppers, malting house and lofts. Glenkinchie Distillery is still in production and makes a fine lowland single malt which, by reason of the whisky being the final traffic on the line, is a suitable drink with which to toast the memory of the Gifford & Garvald!

Finally, there were two other railway systems in the area, both of which were built in connection with the construction of two dams in the foothills of the Lammermuirs. The earliest of these was at Lammerloch, two miles south of Humbie station, where in 1905 Messrs Stirling & Kinniburgh constructed a reservoir for the Prestonpans Water Supply. A Barclay 'pug' engine was used on the system here and, after completion of the contract in September 1906, the 'pug' was offered for sale at Humbie station. The other system to be built was the much later Hopes Reservoir scheme near to Gifford. The contractor was Richard Baillie of Haddington and the main works were carried out between 1929 and 1935. A two and a half mile 3 ft gauge line was built between Quarryford, near Long Yester, where the puddling clay was obtained, to the transhipment point near to Hopes House and the excavation point at the quarry itself. Six or seven 0–4–0T locos were used, although details of these are slight; one of the more interesting aspects of the scheme was the use of stone from the demolished Calton Jail next to Waverley station. The importance of the public water supply to industry in East Lothian is clearly illustrated by the fact that in 1947 of the 1,095 million gallons of water used in the county that year, 67 million gallons were used in connection with the coal mines and 18 million gallons by the LNER.

Edinburgh Colleries Company locomotive No. 8 at the Fleets Colliery in August 1929. This venerable Hudswell, Clarke 4–4–0T began life on the Lynn & Fakenham Railway in 1878 passing to the Midland & Great Northern and the War Department before arriving in East Lothian in 1925, still bearing its original number but by now in a dark grey livery. She remained there until scrapped at the beginning of 1935.

David Bayes Collection

Interior and exterior views of the signal box at Smeaton Junction taken in November 1937; the 1912 extension to the box can be clearly seen and in the foreground are the stairs leading up from the station platform to the road bridge. *Dr I.W. Scrimgeour*

Chapter Twelve

Tickets, Tokens and Telegraphs

SIGNALLING ON THE THREE BRANCH LINES

'A train staff, or train staff ticket indicating that the train staff will follow, must be carried with each train . . .'

LNER General Appendix, 1948

Railway signalling is a complex but fascinating subject and while, of necessity, the following details have been compressed and much of the technical detail omitted, a brief explanation is needed of some of the terms used so that the general reader can understand this chapter. The basic purpose of signalling is to prevent trains from colliding with each other and each line is thus divided up into a number of sections each of which is subject to a form of control. The simplest way to control a single line is the 'one engine in steam' (OES) system whereby only one train at a time is allowed on the stretch of line concerned; in its commonest form this was done by having one 'staff' or 'token' for the section and insisting that every train carried it. This, however, was inflexible in that it required trains to run alternately in each direction. A refinement, allowing two or more trains to run in one direction before one came the opposite way was the 'staff and ticket' system. This involved a staff for the section of railway concerned which each driver had to see before he was allowed to enter the section. If he were the last train in his direction before one returned he was given the staff, otherwise he was shown it and given a ticket, the staff following with a later train. Some companies, in the early days, used the staff in conjunction with a time interval (between trains) but it is thought this method had ceased by the 1880s.

These methods were later refined by having many tokens for each section, electrically locked in special instruments to ensure that only one could be out at a time. There were a number of variants in this theme, the two which were used on the lines covered in this book being the tablet system, which issued tokens in the form of metal discs or tablets, and the electric train staff system (ETS), where the tokens were long metal staffs.

Sidings and loops, when not directly worked from a signal box, were controlled by levers locked by a key on the staff for the section, or by the staff or tablet itself. In this way the staff or tablet could be removed from the lock only when the points were once more set for the main line, giving drivers an assurance that if they had the token, the siding points were all correctly set. A few outlying points which were little used might be released by an 'Annett's' key from the signal box.

On double lines the early method of control relied on time intervals between trains, but later used the block system, where there were instruments to allow adjacent signal boxes to communicate to indicate when the previous train had left the section between the two boxes.

The Haddington Branch

By the 1860s the original primitive system of train signalling had been replaced on the branch by the staff and ticket system, which was thought to

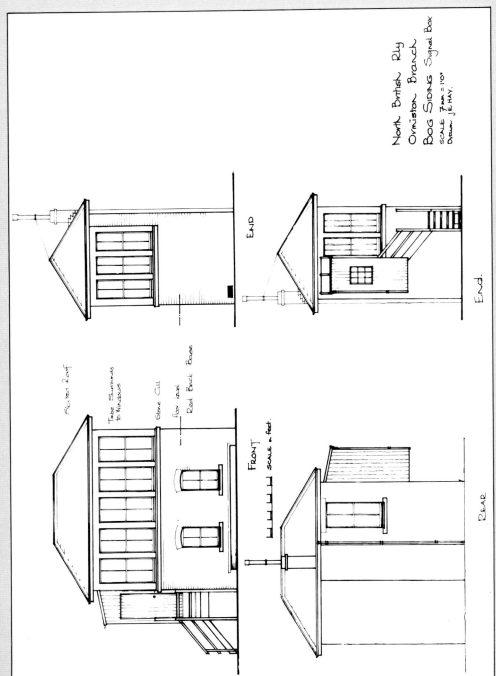

North British Rly
Ormiston Branch
Bog Sidings Signal Box
SCALE 7mm = 1'0"
Drawn J.E. HAY.

END

END.

Slated Roof

Timber Surrounds to Windows

Stone Cill

Floor Level

Red Brick Base

FRONT

SCALE in Feet.

REAR

J.E. Hay

Bog Sidings Signal Box.

The Bog Siding signal box, looking eastwards towards Ormiston in June 1961.
M.B. Smith

Hardengreen Junction, where the Smeaton line joined the Waverley Route; 27th May, 1966.
Dr I.W.G. Scrimgeour

be perfectly safe for use on the by now singled line. In 1892 Tyer's No. 6 tablet working was introduced. This was controlled by the rather squat signal box at Longniddry Junction, which dated from about 1881, and by the Haddington signal box situated on the south side of the line opposite the entrance to the goods yard. This arrangement was authorised by the NBR Board in November 1892 when they also sanctioned alterations to the station sidings and the reconstruction of Coatyburn and Laverocklaw Sidings, the latter two now being worked by a ground frame controlled by tablet lock. The cost of the installation of the block system at Haddington was £134 18s. 7d., while the alterations at Coatyburn cost £58 15s. 11d. and those at Laverocklaw £24 7s. 9d. The signals themselves were of the standard Stevens pattern lower quadrants and there were a couple of particularly fine tall fixed distants on the branch; fortunately there were windlasses for raising and lowering the lamps, so it was only rarely that a man had to go to the top.

Over the years alterations were made and, at Longniddry, the signal box was extended and raised and a Stevens new pattern 5¼ inch frame was installed in 1922, following upon extensive alterations made at the junction. The absolute block system was operated continuously on the main line and Longniddry box was open 24 hours a day on a three shift rota pattern. On 29th January, 1950 the West or Manure Siding was taken out of use and its attendant ground frame removed. After the withdrawal of passenger services on the branch line, Haddington signal box was manned only between 7.30 am and 6.50 pm and the whole section to Longniddry remained controlled by tablet. On 3rd August, 1952 the branch was converted to OES, the tablet instruments were withdrawn and the signals removed (with the exception of the up distant). The sidings were now worked by ground frame controlled by the train staff and a control circuit phone introduced, while the ground frame at the terminal cross-over was removed and the points there fitted with one-way spring levers. Following upon the complete closure of the branch, Longniddry Junction Box was closed on 8th September, 1968, leaving an extended block section of 6 miles 374 yards between St Germains Crossing and Drem Junction boxes.

The Smeaton, Ormiston and Macmerry Line

The branch left the main line at Monktonhall Junction, where a signal box, opened in 1866, was situated on the up side just to the east of the bridge over the River Esk. From here the section extended as far as Smeaton Junction, where there was a signal box on the east side of the line close to the overbridge at the station; this was inspected by the Board of Trade in September 1867 but presumably had been in use for some months prior to then. On 19th March, 1868 train staff regulations were applied between Smeaton Junction and Macmerry (dark blue staff) and Smeaton Junction and Thorneybank (white staff); these were revised on 31st July, 1870 when four separate sections came into use, namely, Monktonhall Junction to Smeaton Junction (red staff), Smeaton Junction to Macmerry (dark blue staff), Smeaton Junction to Thorneybank (white staff) and Thorneybank to Hardengreen (green staff). Thorneybank was a small 5-lever structure which controlled the siding there; it was closed on 29th February, 1896 when Smeaton to Hardengreen became a single section.

The Macmerry line retained fairly primitive signalling until the 1890s, when the Board of Trade used its powers to compel the North British to install proper signalling and the block system. Block instruments were added to the existing staff and ticket working and properly interlocked signal boxes provided or improved at Smeaton, Ormiston and Macmerry. The cost of installing the block was £441 9s. 0d., while at Macmerry £411 2s. 5d. was spent on signalling and £190 6s. 5d. on alterations to the station buildings and platforms. An intermediate 25-lever signal box was provided at Ormiston and here the total cost of the alterations required amounted to £795 4s. 1d. At Smeaton the cost of providing the 35-lever signal box (a replacement for the original signal box) and the other alterations there cost £1,475 5s. 4d., while incidental alterations at Cousland and Bellyford Sidings cost £242 2s. 1d. When Major Marindin inspected the line in December 1893 he was not impressed by what he found and he granted the North British a further extension of time to enable them to comply with the Board of Trade Order.

Increasing traffic justified the installation of tablet working between Smeaton and Ormiston about the turn of the century, but from Ormiston to Macmerry the staff and ticket system was retained along with block instruments. On 8th December, 1901 a signal box was opened at Bog Sidings situated on the south side of the line close to Limeylands Colliery. This box, which broke up the busy section between Ormiston and Smeaton, had first been suggested by the Board of Trade when they had inspected the Elphinstone, or Bog, Siding back in 1876; a 22-lever Stevens old-pattern 5¼ inch frame was fitted. With the opening of the double line from Monktonhall to Smeaton on 15th December, 1912 a new signal box was opened at Monktonhall Junction, while the existing box at Smeaton was extended and a 54-lever frame installed. On 19th May, 1913 the Smeaton to Bog Sidings section was divided when a box was opened opposite Crossgatehall Halt at Dalkeith Colliery, at the junction of (and in control of) the Dalkeith Colliery Branch; this was a difficult location by reason of the signal box being situated at the foot of a steep gradient and special precautions had to be taken against runaways. None of the signal boxes had a loop capable of crossing two passenger trains, although two freight trains or a freight and a passenger train could be crossed at all of them except Dalkeith Colliery, which did not have a loop.

After World War I economies were made and on 30th June, 1925 Macmerry signal box was closed and the section between there and Ormiston Junction worked as OES, while the sidings at Penston, Macmerry and Winton were unlocked by the OES staff. In 1950 Smeaton, Bog Siding and Dalkeith Colliery signal boxes were all open from 6.30 am until 9 pm on weekdays only, there being no Sunday or nightime services. On 12th June, 1956 Ormiston siganl box was closed leaving the whole section east of Bog Siding to be worked OES. On 4th August, 1957 Dalkeith Colliery Box was closed and on 17th November, 1962 Bog Siding succumbed, leaving the surviving section from Humbie, Macmerry and Winton Mine to Smeaton to be worked OES. On 26th June, 1966 Smeaton box was closed and thereafter Monktonhall to Smeaton was worked by 'telephone and notice board'. This line survived long enough to be controlled by colour-light signals from the Edinburgh Signalling Centre at Waverley, following the closure of the Monktonhall Junction signal box on 1st August, 1977.

The Gifford & Garvald Light Railway

The Gifford & Garvald Company initially intended to operate the whole of their line under OES regulations without the aid of telephone or any other form of communication. The North British, however, took exception to this and persuaded the Board of Trade to insist upon the installation of some form of communication or other safeguards at Ormiston. The upshot was the decision to install ETS equipment on sections from Ormiston Junction to Saltoun and Saltoun to Gifford, making the G&G one of the few examples in Scotland of this type of working (others included a handful of NBR lines, the Invergarry & Fort Augustus and the Stranraer & Portpatrick). The instruments were kept in the signal box at Ormiston and in the station offices at Saltoun and Gifford. Signalling was very basic – at Saltoun, for example, there were home signals only with no starters provided. Gifford was provided with a Stevens 7-lever dwarf frame while at Saltoun a similar 9-lever frame was installed. All sidings were worked by ground frames controlled by Annett's key. In 1930 the Gifford signal office was open on a split shift from 7 am until 11.25 am 'or after the departure of the 11.10 am ex-Gifford', and again from 2.30 pm to 4 pm and 4.30 pm to 6.35 pm. On Saturdays, when passenger traffic was heavier, the office was open from 7 am until 11 pm. After 1948, Saltoun to Humbie was worked OES, the Saltoun office being open from 7.30 am until 4.40 pm (2.30 pm on Saturdays). On 12th June, 1956 the ETS equipment was removed from Saltoun and the section Humbie to Bog Siding was worked OES from the latter signal box, ground frames replacing the box at Ormiston. The North British did, incidentally, have a signal box named Humbie but this was on the approaches to the Forth Bridge between Winchburgh and Dalmeny!

A scene near Glenkinchie as the Saltoun goods returns home, April 1964.
G.N. Turnbull

Postscript

It is now more than a quarter of a century since the whistle or horn of a locomotive was heard on four out of the five branch lines that served East Lothian and Gullane, Haddington, Macmerry and Gifford are all bereft of railway communication. As the years pass the memory of those who worked or travelled on the lines keeps them alive in the imagination but to present-day schoolchildren the early days of the reign of Queen Elizabeth, when these country railway lines were past their heyday but still busy, are now as historically remote as the days of Queen Victoria or even David I. Much capital, labour and ingenuity went into the building of these lines and, in many respects, they were the harbingers of the modern age to the isolated countryfolk in the last century. But rapid advances in technology and road transport were soon totally to eclipse them, with the result that what were once lifelines were in the end consigned to acting as the withered limbs of an ailing national railway system.

What positive and permanent benefits did these rural by-ways bring to the inhabitants of the county is a question that is easy to pose but difficult to answer. The railway brought few startling developments or major demographic changes and the industries which were there before it on the whole survived its demise, with the exception of coal mining which, like these lines, barely managed to outlive the steam age. Few communities were radically altered; indeed the county town outwardly changed little since the days when its inhabitants and the railway company were debating the respective merits of the schemes to bring a line to or through the town. The motor bus, on frequent schedules and following a direct route to Edinburgh, was responsible for the rapid demise of the passenger services before it in turn was almost totally superseded by the private car. The motor lorry provided a convenient, if heavily subsidised, alternative to the meandering pick-up goods trains which served remote sidings and yards throughout the county. Of all the places served by the branch lines only North Berwick was changed irretrievably by the North British – the branch line to the burgh enabled it to develop as a holiday resort and pleasant commuter town for those working in Edinburgh. It is perhaps significant that it is this branch line which, alone, has survived, prospered and continues to fulfil its original purposes in an age when the future of both British Rail, and even the county of East Lothian itself, are poised on the hinge of fate.

The past is, indeed, a land which we can never inhabit again but the minor railways of East Lothian, which served such a beautiful and varied stretch of lowland Scotland well for many generations, deserve to be remembered with affection and admiration for the way that they fulfilled all that was expected of them. They used the labour and skill of generations of ordinary railwaymen who continued the proud tradition of the old North British into an era which finally had no use for their work. That little now remains of their endeavours or those of the promoters and builders of the line, is a matter for regret. Standing by the site of the Humbie Viaduct, it is sad to recall the scenes of so much endeavour and activity when men scurried about their construction work, horses toiled, the pug engine laboured up the zig-zags and the Steam Navvy emulated the collie dog crunching his dinner bone. Now, in the words of the old song, 'All things are quite silent, all mortals at rest . . .'

Mileages

Miles	M. Chs	
		Haddington Branch
0.0	0.0	LONGNIDDRY Junction
1.8	1.60	Coatyburn Siding
2.3	2.20	Laverocklaw Siding
4.8	4.60	HADDINGTON Station
		Macmerry and Gifford Branches
0.0	0.00	MONKTONHALL JUNCTION
1.2	1.18	Carberry Branch Junction
1.5	1.39	SMEATON Junction
2.2	2.19	Smeaton Brick Works
2.8	2.62	Thorneybank Siding
4.2	4.12	HARDENGREEN Junction
2.5	2.43	Crossgatehall Halt
3.2	3.19	Cousland (New) Siding
3.9	3.75	Billyford Farm Siding
4.2	4.19	Oxenford Siding
4.4	4.28	Bellyford Colliery
4.9	4.68	Bog Siding Signal Box
5.7	5.57	ORMISTON Junction
6.1	6.10	East Mains Level Crossing
6.4	6.29	Pencaitland Siding
6.9	6.75	Winton Station
7.5	7.43	Penston Colliery Junction
8.1	8.11	MACMERRY Station
5.9	5.70	Meadow Colliery
6.8	6.66	Woodhall Coal Co. Platform
6.9	6.74	Pencaitland (Woodhall) Colliery
7.2	7.18	Brander's (Workshop) Siding
7.4	7.31	Pencaitland Station
8.5	8.34	Lempockwells (Fletcher's) Siding
9.1	9.11	Saltoun Station
10.4	10.29	Highlea (Polwarth's) Siding
11.2	11.13	Humbie Station
11.2	11.19	Gilchriston Level Crossing
11.8	11.66	Saltoun East Level Crossing
12.7	12.52	Marvingston Level Crossing
14.2	14.12	Inglefield Level Crossing
15.0	15.02	GIFFORD Station

Appendix Two

A Brief Chronology

22nd June, 1846	Line from Edinburgh to Berwick and branch to Haddington and stations at Longniddry and Haddington opened.
7th October, 1856	Haddington branch singled.
23rd December, 1866	Monktonhall Junction to Smeaton and Thorneybank line opened to goods traffic.
1st May, 1867	Smeaton to Ormiston line opened to goods.
19th March, 1868	Ormiston to Macmerry line opened to goods.
31st July, 1870	Thorneybank to Hardengreen line opened.
1st May, 1872	Macmerry to Monktonhall line opened to passengers.
14th October, 1901	Ormiston to Gifford line opened.
15th December, 1912	Monktonhall Jn–Smeaton line doubled.
1st August, 1913	Crossgate Halt opened.
1st January, 1917	Crossgatehall Halt closed (wartime economy).
1st February, 1919	Crossgatehall Halt re-opened.
22nd September, 1930	Crossgatehall and Smeaton closed to passengers.
3rd April, 1933	Gifford branch closed to passengers.
11th November, 1934	Smeaton to Hardengreen line closed.
12th August, 1948	Humbie to Gifford line breached and never reinstated.
5th December, 1949	Haddington branch closed to passengers.
1st January, 1959	Gifford station closed.
2nd May, 1960	Humbie to Saltoun and Macmerry to Ormiston lines closed.
23rd March, 1964	Pencaitland and Coatyburn closed.
28th December, 1964	Longniddry closed to goods.
25th May, 1965	Smeaton to Saltoun line closed.
30th March, 1968	Haddington branch closed.
1st February, 1973	Monktonhall–Smeaton line singled.
31st December, 1980	Monktonhall Jn–Smeaton line closed.

BR Standard class '2', 2–6–0 No. 78048 crosses the Humbie Viaduct with a lightly loaded goods on 18th April, 1960.
Rae Montgomery

Selected Timetables

HADDINGTON BRANCH.
May 1872.

Down Trains.

Stations and Sidings.	Distance from Haddington.		WEEK-DAYS												Sundays	
		1	2	3	4	5	6	7	8	9	10	11	12	1	2
		Pass. 1.2.4 Class	Pass. 1.2.3 Class	Fast. Pass. 1.2.3 Class	Mix. Pass. 1.2.3 Class	Pass. 1.2.3 Class	Mix. Pass. 1.2.3 Class.	Pass. 1.2.3 Class	Pass. 1.2.3 Class	Pass. 1.2.3 Class	Goods	Mix. Pass. 1.2.3 Class		Pass. 1.2.4 Class	Pass. 1.2.3 Class
	Mls. Chs.	a.m.	a.m.	a.m.	a.m.	a.m.	p.m.	p.m.	p.m.	p.m.	p.m.	p.m.		a.m.	p.m.
Haddington ... dep.		7.15	8.0	8.56	9.45	10.30	12.25	2.6	2.55	4.20	5.25	6.45		8.31	6.45
Longniddry Junction arr.	4 60	7.30	8.14	9.0	8.10	10.45	12.40	2.20	3.8	4.35	5.40	7.0		8.46	7.0
					Fri days only.										
Edinburgh ... arr.		9.35	9.2	9.46	10.38 1.45 days		1.30		8.45	6.50				10.20 10.45	
Berwick ... „								4.17				7.54 8.47			7.43 8.47

Up Trains.

Stations and Sidings.	Distance from Longniddry.		WEEK-DAYS												Sundays	
		1	2	3	4	5	6	7	8	9	10	11	12	1	2
		Pass. 1.2.4 Class	Pass. 1.2.4 Class	Pass. 1.2.3 Class	Pass. 1.2.3 Class		Mix. Pass. 1.2.3 Class	Mix. Pass. 1.2.3 Class	Pass. 1.2.3 Class	Mix. Pass. 1.2.3 Class	Fast. Pass. 1.2.3 Class	Goods	Mix. Pass. 1.2.3 Class	Pass. 1.2.4 Class	Pass. 1.2.3 Class
	Mls. Chs.	a.m.	a.m.	a.m.	a.m.		a.m.	a.m.	p.m.	p.m.	p.m.	p.m.	p.m.	a.m.	a.m.
Berwick ... dep.			6.5	9.18	8.26		8.26	10.45					5.10	7.45	5.20
Edinburgh ... „		7.0		9.33	10.20 Fri days only.		10.30	1.10	2.5		12.45 4.32		6.30	8.15	6.30
Longniddry Junction dep.		7.37	8.24	9.39	10.5		11.10	12.55	2.35	3.20	5.0	8.10	7.14	9.40	7.6
Haddington ... arr.	4 60	7.50	8.39				11.24		2.47	3.35	5.15	6.25	7.29	9.55	7.21

42

88 — MONKTONHALL AND ORMISTON BRANCHES. — Oct. 1896.

Up Trains.

Stations and Sidings.	Miles. Chns. Distance fr. Edinburgh	Hardengreen Pilot Engine.	1	2 Macmerry Goods	3 Smeaton Goods	4 Pass. 1 3 Class.	5 Macmerry Goods	6 Ormiston Goods Thurs Oct. 29	7 Stores	8 Smeaton Goods	9 Ormiston	10 Pass. Sat. only. 1 3 Class.	11 Ormiston Goods	12 Niddrie West and Hardengreen Goods	13 Pass. 1 3 Class.
			a.m.	a.m.	a.m.	a.m.	a.m.	a.m.	a.m.	a.m.		p.m.	p.m.	p.m.	p.m.
Edinburgh ... ... dep.			...	...	...	7 20	...	...	...	...	Goods	12 30	...	...	4 55
Portobello ... ... ,,	3 0		...	4 45	5 15	7 28	...	7 30	...	...	p.m.	12 39	...	...	5 4
Joppa ... ... ,,	3 53		...	...	...	7 30	...	...	...	...		12 42	...	...	5 6
New Hailes ... ... ,,	4 54		...	...	...	7 34	...	...	...	...		12 46	...	...	5 10
Inveresk Junction dep.	6 40		...	...	5 35	...	8 0	8 30	...	12 10		...	...	...	
Monktonhall Junction ,,	6 12		...	5 10	5 45	7 37	8 10	8 42	9 45	...		12 49	...	...	5 13
Carberry Colliery ... ,,	7 30		...	...	...	...	...	...	...	...		...	...	...	
Smeaton Junction ... arr.	7 51		...	5 15	5 50	7 42	8 15	8 15	9 50	12 15		12 54	...	...	5 18
Smeaton Junc. ... dep.	7 51		...	5 30	...	7 43	7 54	8 40	...	10 45	Stop.	12 55	2 5	...	5 19
Cousland Siding ... ,,	10 11		...	...	...	...	...	...	...	11 0		...	...	...	
Billyford Siding ... ,,	10 40		...	...	...	...	...	...	...	11 15		...	2 20	...	
Bog Sid. & Limeylands Sid,,	10 78		...	...	...	...	...	9 50	...	12 5		...	2 25	...	
Ormiston ... ... ,,	11 71		...	5 45	...	7 54	8 30	9 55	...	12 10		1 6	2 35	...	5 30
Winton ... ... ,,	13 9		...	...	...	7 58	8 45	...	...	...		1 10	2 50	...	5 34
Macmerry (Gladsmuir) arr.	14 25		...	Stop.	...	8 2	8 50	Stop.	...	Stop.		1 15	2 55	...	5 40
Smeaton Junction ... dep.	7 51	5 20	...	...	6 20	...	...	Stop.	8 50	...		...	...	2 10	...
Thorneybank ... ... ,,	8 74	...	...	...	6 35	...	...	...	8 55	...		...	...	2 20	...
Hardengreen Junction arr.	10 43	5 30	...	...	6 40	...	...	...	9 0	...		...	...	2 25	...

No. 2.—Takes full load of Empty Wagons for the Branch from Portobello.
No. 3.—Takes Loaded Wagons for Macmerry Branch. Runs to Polton.
No. 5.—Takes forward Edinburgh and Macmerry Road Van.
No. 6.—Works the Pits in Bog Siding going up. Works Pit Sidings after arrival at Ormiston.

Down Trains.

Stations and Sidings.	Miles. Chns. Distance from Hardengreen.	1 Hardengreen Pilot E'gine.	2 Pass. 1 3 Class.	3 Smeaton Goods	4	5 Macmerry Goods	6 Ormiston Goods.	7 Smeaton Goods	8	9 Pass. Sat. only. 1 3 Class.	10 Niddrie West and Hardengreen Goods	11 Smeaton Goods	12 Ormiston Goods	13 Pass. 1 3 Class.
		a.m.	a.m.	a.m.		a.m.	a.m.	p.m.		p.m.		p.m.	p.m.	p.m.
Hardengreen Junction dep.		5 0	...	8 40	...	...	...	...	...	...	1 50	...	...	...
Thorneybank ... ,,	1 49	...	...	...	...	...	...	...	...	...	1 55	...	...	...
Smeaton Junction ... arr.	2 72	5 10	...	8 50	...	...	...	...	...	...	2 0	...	...	...
Macmerry (Gladsmuir) dep.	9 16	1a Macmerry Goods	8 10	...	...	9 10	...	...	...	Stop. 1 25	...	...	3 10	6 15
Winton ... ... ,,	8 30		8 14	...	...	9 35	...	...	...	1 29	...	...	3 25	6 19
Ormiston ... ... ,,	7 12	5a 50	8 18	...	...	9 55	10 10	12 20	...	1 33	...	...	3 50	6 23
Bog Sid. & Limeylands Sid,,		6 40	...	...	...	...	10 25	12 30	...	...	...	...	4 0	
Smeaton Junction arr.	2 72	7 0	8 27	...	...	10 10	10 40	12 45	...	1 42	...	...	4 35	6 32
Smeaton Junction ... dep.	2 72	Stop.	8 28	9 25	...	10 35	11 20	Stop	...	1 43	...	2 55	5 20	6 33
Carberry Colliery ,,	3 13		...	9 35	...	...	...	...	...	...	...	...	...	
Monktonhall Junction ,,	4 31		3 31	9 40	...	10 45	11 30	...	...	1 47	...	3 5	5 30	6 37
Inveresk Junction arr.	4 59		...	Stop.	...	...	11 35	...	...	...	...	3 10	5 35	...
Do. dep.	4 59		...	...	...	...	Stop.	...	...	...	...	3 15	5 45	...
New Hailes ... ... dep.	5 69		8 34	...	...	...	...	...	...	1 51	...	...	...	6 41
Joppa ... ... ,,	6 70		8 37	...	...	...	...	...	...	1 55	...	...	...	6 45
Portobello ... ... ,,	7 47		8 40	...	...	10 55	...	...	...	2 0	...	3 25	6 0	6 50
Edinburgh ... ... arr.	10 45		8 48	...	...	Stop.	...	...	...	2 10	...	Stop.	Stop.	7 0

No. 1a.—Leaves off but does not shunt its Train at Smeaton, but will arrange Wagons for its return trip to Macmerry. The Wagons left by this Train must be marshalled by 9-45 a.m. Train from Monktonhall to Smeaton.

No. 5.—Starts from Polton.

No. 5.—Works Gladsmuir and Penstone Collieries; also Winton. On Tuesdays takes Live Stock to Inveresk for 6-15 a.m. ex Berwick. The Wagons left at Smeaton by this Train must be marshalled by the 10-10 a.m. Train from Ormiston to Smeaton.

No. 12.—On alternate Mondays takes Live Stock for Haymarket to Portobello on Mondays, to be sent thence by 8-52 p.m. Train from Earleton.

Down Trains must not marshal Traffic at Limeylands Sidings, but they must marshal the Traffic from these places at Smeaton.

Branch Trains to run special from Inveresk or Smeaton to Stations and Sidings on Macmerry Branch if required.

Traffic for the South via Falahill (except wagons for Carlisle, Newcastle and south thereof, which will be carried via Portobello), and for the Polton and Peebles Branches, will be carried via Hardengreen.

Weighing.—The Traffic from these branches will be weighed as under, viz.:—At Smeaton Junction.—All Traffic arising between Macmerry and Smeaton Junction, both inclusive, and all Traffic arising between Hardengreen and Smeaton, going towards Inveresk; also Traffic from Carberry. At Hardengreen.—All Traffic from the Dalkeith Colliery passing of the Branch via Hardengreen.

Deans & Moore's Wagons, when for repairs, must be put into Carberry, and not taken to other Pits.

Gifford and Garvald Light Railway.

The Train Service on the Gifford and Garvald Light Railway will be altered to the following :—

Up Trains.

	Distance from Ormiston.		WEEK-DAYS.				
			1	2	3	4	5
			Pass.	Goods		Goods	Pass.
	Miles.	Chns.	a.m.	a.m.		p.m.	p.m.
Edinburgh (Waverley) ... depart	...	...	7 10			...	4 55
—Ormiston Junction ... depart	...	...	8 7	11 10	...	3 40	5 53
—Pencaitland	1	54	8 13	11 30	...	...	5 59
—Saltoun	3	34	8 21	11 50	...	4 10	6 7
—Humbie	5	36	8 29	12 10	...	...	6 15
—Gifford ... ... arrive	9	20	8 50	12 35	...	4 45	6 36

No. 2.—Carries Road Wagons labelled "Leith Walk and Gifford" and "South Leith and Gifford."

Down Trains.

	Distance from Gifford.		WEEK-DAYS.				
			1	2	3	4	5
			Pass. Mixed	Pass.		Goods	Pass.
	Miles.	Chns.	a.m.	a.m.		p.m.	p.m.
—Gifford ... ... depart	...	...	7 0	9 25	...	2 0	5 0
—Humbie ... ... ,,	3	61	7 31	9 46	...	2 30	5 21
—Saltoun ... ... ,,	5	66	7 40	9 54	...	2 50	5 29
—Pencaitland ... ... ,,	7	46	7 51	10 2	...	3 10	5 37
—Ormiston Junction ... arrive	9	20	7 57	10 8	...	3 20	5 43
Edinburgh (Waverley) ... arrive	...	...	8 48	To	...	...	7 0
				Newhailes.			

No. 4.—Carries Road Wagon labelled "Gifford and Leith Walk."

November 1901.

MONKTONHALL AND ORMISTON BRANCHES AND GIFFORD & GARVALD LIGHT RAILWAY.   May 1914

WEEK-DAYS. UP TRAINS.

Stations and Sidings	Distance from Edinburgh M.	1 Goods	2 Goods (Min. ex Mon 4 & 18 May and 29 June)	3 Goods (Min. ex Mon 4 & 18 May and 29 June)	4 Goods	5 Goods	6 Pass	7 Goods	8 Goods	9	10 Goods (Min. ex Sat 2, 16, 30 May and 13 & 27 June Traffic)	11 Pass	12 Pass	13 Goods	14 Goods	15	16	17	18 Pass	19 Pass S O	20 Goods (Blackford Hill 12.45 p.m.)	21	22 Pass	23 Pass	24 Pass S O
		a.m.	a.m.	a.m.	a.m.	a.m.	a.m.	a.m.	a.m.		a.m.	a.m.	a.m.	a.m.	a.m.				p.m.	p.m.	p.m.		p.m.	p.m.	p.m.
Edinburgh ... dep.	—																								
Portobello ... "																									
Joppa ... "																									
New Hailes ... "																									
Inveresk Junction dep.																									
Monktonhall Junction "																									
Carbery Colliery "																									
Smeaton Junction arr.																									
Smeaton June dep.																									
Crossgatehall (Halt) "																									
Dalkeith Colliery "																									
Cousland Siding "																									
Billyford Siding "																									
Oxenford Siding "																									
Limeylands Siding } "																									
Bog Siding "																									
Ormiston Junction arr.																									
Ormiston Junction... dep.																									
Woodhall Coal Co.'s Plat. "																									
Pencaitland Colliery "																									
Pencaitland "																									
Saltoun "																									
Humbie "																									
Gifford arr.																									
Ormiston Junction dep.																									
Winton "																									
Macmerry (Gladsmuir) arr																									
Smeaton Junction ... dep.																									
Thorneybank "																									
Hardengreen Junction arr.																									

No. 1.—Takes full load for Limeylands and Bog Sidings. † Calls at Oxenford Siding when required to leave off empties.

No. 2.—Calls at Ormiston only to leave Leith Walk and Macmerry Road Van.

No. 5.—Takes forward Edinburgh and Macmerry Road Van.

No. 8.—After arrival at Bog Siding this train will work to orders of Control Master at Portobello till 4.30 a.m.

No. 9.—Puts Empty Wagons into Meadow Pit when required. † Calls at Pencaitland Colliery when required to leave Empty Wagons.

No. 11.—Gifford Branch Traffic to get the preference. † On Tuesdays waits at Smeaton arrival of No. 8 Down.

No. 12.—After arrival at Gifford, Engine and Guard return to Ormiston and work to orders of the Station Agent and the Control-master. Works Water Tank train to Macmerry daily.

No. 13.—Takes full load of Empties for Dalkeith Colliery from Portobello.

No. 19.—Is a Mixed Train from Ormiston to Gifford, but only takes Live Stock and Perishable Traffic.

No. 20.—Takes all Traffic for Ormiston and Gifford Branches. Makes Special Trip to Inveresk Junction or Bog Siding if necessary. † Calls at Cousland Siding when required to lift Traffic.

No. 23.—Empty Vehicles of Macmerry train return immediately from Macmerry to Edinburgh. Empty train to leave Gifford for Ormiston at 10.30 p.m.

Gifford Branch Engine.—This Engine will perform shunting at Ormiston when requested by the Station master there.

South Leith and Smeaton Goods Train.—Leaves South Leith for Smeaton and Limeylands about 6.40 p.m., returning from Limeylands about 8.30 p.m. for South Leith with traffic, lifting also at Oxenford and Smeaton, returning again from South Leith to Smeaton and leaving latter for South Leith about 1.0 a.m., calling at Portobello, and finishing at 3.0 a.m.

Shunting Engine at Smeaton.—This Engine is double-shifted. Starts work at 7.0 a.m. on Mondays and finishes at 1.00 a.m. on Saturdays. Carberry and Dalkeith Collieries.

MONKTONHALL AND ORMISTON BRANCHES AND GIFFORD & GARVALD LIGHT RAILWAY.   May 1914

WEEK-DAYS. DOWN TRAINS.

Stations and Sidings.	Dist'ce fr'm H'denry'n. M.C.	1 Goods a.m.	2 Min.	3	4 Pass. a.m.	5 Goods a.m.	6 Goods a.m.	7	8 Pass. a.m.	9 Goods a.m.	10 Goods p.m.	11 Min.	12	13 Goods p.m.	14	15 Pass. p.m.	16	17	18	19 Goods p.m.	20	21 Goods p.m.	22	23 Pass. p.m.	24
Hardengreen Junction dep.	1 49																								
Thorneybank ″	2 72															8 0						3 30		6 46	
Smeaton Junction arr.					7 56	8 25			9 38							1 34						3 40		6 50	
Macmerry(Jacksmuir)dep.					8 0	8 35			9 48					12 32		1 38			2 30			3 45		6 58	
Winton ″					8 3	8 45			9 55					1 2		1 41			2 45						
Ormiston Junction arr.									10 1					1 17										6 30	
Gifford ... ... dep.				Mixed	7 25			7 50								12 56								6 40	
Humble ... ″					7 35			8 10								1 13								6 47	
Saloun ... ″					7 42			8 30								1 18								6 53	
Pencaitland ″					7 49			8 48								1 19									
Pencaitland Colliery ″																									
Woodhall Coal Co.'s Flat. ″																									
Ormiston Junction arr.					7 55			9 0	10 7				11 30	Stop.		1 25			3 0			4 15		6 59	
Ormiston Junction dep					8 + 6	9 0		9 20	10 10				11 38			1 42			3 40			4 35		7 2	
Bog Siding ″					8 8	9 5			10 13				12 7												
Limeylands Siding ″					†	†							12 15												
Oxenford Siding ″		5 12																							
Dalkeith Colliery ″																									
Crossgatehall (Halt) ″					8 18	9 20			10 17				12 29			1 49			4 15			4 55		7 9	
Smeaton Junction arr.					8 16	10 0			10 20	10 55						1 52			4 35			5 32		7 12	
Smeaton Junction ... dep.		5 50			8 17	10 0		9 35	10 21	11 10	12 40		1 6			1 53								7 13	
Carberry Colliery ″		Stop.			†	10 10			10 44	11 16	11 50					1 56			5 0			5 40			
Monktonhall Junction ″				7 46	8 30	10 10		9 45	10 52	11 26			1 11			2 0						5 45		7 16	
Inveresk Junction arr.																2 4						6 8			
Do. dep.																2 9									
New Hailes ... dep.		5 59			8 28				10 56							2 0						6 15		7 20	
Joppa ... ″		6 70		7 55	8 29	10 20			10 58		1 0	1 23				2 4			5 15			6 16		7 23	
Portobello ... ″		7 48		Stop.	8 34	Stop.			10 32		Stop.	Stop.				2 9			Stop.			Stop.		7 27	
Piershill ... ″					8 37																				
Abbeyhill ... ″					8 40																				
Edinburgh ... arr.		10 48							10 38							2 15								7 33	

Except Mons. 4th and 18th May and 1st, 15th and 29th June.
Except Sats. 2nd, 16th, & 30th May, and 13th and 27th June.
Blackford Hill ... 12-15 p.m.
Gorgie Arrive 10-13 a.m.

NOTES.

† No. 1.—Calls at Oxenford Siding when required to lift traffic.

No. 2.—Runs forward to South Leith if required.

† No. 4.—On Tuesdays leaves Gifford 7-18 a.m. and Humble 7-30 a.m., the other times remaining unaltered. ‡ Leaves the Platform at Ormiston at 8-4 in order to attach the Gifford portion. Arrives at No. 3 Platform at Waverley.

No. 5.—Works Penstone Colliery ; also Winton. On Tuesdays works Live Stock from Macmerry and Winton to connect with Gifford Special when run, or runs forward to Monktonhall Junction on arrival at Smeaton to connect with 6-28 a.m. from Berwick, thereafter returning to Smeaton to take up booked working. † Calls at Oxenford Siding when required.

No. 6.—Connects at Ormiston with No. 5.

† No. 18.—On Saturdays follows from Gifford No. 18.

No. 21.—Works Meadow Pit. Works Penstone Colliery when required. If necessary, makes run to Niddrie West, Granton, or North or South Leith. On Mondays takes Live Stock for Gorgie to Portobello.

No. 28.—Gifford Branch Engine and Guard return at once from Ormiston to Gifford.

Branch Trains to run special from Inveresk or Smeaton to Stations and Sidings on Macmerry Branch if required.

Limeylands Siding.—All Down Ordinary Goods Trains must call to lift at Limeylands when required by the Station-master at Ormiston.

Smeaton Branch Mineral Trains.—These Trains will run to Portobello, Niddrie West, Leith, or Granton, as instructed by the Control Master, Portobello.

HADDINGTON BRANCH.

May 1914.

UP TRAINS.

Stations.	Distance from Longniddry. Mi. Ch.	1 Goods	2 Pass.	3 Pass. Commences 1st June	4 Pass. Ceases after 30th May	5 Pass.	6 Pass.	7 Pass. Edinburgh 10 42 FO	8 Pass.	9 Goods Mon. May 11 & 25 8 & June 22 only. Portobello 10.34	10	11 Goods Portobello a.m. 11 48	12 Goods	13 Pass.	14 Goods	15 Pass.	16 Pass. Ceases after 30th May	17 Pass. Commences 1st June	18 Pass.	19 Pass. (Mix.)	20 Pass. SO	21 Pass. SO THO	Sundays 1 Pass.	Sundays 2 Pass.	Sundays 3 Pass.
Departs from ...																									
Longniddry ... dep.	—	a.m. 6 0	7 50	8 32	8 38	9 18	9 56	11 52		p.m. 12 3		1 15		2 27	3 38	4 45	4 58	6 2	6 20	8 48	10 51	11 27		a.m. 9 52	p.m. 7 20
Haddington ... arr.	4 60	a.m. 6 15	8 0	8 42	8 48	9 28	10 6	11 24		p.m. 12 18		1 35		2 37	3 53	4 55	5 6	6 12	7 30	9 0	11 3	11 37		a.m. 10 2	p.m. 7 30

No. 19.—Conveys only Live Stock and urgent Goods Wagons.

No. 21.—Empty Vehicles leave Haddington for Longniddry at 11-0 p.m.

DOWN TRAINS.

Stations and Sidings.	Distance from Haddington. Mi. Ch.	1 Pass.	2 Pass. Commences 1st June	3 Pass.	4 Pass. Ceases after 30th May	5 Pass.	6 Goods TO	7 Pass.	8 Pass.	9 Pass.	10 Goods MO FO Edinburgh	11 Pass. FO	12 Goods M	13 Pass.	14 Pass. Cattle Mon. May 11 & 25 & June 8 & 22 only.	15 Pass.	16 Pass. Ceases after 30th May	17 Pass. Commences 1st June	18 Pass.	19 Goods (Mix.) Portobello	20 Pass. (Mix.)	21 Pass. SO	22 Pass.	Sundays 1 Pass.	Sundays 2 Pass.
Haddington ... dep.	—	a.m. 7 5	8 10	8 18	8 58	9 38	10 15	11 28		p.m. 1 52	2 40	2 49	2 58		3 55	4 20	5 30	5 35	5 40	7 40	8 20	9 20		a.m. 8 50	p.m. 6 45
Laverocklaw ... "	2 40																								
Coatyburn Sid. ... "	3 0												3 25												
Longniddry Jc. ... arr.	4 60	a.m. 7 14	8 19	8 27	9 7	9 42	10 30	11 37		p.m. 2 1		2 55	3 25		4 9	4 29	5 39	5 44	5 49	7 55	8 32	9 29		a.m. 8 59	p.m. 6 54
Arrives at destination											Edinburgh 3 22				Gorgie 5 55						Portobello 8 55				

No. 6.—Leaves Live Stock for Edinburgh at Longniddry for 6-28 a.m. Train from Berwick. Engine, with Guard and Van, returns from Longniddry to Haddington.

No. 7.—Haddington must wire Dunbar particulars of any Extra Vehicles on this Train to go on from Longniddry by 11-6 a.m. Train, Dunbar to Edinburgh.

No. 10 and 12.—The Station Master at Longniddry will advise the Station Master at Haddington when this Trip is required to be made.

No. 19.—Haddington will arrange to run a Special to Longniddry about 6-5 p.m. with any Live Stock for Berwick to go forward by 6-40 p.m. Goods Train from Portobello.

† Coatyburn and Laverocklaw Sidings.—The Train marked thus (†) are intended to work Coatyburn and Laverocklaw Sidings when there is Traffic to lift or leave off, but these Sidings cannot be worked on Sale Mondays.

Haddington Branch Engine turns out at Longniddry at 6-0 a.m. to do shunting work.

No. 5.—MONKTONHALL JUNCTION TO MACMERRY AND GIFFORD.

MONKTONHALL JUNCTION TO SMEATON JUNCTION.—Worked by Block Telegraph.

Carberry Colliery Branch.—Worked from Smeaton Junction under following instructions:—

(1) The Smeaton and Carberry Train Staff Section terminates at a point about 100 yards east from the Public Road crossing where a board lettered as follows has been erected on the Driver's right hand.

On the West Side—End of Train Staff Section, beginning of Yard Working Section.

On the East Side—Beginning of Train Staff Section.

The Sidings on the east side of the board are worked as a yard, and Drivers must therefore keep a sharp lookout and be prepared to stop clear of any obstruction which may be in front of them.

(2) A Brake Van must invariably be at the rear of wagons when drawing them to and from Carberry Colliery Sidings.

(3) **Bell Communication between Smeaton Junction and Smeaton Shaw Level Crossing.—**All Trains and Engines must be signalled to the Crossing, as follows:—

When leaving Smeaton Junction, 1 ring. | When leaving Dalkeith Colliery, 2 rings.

SMEATON JUNCTION TO ORMISTON JUNCTION.—Worked by Tablet No. 6.

ORMISTON JUNCTION TO MACMERRY.—Worked by Tyer's Single Line Block Staff (No. 1) and Ticket (colour Yellow).

(8) **Dalkeith Colliery—Trains from Dalkeith Colliery to Smeaton.—**In the case of trains going from Dalkeith Colliery to any point in the direction of Smeaton, the Signalman must not reverse the Points for the Main Line until he has received a Whistle from the Driver, which must be taken as an indication that sufficient Wagon, &c., Brake Power has been applied, and that the Train is ready to proceed downhill towards Smeaton.

(4) **Cousland Sidings.—Worked by Tablet Lock.—**Owing to the steepness of the gradient, these Sidings are worked by Up Trains only ; and, during the shunting operations the Engine must be at the Ormiston end of the Wagons.

Billyford Siding.—Worked by Tablet Lock.

(5) **Oxenford Siding.—Worked by Tablet Lock.—**Down Trains working the Sidings must always be drawn clear of the trap points, placed 200 yards east from the Up facing connection, and the Engine or wagons must not be uncoupled until these trap points are opened to prevent any part of the Train running away in the direction of Bog.

Limeylands Sidings.—Worked from Bog Signal-box.

(G) Bog Siding.

(6a) **Bog Train Refuge Sidings (West End).—**Worked by Tablet Lock—Engines of Up Trains when shunting at Bog Sidings and Junction must be at the Ormiston end of the Wagons owing to steepness of the gradient.

(b) Before any shunting operations are commenced at Bog Siding with a Down Train, the entire Train, including, of course, the Guard's Van, must be shunted off the Main Line into the Siding, so as to admit of the shunting operations being performed safely, and in such a way as will ensure against the possibility of any portion of the Train or any other Vehicle running away on the Main Line down the Incline.

(c) Wagons from other Sidings must not be inter-marshalled in Bog Sidings with Wagons uplifted there.

(d) The Sidings at Bog are worked as a Yard. Drivers must keep a sharp lookout and be prepared to stop clear of any obstruction which may be in front of them.

(7) **Fleets Colliery.—Worked from Bog Signal-box.—**The Fleets Branch is worked by the Edinburgh Collieries' Pug Engine.

(P) **Ormiston Junction.—**(From the direction of Macmerry and Gifford).

(G) **Ormiston Junction.—**(From Smeaton Junction direction).

(8) **Winton Station.—**Guards of Up Trains working Winton Station must be careful not to uncouple their Engines from the Train until the rear brake van is drawn clear of the Public Level Crossing.

ORMISTON JUNCTION TO GIFFORD.—Worked by Electric Train Staff.

(9) **Meadow Pit Siding.—Worked by Electric Train Staff.—**This Siding is on the Gifford Line, about 100 yards out from the Junction with the Macmerry Branch. The points, which are facing to Up Trains, are worked from a Ground Frame and secured by an Annett Lock, the key of which is affixed to the Electric Staff for the Saltoun Section. It is worked from Ormiston, and Guards must, in every case, have the points open for the Siding before bringing the Train or lift of wagons over the Junction.

(10a) **Woodhall Colliery Sidings—Pencaitland.—Worked by Electric Train Staff.—**Trains working these Sidings must be brought to a stand on the level part of the Line between the Up and Down Facing Points, so that the Engine will always be at the lower end of the Wagons when lifting or leaving Traffic.

(b) Not more than twenty Wagons must be propelled at one time into these Sidings.

(11) SIDINGS WORKED BY ELECTRIC TRAIN STAFF.—

Pencaitland Station Sidings.	Highlee Siding (Lord Polwarth's).
Lempockwells Siding	Humbie Station Sidings.

(P) Saltoun.

No. 7.—HADDINGTON, GULLANE, AND NORTH BERWICK BRANCHES.

LONGNIDDRY JUNCTION TO HADDINGTON.—Worked by Tablet No. 6.

Coatyburn and Laverocklaw Sidings—Worked by Tablet Lock—Owing to the steepness of the gradient, no shunting is to be done on the Main Line at these Sidings unless the Engine is at the Longniddry end of the wagons, and the Sidings must only be shunted by *Down Trains*.

NBR Working Timetable, October 1922.

WEEK-DAYS.

DOWN TRAINS.

Stations and Sidings. Departs from :—	Dist. from Gifford (Mls / Chns)	Dist. from Macmerry (Miles / Chns)	1 Min.	3 Pas.	5 Min.	6 Pas.	7 Goods	8 Min.	9 Goods	10 Goods	11 Pas.	12	13 Goods	14 Goods	15	17 Goods	18 Goods	19 Min.	20 Pas.	21 Pas.	22	23 Min.	24 Min.
			Porto-bello a.m. 4 55	a.m.	Ormiston a.m. 7 45 TX	Porto-bello a.m.	Goods a.m. 5 15	Min.	a.m.	a.m.	p.m.		Ormiston p.m. 1 10	Goods p.m.		Porto-bello a.m. 11 5	Porto-bello p.m. 2 15	Porto-bello p.m.	Pas.	Pas.	South Leith p.m. 4 15	Min.	Smeaton p.m. 8 10
Macmerry (Gif'd V'y) dep.	...	...			TX 8 30		TO 8 20	TO	11 10		p.m.		8 X 8 X	8 O		TO	16 X	8 X	8 O	8 X	8 X		8 X
Winton "	... 16	1 ...			8 45		8 30		11 40		1 14												
Ormiston Junction arr.	... 34	2 ...			8 55		8 50		12 10		1 36												
Gifford dep	...	...		7 40		9 44																	
Humble "	... 69	...		7 51		9 55					1 25								5 39	6 22			
Saltoun "	... 71	...		7 58		10 6							2 15						5 50	6 33			
Pencaitland Colly. "	... 51	...	7 20	8 4		10 12			12 30		1 42		1 45 2 40					5 0	5 57	6 40			
Woodhall Coal Co.'s Platform	... 28	...						11 50											6 3	6 46			
Ormiston Junc. arr.	... 36	8 ...	7 30	8 10		10 18		12	12 40		1 48		2 0			3 20	6 35	5 0	6 9	6 52			
Ormiston Junction dep.	... 25	9 ...	9 55	8 12		10 19	10 35	12 0			1 50					3 30	8 10	5 10	6 9	6 53			9 0
Bog Siding	... 14	10 ...														4 0						7 15	
Limeylands Siding	... 19	10 ...	10 40													4 45		K 35					9 0
Oxenford Siding	... 65	10 ...									2 01					4 40							
Dalkeith Colliery	... 41	11 ...	11 5					12 40			2 08					5 30							
Smeaton Junc. arr.	... 45	13 ...		8 21							2 09						6 30						
Smeaton Junc. dep.	... 66	13 ...		8 25			10 28				2 10					4 07				7 7		7 40	
Carberry Colliery	... 4	15 ...		8 28							2 12							6 25	6 18	7 8			9 25
Monktonhall Junc.	... 2	16 ...		8 31			10 35				2 15					6 23							
New Hailes	... 43	17 ...																	6 25				
Jeppa	... 25	11 ...																					
Portobello	...	...																	6 31	7 14			
Piershill	...	...																					
Abbeyhill	...	...																					
Edinburgh arr.	... 16	21 ...		8 37		10 41																	
Arrives at ...	... 25	14 ...	Finishing 12.10 p.m. Thereafter works to orders of Control		Smeaton 11 8 X		Thereafter to orders of Control finishing at 12.30 a.m.	Thereafter to orders of Control finishing at 4.30 p.m.	Sat. 1.35 8 X			Oğa U/ld f'ord 3 30 3 25	Gifford Branch Engine.		Thereafter to orders of Control finishing at 8.30 p.m.	Thereafter to orders of Control finishing at 8.15 p.m.			Bog Siding 8 30			

Notes

No. 4.—Performs necessary shunting at Ormiston Junction and prepares traffic for Gifford Branch train. ‡ Works 7.45 a.m. T X Ormiston to Macmerry and 8.30 a.m. T X Macmerry to Ormiston.

No. 2.—Gifford men to work to Edinburgh and back with No. 5 Up. † On Tuesdays leaves Gifford 7.53, Humble 7.45, and Saltoun 7.55 a.m., thereafter as booked.

No. 6.—‡ Calls at Woodhall Colliery Platform to pick up Manager of Woodhall Coal Co., if intimated. Being made to the Pencaitland or Ormiston Station-master.

No. 9.—On Saturdays, Engine and Guard return direct to Gifford to work No. 11.

No. 11.—Trainmen change trains at Saltoun with trainmen of 12.11 p.m. S O ex Edinburgh.

No. 12.—Vegetable traffic to connect with the 10.0 p.m. S X Portobello and High Street Goods train to be marshalled next engine.

HADDINGTON BRANCH. 61

WEEK-DAYS.

UP TRAINS.	Distance from Longniddry	1	2	3	4	6	7	8	9	10 Live Stock	11	12
		Goods	O.P.	O.P.	O.P.	O.P.			O.P.	O.P.	A	O.P.	O.P.
CLASS		D	...	...	...	...		...	...		...	...
Departs from								Edinburgh a.m. 10 45	Suspended	Portobello a.m. 11 40		
			...								...		
								FX a.m.	FO a.m.	MO p.m.	8 X p.m.	8 O p.m.
—Longniddry Junction dep.	M. — 4	a.m. 6 24	a.m. 6 39	a.m. 7 20	a.m. 8 14	a.m. 8 39	9 57	11 8	11 11	12 40	1 33	1 38
—Haddington ... ... arr.	C. 60	6 39	7 28	8 22	8 47	10 5	......	11 16	11 19	1 0	1 41	1 46

WEEK-DAYS.

UP TRAINS.	13	14	15	16	17	18	19	20	21	22	23	24	25	27
	O.P.	...	Goods	Goods	O.P.	O.P.	O.P.	O.P.	O.P.	O.P.	O.P.	O.P.	O.P.	O.P.
CLASS	...	...	D	D	...	...	...	...	...	...			...	...
Departs from			Portobello a.m. 11 55	Portobello p.m. 12 30								8 X after July 3.	Commences July 10.	
	...	...			...	...		...	...	...	...		...	...
			8 O p.m.	8 X p.m.		8 X p.m.	8 O p.m.	8 X p.m.				8 O p.m.	Th 8 O p.m.	8 O p.m.
—Longniddry Junction dep.	p.m. 2 38	...	3 20	3 45	4 22	5 22	6 0	6 10	6 53	7 55	9 8	9 16	10 10	11 48
—Haddington ... ... arr.	2 46	...	3 40	4 0	4 30	5 30	6 8	6 18	7 2	8 3	9 16	9 24	10 18	11 54

No. 10 (Suspended).—Runs on Haddington Live Stock Sale days.

Haddington Branch Passenger Engine.—Will turn out at Longniddry at 6.0 a.m. to shunt out Road Van and other important traffic for Haddington, leaving Longniddry at 6.24 a.m., as booked ; shunts as required at Haddington during the day ; makes trip, Mondays, Wednesdays and Fridays, Haddington to Longniddry and back, leaving Haddington at 12.0 noon, working Sidings as required on the Branch, and performing any necessary shunting work required at Longniddry. On Tuesdays, after arrival at Longniddry at 8.59 a.m., returns to Haddington for Live Stock for Gorgie, leaving Haddington at 9.20 a.m. for Longniddry, to connect with the 5.10 a.m. T O Cattle train ex Berwick.

WEEK-DAYS.

DOWN TRAINS.	Distance from Haddington.	1	2	3	4	5	6	7	8	9	10	11	12
		O.P.	O.P.		O.P.	O.P.		O.P.	O.P.		O.P.	O.P.	
CLASS		...	...		...	...		...	...	...	...	...	...
												F O	
—Haddington ... dep.	M. —	a.m. 7 5	a.m. 8 1		a.m. 8 26	a.m. 8 51		a.m. 10 25	p.m. 1 14		p.m. 2 25	p.m. 3 27	...
Laverocklaw ... ,,	2 40	......	......	......	......	......		......	......		......	......	......
Coatyburn Siding ... ,,	3 0	......	......	......	......	......		......	......		......	......	......
—Longniddry Junction arr.	4 60	7 13	8 9		8 34	8 59		10 33	1 22		2 33	3 35	......
Arrives at												Edinburgh 3 59	...

WEEK-DAYS.

DOWN TRAINS.	13	14	15 Live Stock	16	17	18	19	20‡	21‡	22	23	24	25
	O.P.	O.P.	A	Goods	O.P.	Goods	O.P.	O.P.	O.P.	O.P.	O.P.	O.P.	O.P.
CLASS			A	D	...	D	...	...	...	...	...	...	...
			MO	8 O	8 X	8 X					8 O	Th O	8 O
—Haddington ... dep.	p.m. 4 5	p.m. 5 5	p.m. 5 5	p.m. 5 17	p.m. 5 45	p.m. 6 20	p.m. 6 40	p.m. 7 A17	p.m. 7 27	p.m. 8 48	p.m. 9 42	p.m. 9 55	p.m. 11 30
Laverocklaw ... ,,	......	......		......	......	......		......	......		......	......	......
Coatyburn Siding ... ,,	...	...		...	...	...		...	...		...	...	...
—Longniddry Junction arr.	4 13	5 13	5 18	5 30	5 53	6 32	6 48	7 A25	7 35	8 56	9 50	10 3	11 38
Arrives at			Gorgie 7 25	Portobello 7 25	...	Portobello 8 15	...	...	...	...	...	...	...

No. 20.—‡ Commences July 5.   A On Saturdays until September 11 inclusive runs 20 minutes later.

No. 21.—‡ Ceases after July 3.

3rd May, 1937 until further notice.

60 MACMERRY and GIFFORD BRANCHES.

UP TRAINS.

CLASS	Distance from Portobello	1 Min. D	2 Live Stock A	3	4 Min. D	5 Goods D	6 Goods D	7 Min. D	8 Min. D	9 Min. D	10	11	12
Departs from					Pencaitland 7a20					South Leith p.m. 4 45	...	...	...
	M. C.	a.m.	a.m.	T O	T X a.m.	S O a.m.	S X a.m.	a.m.	p.m.	p.m.			
—Portobello ... ...dep.	...	4 55	6 0		...	8 23	10 50	11 26					
Joppa ... ... ,,	... 53				...	8 33	11 5		1 50				
—Monktonhall Junc. ... ,,	3 12	5 7	6 12		9...	8 47	11 19	11 42	2 1	5 15			
Carberry Colliery ... ,,	4 30												
—Smeaton Junction { arr.	4 51	5 19	6 25		...	8 57	11 28	11 51					
{ dep.	...	5 35	6 40		...	9 4	11 35	12 0	2 9	6 10			
—Dalkeith Colliery ... ,,	5 55				...	...	...						
Cousland Siding ... ,,	6 31				...	...	1 30		...				
Billyford Siding ... ,,	7 6				...	...	...		...				
Oxenford Siding ... ,,	7 31				...	...	...		...				
Limeylands Siding ,,	7 77				...	...	...		...				
—Bog Siding } ,,	8 2				...	...	...		2 43	6 30			
—Ormiston Junction arr.	8 71	6 5	7 10		...	9 34	12 5	2 0	2 51				
—Ormiston Junc. ... dep.	...	6 15	7 30		...	9 50	1 10		3 3				
Pencaitland Colly. ,,	9 68	6 25			...	10 25			3 13				
Pencaitland ... ,,	10 45		7 40		...	10 43	1 30						
—Saltoun ... ,,	12 25		8 0		...	11 8	1 55		...				
Humbie ... ,,	14 27		8 20		...	11 30	2 15		...				
Gifford ... ... arr.	18 16		8 35		...	11 45	2 30		...				
Ormiston Junction dep.	...				7 45			2 30					
Winton ... ... ,,	10 9				8 5			2 50					
Macmerry (Gladsm'ir) arr.	11 25				8 15			3 0					
Arrives at... {		Smeaton 11 5	Gorgie 11 55		Ormiston 8 55	Portobello 4 0	Portobello 8 22	Portobello 7 33	Smeaton 6 5	Smeaton 8 10	...	...	...

No. 1.—Except on Tuesdays works Water Tank from Ormiston. Also Road Van daily from Leith Walk to Macmerry ; also South Leith and Gifford Road Van—latter to be lifted from Ormiston by 10.50 a.m., Portobello and Gifford. On Tuesdays will leave Ormiston at 6.51 a.m. and arrive Pencaitland Colliery at 7.1 a.m., thereafter makes trip to Macmerry to lift L.S. for Gorgie to connect with 8.55 a.m. T O, Gifford to Gorgie.

Nos. 5 and 6.—Calls at Joppa Passenger Station to uplift Parcel traffic for Macmerry and Gifford Branches. Conveys Leith Walk and Gifford Road Van from Portobello. Lifts South Leith and Gifford Road Van at Ormiston.

No. 7.—Works Fordel Mains Colliery. Worked by Trainmen of 2.35 p.m. Portobello daily Special.

No. 9.—Finishes 11.30 p.m.

DOWN TRAINS.

CLASS	Distance from Gifford.	Distance from Macmerry.	1 Min. D	2 Live Stock A	3	4 Min. D	5 Goods D	6 Goods D	7 Goods D	8 Min. D	9 Min. D	10 Min. D
Departs from			Portobello a.m. 4 55	Portobello a.m. 6 0		Ormiston a.m. 7 45	Portobello a.m. 8 23	Portobello a.m. 10 50	Joppa p.m. 1 50	Portobello p.m. 11 26	South Leith p.m. 4 45	...
	M. C.	M. C.	a.m.	a.m.	T O	T X p.m.	S O p.m.	S X p.m.	p.m.	p.m.	p.m.	
Macmerry (Gladsm'ir) dep.	...	...	...	...		...	8 30			3 15		
Winton ... ,,	...	1 16				...	8 45			3 30		
—Ormiston Junction arr.	...	2 34				...	8 55			3 40		
Gifford ... ...dep.	...	...				8 55		12 15	3 0			
Humbie ... ,,	3 69	...				9 5		12 40	3 25			
—Saltoun ... ,,	5 71	...				9 30		1 10	3 45			
Pencaitland ,,	7 51	...				9 50		1 30	4 5			
Pencaitland Colly. ,,	8 28	...	7 20					2 20		5 0		
—Ormiston Junc. arr.	9 25	...	7:30					2 25	4 15	5 10		
—Ormiston Junction dep.	...	...	10 0	10 25				3 0	4 45	5 35	4 5	
—Bog Siding ... }	10	3 23		10 40							5 45	
Limeylands Siding } ,,	10 19	3 28										7 45
Oxenford Siding ,,	10 65	3 74										
—Dalkeith Colliery ,,	12 41	5 50										
—Smeaton Junc. { arr.	13 45	6 54	11 5					3 36	5 15	6 5	6 15	8 10
{ dep.	...	...				10 50			6 0		6 55	
Carberry Colliery ,,	13 66	6 75										
—Monktonhall Junc. ,,	15 4	8 13				11:20		3 43	6 5		7:15	
—Newhailes Junc. ,,	16 42	9 51						3:52	8:14			
—Joppa ... ,,	17 43	10 52									7:28	
—Portobello ... arr.	18 16	1! 25						4 0	6 22		7:33	
Arrives at... {				Gorgie 11 55		Smeaton 11 5						

No. 1.—Performs necessary shunting at Ormiston Junction. ‡ Works 7.45 a.m. T X, Ormiston to Macmerry, and 8.30 a.m. T X, Macmerry to Ormiston. After arrival Smeaton works to Control orders. Finishes 12.10 p.m.

No. 2.—‡ Lifts traffic from Inveresk.

Nos. 5 & 6.—‡ Call Newhailes Passenger Platform to leave off Parcel traffic when required. Convey Road Van, Gifford to Leith Walk.

No. 7.—After arrival Smeaton works to Control orders. Finishes 9.15 p.m.

No. 8.—After arrival Smeaton works to Control orders. ‡ On Saturdays, commencing July 10, runs ten minutes later. Finishes at 11.30 p.m.

3rd May, 1937 until further notice.

56   **MACMERRY and GIFFORD BRANCHES.**

UP TRAINS.

CLASS	Distance from Portobello	1 Live Stock A	2	3	4	5 Goods D	6 Goods D	7 Min. D	8	9	10	11	12
Departs from ...			...		...				...		...		
	M. C.	T O a.m.				S O a.m.	S X a.m.	a.m.					
—Portobello ... ...dep.	... ...	6 10	...	...	...	8 23	10 50	11 26	...	...	...	...	
—Joppa — ,,	... 53					8 33	11½ 5						
—Monktonhall June. ... ,,	3 12	6 20				8 47	11 19	11 42					
Carberry Colliery ... ,,	4 30		...	...		...	...	...					
—Smeaton Junction { arr.	4 51		...	...		8 57	11 28	11 51					
{ dep.		6 33				9 4	11 35	12 0					
—Dalkeith Colliery ... ,,	5 55		...	...		...	...	...					
Cousland Siding ... ,,	6 31							1 30					
Billyford Siding ... ,,	7 6		...	...		...	...	...					
Oxenford Siding ... ,,	7 31		...	...		...	...	...					
Limeylands Siding } ,,	7 77		...	...		...	...	...					
—Bog Siding } ,,	8 2	7 10				...	...	...					
—Ormiston Junction arr.	8 71	7 13	...			9 34	12 5	2 0					
—Ormiston June. ... dep.	.. .	7 20	...	...		9 50	1 10						
Pencaitland Colly. ,,	9 68					10 25							
Pencaitland ... ,,	10 45					10 43	1 30						
—Saltoun ... ... ,,	12 25					11 8	1 55						
Humbie ... ... ,,	14 27					11 30	2 15						
Gifford ... ... arr.	18 16	7 55				11 45	2 30						
—Ormiston Junction dep.	... .		...	...		...	...	2 30					
Winton ... ... ,,	10 9					...	...	2 50					
Macmerry (Gladsm'ir) arr.	11 25					...	...	3 0					
Arrives at... ... {		Gorgie 11 13				Porto-bello 4 4	Porto-bello 7 6	Porto-bello 7 35					

6.0 a.m. T X (6.33 a.m. T O) Portobello and Macmerry Conditional Train will, except on Tuesdays, work Water Tank from Ormiston. Also Road Van daily from Leith Walk to Macmerry; also South Leith and Gifford Road Van—latter to be lifted from Ormiston by 10.50 a.m., Portobello and Gifford. On Tuesdays will leave Ormiston at 6.51 a.m. and arrive Pencaitland Colliery at 7.1 a.m., thereafter makes trip to Macmerry to lift L.S. for Gorgie to connect with 8.35 a.m. T O, Gifford to Gorgie.

Nos. 5 and 6.—‡ Calls at Joppa Passenger Station to uplift Parcel traffic for Macmerry and Gifford Branches. Conveys Leith Walk and Gifford Road Van from Portobello. Lifts South Leith and Gifford Road Van at Ormiston.

No. 7.—Works Fordel Mains Colliery.

DOWN TRAINS.

CLASS	Distance from Gifford.	Distance from Macmerry.	1	2	3	4 Live Stock A	5 Goods D	6 Goods D	7	8 Min. D	9	10
Departs from ...				...		Porto-bello a.m. 6 10	Porto-bello a.m. 8 23	Porto-bello a.m. 10 50		Porto-bello a.m. 11 26	...	..
	M. C.	M. C.				T O a.m.	S O p.m.	S X p.m.		p.m.		
Macmerry(Gladsm'ir)dep	... ...	... ...	...	...		...	...	...	•	3 15	...	...
Winton ... ... ,,	... ...	1 16	...							3 30	...	...
—Ormiston Junction arr.	... ...	2 34	...							3 40	...	...
Gifford ... ...dep.	... ...	... ...	...				8 35	12 15	3 0	...	...	...
Humbie ... ... ,,	4 69	... ...	...				8 53	12 40	3 25	...	...	...
—Saltoun ... ... ,,	5 71	... ...	...				9 11	1 10	3 45	...	...	...
Pencaitland ... ,,	7 51	... ...	...				9 26	1 30	4 5	...	...	...
Pencaitland Colly. ,,	8 28	... ...	...					2 20		...	...	...
—Ormiston Junc. arr.	9 25	... ...	...				9W34	2 25	4 15	...	...	...
—Ormiston Junction dep.		... ...	...				9 50	3 0	4 45	...	4 5	...
—Bog Siding } ,,	10 14	3 23	...				...	...	...		5 45	...
Limeylands Siding } ,,	10 19	3 28	...				...	...	...		...	...
Oxenford Siding ... ,,	10 65	3 74	...		...		...	...	...		...	...
—Dalkeith Colliery ... ,,	12 41	5 60	...				...	...	...		...	...
—Smeaton Junc. { arr.	13 45	6 54	...				10 8	...	5 15		6 15	...
{ dep.			...				10 18	3 36	6 0		6 55	...
Carberry Colliery ... ,,	13 66	6 75	...				...	...	...		...	...
—Monktonhall June. ... ,,	15 4	8 13	...				10¦40	3 43	6 46		7 17	...
—Newhailes Junc. ... ,,	16 42	9 51	...				...	3¦56	6¦56		...	...
—Joppa ... ,,	17 43	10 52	...				...	...	...		7 30	...
—Portobello ... arr.	18 16	11 25	...				...	4 4	7 6		7 35	...
Arrives at... ... {			...				Gorgie 11 13	...	...		...	...

No. 4.—‡ Lifts L.S. traffic from Inveresk.
Nos. 5 & 6.—‡ Call Newhailes Passenger Platform to leave off Parcel traffic when required. Convey Road Van, Gifford to Leith Walk.

The pattern of war-time services; 1st October, 1944 until further notice.

HADDINGTON BRANCH.   57

UP TRAINS — WEEK-DAYS

UP TRAINS.	Distance from Longniddry		1	2	3	4	5	6	7	8	9	10	11
			Goods	Goods	O.P.	O.P.		E.C.S.		O.P.		O.P.	
CLASS			D	D	...	...				...		...	...
Departs from								To work No. 7 Down.					
					...	...				...	...	Y	
	M.	C.	S X a.m.	S O a.m.	Z a.m.	Z a.m.		a.m.		a.m.		S O p.m.	
—Longniddry Junction dep.	...	...	6 0	6 24	7 22	8 17	...	10 30		11 8		1 30	...
—Haddington ... ... arr.	4	60	6 15	6 39	7 31	8 26	......	10 40		11 17	......	1 39	......

UP TRAINS — WEEK-DAYS

UP TRAINS.	13	14	15	16	17	18	19	20	21	22	23	24	25	27
	O.P.			Goods	O.P.	O.P.		O.P.	O.P.	O.P.		O.P.		
CLASS	...		...	D	...	...	...	...	...	...		...	...	.
Departs from				Porto-bello p.m. 12 30	...	...	...	...	...	...		...		
		...	...			V		V				S O		
	S O p.m.			p.m.	V p.m.	S X p.m.		V p.m.	p.m.	p.m.		S O p.m.		
—Longniddry Junction dep.	2 10	...	...	3 45	4 28	5 35		6 10	7 10	8 38		11 20	...	...
—Haddington ... ... arr.	2 19	...	...	4 0	4 37	5 44	......	6 19	7 19	8 47		11 29	......	...

Haddington Branch Passenger Engine.—Will turn out at Longniddry at 5.30 a.m. S X (6.0 a.m. S O) to shunt out Road Van and other traffic for Haddington, leaving Longniddry at 6.0 a.m. S X (6.24 a.m. S O), for Haddington; shunts as required at Haddington and Longniddry during the day ; makes trip, Mondays, Wednesdays and Fridays, Haddington to Longniddry and back, leaving Haddington at 12.0 noon, working Sidings as required on the Branch, and performing any necessary shunting work required at Longniddry. After arrival at Longniddry at 8.46 a.m., makes trip S X to Gullane, leaving 9.0 a.m.

DOWN TRAINS — WEEK-DAYS

DOWN TRAINS.	Distance from Hadding-ton.		1	2	3	4	5	6	7	8	9	10	11	12
			O.P.	O.P.				O.P.		O.P.		O.P.		O.P.
CLASS			Z	Z		...			...		Y	...	Y	
											S O		S O	
	M.	C.	a.m.	a.m.			a.m.		a.m.		p.m.		p.m.	
—Haddington ... ...dep.	...	...	6 52	7 59	...	......	8 37	...	10 50	...	12 57	...	1 50	—
Laverocklaw ... ... ,,	2	40	......	......	......	......	......	......	......	......	......	......	......	—
Coatyburn Siding ... ,,	3	0	......	......	......	......	......	......	......	......	......	......	......	
—Longniddry Junction arr.	4	60	7 1	8 8	......	......	8 46	......	10 59	......	1 6	......	1 59	......

DOWN TRAINS — WEEK-DAYS

DOWN TRAINS.	13	14	15	16	17	18	19	20	21	22	23	24	25
	O.P.	O.P.			O.P.	Goods	O.P.	O.P.	O.P.				
CLASS	V	V	.	...	...	D	...	...	...	...	..	...	...
		S X			V				S O				
	p.m.	p.m.			p.m.	p.m.	p.m.	p.m.	p.m.				
—Haddington ... ...dep.	4 5	5 10	......	......	5 50	6 20	6 38	7 35	10 30	......	...	...	...
Laverocklaw ... ... ,,	......	......	......	......	......	......	......	......	......	......		...	
Coatyburn Siding ... ,,	......	......	......	......	......	......	......	......	......	......			
—Longniddry Junction arr.	4 14	5 19	......	......	5 59	6 33	6 47	7 44	10 39	......	...	...	...
Arrives at	...	...	...	...	Porto-bello 8 10	...	...	...	...	...		...	.

1st October, 1944 until further notice.

UP TRAINS — HADDINGTON BRANCH — WEEKDAYS

No.	Distance from Longniddry	664	599	664	599					
Description										
Class		K	K	K	K					
Departs from		Prestonpans 7.38 a.m.	Portobello 11.35 a.m.	Prestonpans Pilot						
	M. C.	am	SX PM	SO PM	SX PM					
Longniddry Jct. ⊕	.....	7 50	..... 12 20	..... 2 30	..... 3 35	.....				
Haddington.. ⊕	4.60 ..	8 8	.. 12 38	.. 2 50	.. 3 53	..	..	..	..	..

HADDINGTON BRANCH — DOWN TRAINS — WEEKDAYS

No.	Distance from Haddington	664	664	599	664	599				
Description										
Class		K	K	K	K	K				
	M. C.	SO am	SX am	SX PM	SO PM	SX PM				
Haddington ....⊕		..... 9 15	..... 9 30	..... 1 30	..... 3 40	..... 5 40	.....		..	..
Laverocklaw ..	2 40	.. ..	.. ..	.. ..	.. ..	.. ..	..	..	..	..
Coatyburn Siding	3 0									
Longniddry Junction ⊕	4 60 ..	9 35	.. 9 50	.. 1 45	.. 4 0	.. 6 5	..	..	..	..
Arrives at			Prestonpans 10.28a EBV	Gullane 2.30 p.m.	Portobello 6.3 p.m.	Portobello 7.6 p.m.				

No. 599—Conveys Parcels Van for Edinburgh to Prestonpans.

No. 664—SX On Tuesdays, after arrival at Longniddry, runs to Gullane or Aberlady to work Live Stock to Prestonpans.

October 1951 until further notice.

MONKTONHALL JN.

MONKTONHALL JN. TO SMEATON (GOODS LINES)

This branch is worked by telephone and notice board between Monktonhall Jn. and Smeaton.

At Monktonhall Jn. trains must not exceed 20 m.p.h. going through junction from Smeaton. The speed of trains on the branch must not exceed 40 m.p.h.

Catch points worked from Monktonhall Jn. box exist on the Up branch line, 520 yards before reaching the Up branch starting signal—gradient 1 in 75. Spring catch points exist on the Up branch line, 606 yards before reaching the illuminated notice board worded: "End of telephone section. Commencement of yard working"—gradient 1 in 75.

The instructions (Stop. Departing trains to telephone for instructions) on the Smeaton side of the double sided notice board at the West sidings end of the connection to the Down line apply only to trains ready to depart for Monktonhall Jn. Shunting movement beyond this notice board in the Monktonhall Jn. direction may be made without reference to the Signalman.

SMEATON

N.C.B. sdgs.—Lifting Barriers are provided at the level crossing at the entrance to the branch. A National Coal Board Crossing Keeper, when he is in attendance, will operate the barriers and will control the movement of road vehicles over the crossing. When there is no Crossing Keeper in attendance the barriers will be operated by road users. Trainmen must keep a good lookout when approaching the crossing and be prepared to stop in the event of any obstruction.

N.C.B. Preparation Plant.—Wagons must be propelled to the Preparation Plant inwards sidings off the Thorneybank branch only after the Guard or Shunter has contacted the National Coal Board's wagon runner and agreed with him as to what is to be done. Any wagons already in the sidings must be closed up and secured.

The number of wagons to be propelled must not exceed 20, and care must be taken to prevent any wagons being moved foul of the tippers.

From BR Sectional Appendix, 1969.

Smeaton station, looking north towards Monktonhall Junction, 4th October, 1953.

A.G. Ellis

Appendix Four
Statistics, Facts and Figures

(i) Returns and staff records for Haddington and Longniddry stations, January 1856

HADDINGTON (including Coatyburn and Laverocklaw Sidings)

Staff	Salary/Wages
George Tait, Agent	£80
John Lees, Clerk	12/-
Alexander Tait, Clerk	£10
Andrew Blackwood, Porter	15/-
James Donaldson, Porter	14/-
Thomas Bell, Porter	14/-
James Edmonds, Porter	14/-
James Ochiltree, Watchman	14/-

Traffic Receipts at station for half-year ending 31st January, 1856:

GOODS	Outwards (tons)	Inwards (tons)	Total (tons)	Receipts: £	s.	d.
merchandise	5,683	3,520	9,173	2464	11	6
minerals		1,153	1,153	129	2	8
live stock				85	9	8
total	5,653	4,673	10,326	2679	3	10
average per week	217.4	179.7	397.1	103	0	11

Actual receipts at station £1,824 1s. 9d.; average per week £70 3s. 1d.

PASSENGERS

Total: 14,045, average per week 540.
Receipts £1,379 1s. 11d.; actual receipts at station £1,406 3s. 10d., average per week £54 1s. 8d.

Total average weekly receipts at station from all traffic: £124 4s. 9d.

LONGNIDDRY (including Seton, St Germains, Seton Mains, Manure and Spittal Sidings)

Staff	Salary/Wages
Edwin Sladen, Agent	£60
George Neill, Clerk	£25
Thomas Sibbald, Porter	13/-
Robert Lees, Porter	14/-
James Bridges, van driver	15/-
William Wilson, Pointsman	14/-
Donald McDonald, Gatekeeper	13/-

Traffic Receipts at station for half-year ending 31st January, 1856:

GOODS	Outwards (tons)	Inwards (tons)	Total (tons)	Receipts: £	s.	d.
merchandise	4,112	2,172	6,284	1031	16	7
minerals	12,054	5	12,059	1710	4	6
live stock				25	0	0
total	16,166	2,177	18,343	2767	1	1

Actual receipts at station £25 7s. 10d.; average per week £9 18s. 1d.

PASSENGERS

Total: 6,034, average per week 232; receipts £417 14s. 6d.
Actual receipts at station £417 14s. 6d., aver per week £16 1s. 4d.
Total average weekly receipts at station from all traffic: £26 0s. 1d.

(ii) Passengers booked to and from stations 1901–1932

Year Ending:	Longniddry	Haddington	Smeaton	Crossgatehall	Ormiston	Winton	Macmerry	Pencaitland	Saltoun	Humbie	Gifford
01.1901	35,009	72,299	2,132	–	23,146	9,163	4,684	–	–	–	–
01.1902	34,456	72,717	2,387	–	13,048	7,601	4,559	857	1,392	1,023	1,442
01.1903	34,607	66,743	2,939	–	11,831	2,671	3,681	4,750	5,747	4,420	5,293
01.1904	36,389	70,584	3,190	–	12,691	2,467	3,638	5,032	6,247	5,746	6,013
01.1905	33,593	69,942	3,175	–	13,221	2,740	3,263	5,243	6,555	6,307	6,363
01.1906	30,729	65,415	3,702	–	13,150	2,506	2,947	5,779	6,428	6,199	6,195
01.1907	29,949	62,178	3,679	–	13,184	2,256	2,558	6,434	5,873	6,171	6,130
01.1908	28,939	66,588	3,198	–	22,462	2,942	3,111	7,941	6,326	6,249	6,274
01.1909	28,185	69,659	3,544	–	15,765	2,443	3,138	8,835	6,220	5,636	6,786
01.1910	28,330	65,195	3,488	–	12,246	1,944	2,325	7,863	5,971	5,695	6,460
01.1911	26,477	66,928	3,106	–	13,821	1,992	2,160	8,031	6,065	6,224	7,077
01.1912	25,545	67,554	3,936	–	13,200	1,933	2,197	7,795	5,663	6,698	6,783
12.1912*	21,056	57,346	3,355	–	13,119	1,953	2,006	6,651	5,241	5,866	6,021
12.1913	26,004	74,836	3,975	2,298	19,022	2,740	2,684	9,756	7,263	6,405	6,961
12.1914	24,569	82,369	2,608	6,435	17,627	2,508	2,606	9,754	6,941	6,167	6,463
12.1915	23,744	83,131	1,938	6,383	16,970	2,150	2,102	8,215	5,890	5,264	5,968
12.1916	21,887	80,489	2,152	7,475	16,613	1,897	2,037	8,040	6,035	5,091	6,214
12.1917	20,569	45,775	4,149	–	10,977	1,454	1,347	5,759	4,503	3,668	4,163
12.1918	18,071	56,443	4,493	–	13,748	2,412	1,686	6,483	4,797	4,138	5,674
12.1919	21,689	76,097	3,458	7,257	18,086	2,416	2,046	7,699	6,612	4,959	7,307
12.1920	33,787	68,075	3,112	11,093	20,933	2,622	2,257	10,123	7,708	6,270	7,047
12.1921	27,408	42,821	1,829	6,809	12,005	1,726	670	7,236	5,808	4,953	6,197
12.1922	34,642	54,011	2,058	7,358	10,863	1,418	409	8,027	6,903	5,502	7,418
12.1923	38,116	66,809	1,991	10,254	17,020	2,124	476	11,527	8,015	5,845	8,165
12.1924	39,418	72,428	2,140	9,469	13,922	1,856	539	9,684	7,300	5,303	7,167
12.1925	35,803	72,637	1,468	8,358	13,331	776	231	12,267	8,000	5,553	7,628
12.1926	28,928	48,518	1,166	6,308	6,835	–	–	6,743	5,927	4,582	7,258
12.1927	34,010	52,501	1,017	6,023	5,937	–	–	6,699	6,250	4,989	6,839
12.1928	31,669	49,529	605	1,819	4,891	–	–	6,388	4,730	6,839	5,783
12.1929	25,479	54,021	624	1,456	10,374	–	–	6,829	4,799	5,049	2,880
12.1930	26,727	52,898	382	1,107	10,139	–	–	6,522	3,959	5,857	3,389
12.1931	26,038	49,760	–	–	12,088	–	–	7,545	3,855	4,329	3,220
12.1932	27,107	45,600	–	–	10,543	–	–	7,421	3,631	4,416	3,213

*11 month period from 1 Feb. 1912 to 31 Dec. 1912.

(iii) Goods statistics for selected years, 1903–1932

Year Ending 31st Jan., 1903:

	Goods (tons)	Minerals (tons)	Coal (tons)	Livestock (head)
Longniddry	6,757	8,688	20,433	12,774
Haddington	32,230	6,952	9,626	38,310
Smeaton	1,980	7,339	203,880	–
Ormiston	6,303	4,734	2,003	3,156
Winton	2,777	2,284	442	3,980
Macmerry	3,250	3,880	89	4,228
Pencaitland	2,167	996	46	2,093
Saltoun	4,002	823	752	2,924
Humbie	3,164	206	966	3,042
Gifford	2,386	739	3,140	3,472

Year Ending 31st Dec., 1913:

	Goods (tons)	Minerals (tons)	Coal (tons)	Livestock (head)
Longniddry	8,073	8,658	28,235	18,337
Haddington	40,001	4,473	10,819	48,239
Smeaton	11,637	7,616	765,065	–
Ormiston	9,199	6,379	938	8,173
Winton	2,638	912	154	3,374
Macmerry	5,446	717	1,475	4,932
Pencaitland	1,680	884	34	3,476
Saltoun	7,749	1,421	1,173	8,896
Humbie	3,641	405	1,412	7,746
Gifford	4,873	227	2,264	8,253

Year Ending 31st Dec., 1932:

	Goods (tons)	Minerals (tons)	Coal (tons)	Livestock (head)
Longniddry	3,916	1,127	7,277	5,882
Haddington	17,658	4,737	7,985	49,236
Smeaton	5,119	68	672,360	–
Ormiston	10,059	55,230	5,491	11,561
Winton (a)	2,317	3,766	98	4,175
Macmerry (b)	2,262	209	63	3,224
Pencaitland (b)	834	262	6	2,434
Saltoun	1,880	182	632	12,854
Humbie (a)	1,126	139	655	6,878
Gifford (c)	1,849	343	1,423	9,169

Notes: (a) Year ending 30th June, 1931; (b) y/e 31st Dec., 1930; (c) y/e 30th Dec., 1929.

(iv) Traffic Receipts for Saltoun, Humbie and Macmerry, 1950/1 and 1955/6.

(From BR Report on Gifford and Macmerry branch lines, 30th July, 1956.)

Saltoun Station

	1950–1951		1955–1956	
	No.	Receipts	No.	Receipts
Passenger train traffic:				
Forwarded:				
Parcels, etc.	137	£36	24	£5
Livestock (head)	17	£152	16	£157
Received:				
Parcels, etc.	not known		68	£68
Livestock	nil		10	£44
		£188		£274
Goods train traffic:				
Forwarded:				
Sundries (tons)	26	£70	36	£175
Full loads (tons)	1979	£4867	2158	£6796
Minerals (tons)	9	£7	—	—
Livestock (head)	414	£119	—	—
		£5063		£6971
Received:				
Sundries (tons)	24	£86	6	£41
Full loads (tons)	737	£2057	373	£1149
Minerals (tons)	343	£396	112	£151
Coal (tons)	2061	£732	2469	£1275
Livestock (head)	342	£90	699	£409
		£3361		£3025
GROSS TOTAL:		£8424		£9996

Humbie

| | 1950–1951 | | 1955–1956 | |
	No.	Receipts	No.	Receipts
Passenger train traffic:				
Forwarded Parcels	68	£14	18	£4
Received Parcels	not known		30	£9
		£14		£13
Goods train traffic:				
Forwarded:				
Sundries (tons)	3	£9	2	£10
Full loads (tons)	1034	£2633	491	£1348
Minerals (tons)	–	–	85	£103
Livestock (head)	320	£21	–	–
		£2663		£1461
Received:				
Sundries (tons)	32	£144	14	£171
Full loads (tons)	184	£396	84	£318
Minerals (tons)	414	£642	505	£1142
Coal (tons)	160	£62	–	–
Livestock (head)	237	£65	4	£5
		£1309		£1636
GROSS TOTAL:		£3986		£3110

Macmerry

| | 1950–1951 | | 1955–1956 | |
	No.	Receipts	No.	Receipts
Goods train traffic:				
Forwarded:				
Sundries (tons)	2	£18	1	£6
Full loads (tons)	1100	£3590	325	£954
Minerals (tons)	381	£268	235	£257
	1483	£3876	561	£1217
Received:				
Sundries (tons)	4	£19	3	£20
Full loads (tons)	445	£1190	48	£163
Minerals (tons)	37	£91	78	£194
Coal (tons)	49	£18	23	£31
Livestock (head)	140	£46	–	–
		£1364		£408
GROSS TOTAL:		£5240		£1625

(v) Haddington branch traffic and receipts for year ending 31st August, 1958.

Passenger train traffic:	No.	Recpts.
Parcels forwarded	4,712	£3,391
Parcels received	12,708	£3,177
	17,420	£6,568

Goods train traffic:	Forwarded		Received		Total	
	Tons	Rects.	Tons	Rects.	Tons	Rects.
Goods	3,290	£13,872	3,678	£9,510	6,968	£23,382
Minerals	2,870	£3,364	152	£341	3,022	£3,705
Coal			6,231	£3,427	6,231	£3,427
Livestock (wagons)			45	£409		£409
	6,160	£17,236	10,061	£13,687	16,221	£30,923

(vi) Haddington station: staff particulars, October 1958.

	Rate:	Hours:	Duties:
Operating appointments			
Station master (Gr.1)	£763	8.30am–5.30pmSX 8.30am–12.15pmSO	General supervision; paybills (13 men), wagon report, cartage returns, demurrage, special duties.
Porter	156/-	9am–6pmSX 12noon–4pmSO	Cleans stationmaster's and parcels office, fires in winter, loads and bags vulnerable traffic, attends to forwarded and received parcels throughout day, SO: washes parcels, goods and station master's office floors and attends goods train.
Commercial appointments:			
Goods clerk (Grade 2)	£660	8am–5.30pmMWF 8am–5pmTuTh 8am–12.30SO	Office supervision, sack accountancy, checking forwarded consignment notes, general bookkeeping; current account. Off duty every 3rd Sat in rotation.
Goods clerk (Grade 3)	£590	8.30am–5.30pmMWF 9am–5pmTuTh 8.30–1pmSO	Forwarding invoicing; charging; compiles accounts for railhead stations; correspondence. Off duty every 3rd Sat in rotation.
Goods clerk (Grade 4)	£521	8am–5.30pmMWF 8am–5pmTuTh 8am–12.30pmSO	(Winter appointment, 1st Oct to 31st Mar.) Received warehouse book, advising, checks forwarded rates & charges, records delivery sheets, correspondence, assists forwarding during seed season, Silcock's returns. Off duty every 3rd Sat in rotation.
Working foreman	184/-	8am–5pmSX 8am–12noonSO	Supervision of outdoor staff, delivery sheets, sundries, loading, sheeting, ticketing wagons, assist Silcock's store.

Goods Porter	156/-	7.30am–5pmSX 7.30–11.30amSO	Opens station gates, cleans goods office, fire in winter, cleans mess room, assists unloading sundries vans, loading sundries and full wagon loads.
Goods Porter	156/-	8am–5pmSX 8am–12noonSO	Empties parcels van ex-Edinburgh Waverley weighs parcels; splits for delivery country and town, loading sundries and full wagon loads.
Goods Porter	156/-	8am–5pmSX 8am–12noonSO	Silcock's store, assists generally as and when available.
Junior weigher	104/6	8am–5pmSX 8am–12noonSO	Weighing, calls off parcels to Parcels Clerk records received wagons, demurrage clerk, records forwarded wagon numbers.
Motor driver (2-ton rigid)	169/-	8.30am–5.30pmSX 8.30am–12.30pmSO	Operates service to Garvald, Gifford, Humbie, Saltoun, Macmerry, Pencaitland and Ormiston.
Motor driver (6-ton arctic)	171/6	8am–5pmSX 8am–12noonSO	Goods C&D, town and local area; also heavy work.
Motor driver (1.5-ton Jensen)	169/-	8.30am–5.30pmSX 8.30am–12.30SO	Parcels C&D, also trunk services Haddington/Longniddry 10.30 am and 3.30pm.
Parcels clerk (Gr.4)	£521	8.30am–5.30pmSX 8.30am–1pmSO	Books forwarded and delivery sheets received parcels, loading lists, vulnerable lists, telegraph instrument, phone and personal enquiries.

Sources, Bibliography and Acknowledgements

Little has previously been written on the subject of the railways, mines and industry of East Lothian and the principal sources used by the present author have been the contemporary primary sources found in the following documents and record held in the Scottish Record Office in Edinburgh and the Public Record Office at Kew and in private collections: The minute books, correspondence, general manager's files, traffic books, working and public timetables, sectional and general appendices, traffic notices, trip working notices, traffic note books, share registers, sidings registers, signalling diagrams and notices and a large number of miscellaneous official material relating to the North British Railway, the Gifford & Garvald Railway, the LNER Southern Scottish Area and British Railways Scottish Region. Also consulted were the reports, records, accident reports and other documentation of the Board of Trade and Railway Commission and in other public collections Ordnance Survey maps, trade and mining directories and the contemporary reports of *The Scotsman, The Edinburgh Evening Courant, The Haddingtonshire/East Lothian Courier, The Haddingtonshire Advertiser, The Dalkeith Advertiser, The Railway Magazine, The Stephenson Locomotive Society Journal, The Railway Observer* and *Blastpipe.* Last, but by no means least, is that valuable but often overlooked source namely former railwaymen and the inhabitants of places formerly served by the lines and much of the human interest element in this book derives from the many fascinating conversations which the author was able to enjoy throughout the county to whom the Haddington, Macmerry and Gifford lines had been not merely a chapter of local history but a very real part of their own lives.

The following bibliography lists some books which may be of interest to those readers who wish to know more about certain aspects covered in this work.

Local history and topography.

The New Statistical Account of Scotland – I.Edinburghshire, (1845).
The New Statistical Account of Scotland – II.Haddingtonshire, (1845).
Political & Social Movements in Dalkeith, A. Mitchell, (1886).
Mining in Mid and East Lothian, A. Cunningham, (1925).
Humbie, C. Nisbet, (1938).
A Short History of Haddington, W. Gray, (1944).
Report of the Scottish Coalfields Committee, (1944).
Picturesque Pencaitland, Whitehead (1953).
The Third Statistical Account of Scotland: East Lothian, (1953).
Pencaitland Railway Walk Management Plan, E. Lothian C.C., (1972)
Longniddry, D. Robertson, (1975).
Penguin Buildings of Scotland: Lothian Except Edinburgh, C. McWilliam, (1979).
Third Statistical Account of Scotland: Midlothian, (1985).
Social Life in Gifford, ed. R. Hamilton, (1989).

Railways and transport:

The First Railway Across the Border, G. Dow, (1946).
The North British Railway, C. Hamilton Ellis, (1955).
The North British Railway, J. Thomas, (2 vols., 1969, 1975).
Locomotives of the NBR 1846–1882, SLS, (1970).
Locomotives of the LNER, Parts 4,5,7,8A & 8B, RCTS (1963 onwards).
Industrial Locomotives of Scotland, Industrial Railway Society, (1976).
A History of the LNER, M. Bonavia, (1983).
From SMT to Eastern Scottish, D. Hunter, (1985).
Contractor's Steam Locomotives of Scotland, R. Wear & M. Cook, (1990).
Early Railways in the Lothians, M. Worling, (1991).
The North Berwick & Gullane Branch Lines, A. Hajducki, (1992).

The following articles have appeared in periodicals:

The NBR in Haddingtonshire, T. Moffat, Railway Magazine, July 1912.
Town development and transport: North Berwick and Haddington, J. Macgregor, Scottish Geographical Magazine, September 1949.
Deluge over the Border, G. Dow, Railway World, September–November 1968 (the story of the 1948 floods).
Narrow-gauge in the Lammermuirs, H.D. Bowtell, Stephenson Locomotive Society Journal, April 1971 (the Hopes Reservoir Railway).

The Historical Geography of the Gifford & Garvald Light Railway, Dr I. Adams, Transactions of the E. Lothian Antiquarian & Field Naturalists Society, 1982.

The Gifford & Garvald Light Railway, N. Ferguson, NBRSG Journal, 1982.

The Gifford Goods, 'The Ile Inspector', NBRSG Journal, 1985.

The Widha', 'The Ile Inspector', NBRSG Journal, 1989.

The Saving of Saltoun, C. Chillies, Blastpipe, 1991.

The author owes a great debt to the many persons and organisations which have provided information, encouragement and assistance in the research and writing of this book. Among the organisations whose officials and employees willingly helped were the Scottish Library at the Edinburgh Central Library, the East Lothian county archive at Haddington, the Midlothian local history centre at Roslin, the National Library of Scotland and its map room, the Royal Commission on Ancient & Historical Monuments for Scotland, the Glenkinchie Distillery and the Planning Department of the East Lothian District Council. Individuals whose assistance was particularly appreciated include George Angus, Harold Bowtell, Jack Burrell, Neil Clark, John Denning, David Easton, Bruce Ellis, Jim Hay, David Heathcote, Willie Hennigan, David Hunter, Jeffrey Hurst, Bill Lynn, Alexander Macdonald, Rae Montgomery, Ed Nicoll, Alex Rankine, Stuart Sellar, Alan Simpson, Mike Smith, David Stirling, Norman Turnbull, Frances Voisey and Veronica Wallace and despite all their help any errors or omissions remain the responsibility of the author. To those whose photographs have been used, the author owes a special vote of thanks and apologies where credit is inadvertently omitted – one of the problems being that the provenance of many of the illustrations was, unfortunately, not readily ascertainable. Thanks is given to George McLeod of Churchill Photography, Edinburgh for his patience and expertise in rendering many old prints and negatives into a suitable form for publication and also to the author's brother, S.M. Hajducki, for redrawing the seal of the Gifford & Garvald Company. The author would welcome via his publishers any comments, corrections, criticisms or photographs (particularly of Crossgatehall Halt!). A final word – the writing of any book dealing with Scotland's premier railway company is greatly helped by the existence of a society whose members are not only knowledgeable but also willing to assist and any serious enquirer into any aspect of the affairs of the NBR, its predecessors and successors, would be well advised to contact Bill Lynn, the Membership Secretary and Treasurer of the North British Railway Study Group, at 2 Brecken Court, Saltwell Road South, Low Fell, Gateshead NE9 6EY.

Index